GLOBALIZATION AND EVERYDAY LIFE

Since the early 1990s 'globalization' has entered public and academic debate within a wide range of disciplines. However, the meaning and significance of globalization remains unclear. Is it an *outcome* of complex socio-economic developments or an emergent process in its own right? How should we evaluate the debate between 'optimists' versus 'pessimists' and 'critics', and between sceptics and radicals? How does globalization theory relate to earlier theories of convergence and world systems? Does sociology have the theoretical and conceptual tools to analyse globalization or are new approaches needed? Much of this debate has become circular and is proving difficult to resolve.

Globalization and Everyday Life provides an accessible account of globalization by developing two themes in particular. First, globalization is an outcome of structural and cultural processes that manifest in different ways in the economy, politics, culture and organizations. So the globalized world is increasingly heterogeneous, unequal and conflictual rather than integrated and ordered. Second, globalization is sustained and created by the everyday actions of people and institutions. Both of these have far-reaching consequences for everyday life and are fully explored in this volume.

Larry Ray skilfully guides students through the various aspects of the globalization debate and illustrates key arguments with reference to specific topics including nation, state and cosmopolitanism, virtual societies, transnationals and development. This innovative book provides this information in a clear and concise manner suitable for the undergraduate student studying sociology, social geography, globalization and development studies.

Larry Ray is Professor of Sociology at the University of Kent. His research interests include social theory, globalization, postcommunism, race, ethnicity and violence. Recent books include *Social Theory and Postcommunism* with William Outhwaite (2005) and *Theorizing Classical Sociology* (1999).

THE NEW SOCIOLOGY

SERIES EDITOR: ANTHONY ELLIOTT, FLINDERS UNIVERSITY, AUSTRALIA

The New Sociology is a book series designed to introduce students to new issues and themes in social sciences today. What makes the series distinctive, as compared to other competing introductory textbooks, is a strong emphasis not just on key concepts and ideas but on how these play out in everyday life – on how theories and concepts are lived at the level of selfhood and cultural identities, how they are embedded in interpersonal relationships, and how they are shaped by, and shape, broader social processes.

Forthcoming in the series:

Religion and Everyday Life
STEPHEN HUNT (2006)

Culture and Everyday Life
DAVID INGLIS (2006)

Community and Everyday Life
GRAHAM DAY (2006)

Consumption and Everyday Life
MARK W. D. PATERSON (2006)

Ethnicity and Everyday Life
CHRISTIAN KARNER (2007)

Globalization and Everyday Life
LARRY RAY (2007)

Self-Identity and Everyday Life
HARVIE FERGUSON (2007)

The Body and Everyday Life
HELEN THOMAS (2008)

Nationalism and Everyday Life
JANE HINDLEY (2007)

Risk, Vulnerability and Everyday Life
IAIN WILKINSON (2007)

Cities and Everyday Life
DAVID PARKER (2007)

EVERYDAY VIOLENCE

LARRY RAY

Routledge
Taylor & Francis Group

LONDON AND NEW YORK

First published 2007
by Routledge
2 Park Square, Milton Park, Abingdon, Oxon OX14 4RN

Simultaneously published in the USA and Canada
by Routledge
270 Madison Ave, New York, NY 10016

*Routledge is an imprint of the Taylor & Francis Group, an
informa business*

Typeset in Garamond and Scala Sans by
Florence Production Ltd, Stoodleigh, Devon
Printed and bound in Great Britain by
T J International Ltd, Padstow, Cornwall

British Library Cataloguing in Publication Data
A catalogue record for this book is available from
the British Library

Library of Congress Cataloging in Publication Data
Ray, Larry J.
   Globalization and everyday life/Larry Ray.
      p. cm
   Includes bibliographical references
   1. Globalization – Philosophy.   2. Sociology – Philosophy.
   I. Title.
   JZ1318.R39 2007
   303.48'201 – dc22   2006037348

ISBN10: 0–415–34095–0 (hbk)
ISBN10: 0–415–34094–2 (pbk)
ISBN10: 0–203–46334–X (ebk)

ISBN13: 978–0–415–34095–3 (hbk)
ISBN13: 978–0–415–34094–6 (pbk)
ISBN13: 978–0–203–46334–5 (ebk)

To Solomon Alexander Ray

CONTENTS

LIST OF FIGURES AND TABLES   VIII
SERIES EDITOR'S FOREWORD   IX
PREFACE   XIII
ACKNOWLEDGEMENTS   XVI
ABBREVIATIONS   XVII

    Introduction: what is globalization?   1

1   What's new about globalization?   15

2   Globalization and the social   45

3   Beyond the nation state?   74

4   Virtual sociality   104

5   Global inequalities and everyday life   139

6   Global terrors and risks   172

    Conclusions   200

    NOTES   207
    BIBLIOGRAPHY   217
    INDEX   235

FIGURES AND TABLES

FIGURES

1.1	Foreign direct investment, inflows and outflows, by region 1970–2001	26
2.1	Dimensions of embeddedness	73
5.1	Global distribution of wealth (%)	144
5.2	Trade in manufactures of OECD countries with developing countries 1980–99	152

TABLES

2.1	First modern societies and second modernity	53
4.1	Sketch of the development of human communication across space	112
4.2	Internet usage 2004	115
5.1	Prices of selected primary commodities between 1980 and 2001	161

SERIES EDITOR'S FOREWORD

'The New Sociology' is a series that takes its cue from massive social transformations currently sweeping the globe. Globalization, new information technologies, the techno-industrialization of warfare and terrorism, the privatization of public resources, the dominance of consumerist values: these developments involve major change to the ways people live their personal and social lives today. Moreover, such developments impact considerably on the tasks of sociology, and the social sciences more generally. Yet, for the most part, the ways in which global institutional transformations are influencing the subject matter and focus of sociology have been discussed only in the more advanced, specialized literature of the discipline. I was prompted to develop this series, therefore, in order to introduce students – as well as general readers who are seeking to come to terms with the practical circumstances of their daily lives – to the various ways in which sociology reflects the transformed conditions and axes of our globalizing world.

Perhaps the central claim of the series is that sociology is fundamentally linked to the practical and moral concerns of everyday life. The authors in this series – examining topics all the way from the body to globalization, from self-identity to consumption – seek to demonstrate the complex, contradictory ways in which sociology is a necessary and very practical aspect of our personal and public lives. From one angle, this may seem uncontroversial. After all, many classical sociological analysts as well as those associated with the classics of social theory emphasized the practical basis of human knowledge, notably Emile Durkheim, Karl Marx, Max Weber, Sigmund Freud and George Simmel, among many others. And yet there are major respects in which the professionalization of academic sociology during the latter period of the twentieth century led to a retreat from the everyday issues and moral basis of sociology itself. (For an excellent discussion of the changing relations between practical and professional sociologies see Charles Lemert, *Sociology After the Crisis*, second edition, Boulder: Paradigm, 2004.) As worrying as such a retreat from the practical and moral grounds of the discipline is, one of the main consequences of recent global transformations in the field of sociology has been a renewed emphasis on the mediation of everyday events and experiences by distant social forces, the intermeshing of the local and global in the production of social practices, and on ethics and moral responsibility at both the individual and collective levels. 'The New Sociology' series traces out these concerns across the terrain of various themes and thematics, situating everyday social practices in the broader context of life in a globalizing world.

It is certainly arguable that nowhere today do we see the impact of big social changes restructuring the terrain of everyday lived experience as well as the intellectual preoccupations of disciplinary sociology than in processes of contemporary globalization. The 'great globalization debate' has, in an amazingly short span of time, colonized both academic and public political debate about the state of the world. As one of the key buzzwords of our age, references to globalization are increasingly inescapable – the term appears, and daily, in newspapers, business magazines, radio, television, universities and what remains of the public spheres in the various regions of the states of the European Diaspora. In *Globalization and Everyday Life*, Larry Ray sets out a provocative account of our global times, of the social forces driving globalization, of its complex yet distinctive patterns of personal dislocation and cultural dispersal, and of the various crises – socio-economic, cultural and political – that face the planet as a consequence of intensifying globalism.

No one can work upon core problems in the social sciences today without entering seriously into dialogue with global perspectives and issues, and one of the great merits of Larry Ray's erudite appraisal of the globalization debate is to have demonstrated why sociology remains as relevant as ever for engaging with the current age. Among the many lines of analysis of globalism and its consequences that Ray undertakes, one overriding theme concerns the utter centrality of globalization processes to the production and reproduction of human agency, as well as of the analytical focus that sociology should accord to the coordination of social action both locally and across global spaces. Yet, the question remains, what social processes are driving globalization? Ray rehearses the debate over globalization through careful appraisal of existing sociological theories, on the one hand, and by connecting these social theories of globalism to some of the most pressing political issues of the day, on the other. Globalization as a term, as Ray indicates, is often used very vaguely in the social sciences; he argues – rightly in my view – that the complexity of the phenomenon eludes any simplistic appraisal either 'for' or 'against' the socio-political impacts of globalization. When we come to consider how globalization enters into personal and social experience today, and to consider its restructuring and transformation of social institutions, it is important to recognize the degree to which sociological assessments have altered in recent years. On a very general level, it can be said that when social analysts first started to speak of the globalizing implications of modernity – that is, the Globalization I debate of the early and mid-1990s – many sociologists were sceptical. The idea that the historical trajectory of modernity marked an overall movement towards 'one world', even though the proponents of globalization never quite expressed it thus, was considered fatally flawed – not only by academics but by various policy analysts and politicians as well. The sceptics were unconvinced, citing trade and investment figures from the late nineteenth century to question the idea that national economic interdependence had entered a historically unprecedented stage in the late twentieth century. Regionalization rather than globalization, it was said, defined the shape of the worldwide economy. Some went so far as to claim that, because of the heavy regionalization of such trading blocs as the European Union and North America, the world economy was becoming less, not more, global. Most agreed, at any rate, that nation states were not becoming progressively less sovereign –

on the contrary, internationalization was regarded as fundamentally dependant on the regulatory control of national governments.

When the Globalization I debate raged some ten years ago, few could have anticipated just how quickly the spread of a 'borderless' world was to occur – and Ray (attentive as he is to the end of the Cold War, postcommunism and the attendant restructuring of East/West boundaries) is an expert guide on these various aspects of the politics of globalization. This in turn connects to the rise of Globalization II – the recognition, on a general level, that globalism should not be equated with Americanization or homogenization and that, in contrast, globalization is constitutive of socio-cultural processes of hybridity, dispersal, dislocation and differentiation. Analysis of globalism today, as a result of these theoretical developments, can in some part be distinguished from the influence of the 'colonization' model of personality and society formation as portrayed in theories associated with Globalization I. In reviewing the most recent sociological research on globalization, Ray highlights the importance of richer, multidimensional frameworks for grappling with the facts, fears and forebodings of contemporary globalization – from the rise of religious extremism to the war on terror.

Anthony Elliott
Adelaide, 2006

PREFACE

The sociologist C. Wright Mills said that when the pace of change outstrips our ability to act in accord with cherished values we feel that older ways of thinking have collapsed while newer beginnings are morally ambiguous. What we need, Mills argues, is a 'sociological imagination', that is, a quality of mind that enables us to use our reasoning plus vast amounts of information to discover a central insight about social life – that our personal troubles are often not just personal but public issues affecting many people and maybe an entire society. In the late twentieth and early twenty-first centuries the pace of change associated with globalization has posed new challenges for the understanding of everyday life and the practice of sociology itself. Many sociologists also feel that the old ways of doing things are no longer valid in the face of profound changes in spatial, organizational, personal, economic and political relationships. This book explores both the ways of understanding the changes brought by globalization and the reactions to these among the sociological community itself.

There is hardly any topical issue – global terror, world debt, the mass media, employment trends, production and consumption chains and social welfare – that is not informed by discussion of globalization. During the latter part of the twentieth century the world became increasingly interconnected by fast modes of communication facilitating global flows of money, ideas, goods, people and cultural styles. Globalization has challenged much established thinking in sociology about the nature of space, locality and social processes, yet there is a still little agreement about its meaning and impact. In the 1990s, especially following the fall of the Berlin Wall, the enthusiasm for globalization spread. But this was seriously challenged by the shock of September 11, 2001 and new uncertainties about terrorism and economic insecurity. Fast communications, the compression of time and space and the global reach of multinational corporations does not necessarily create a homogenous world, and certainly not a harmonious one, but rather increasing diversity and conflict. Globalization is clearly a highly controversial process, but this book is neither a defence nor a critique of globalization – there are many of each of these available already and, anyway, I will argue that the very diversity of the globalization eludes simple judgements 'for' or 'against'. The consequences and meanings of globalization are, as with other forms of sociality are highly diverse. The core issue that will be explored here is how human society depends on the capacity to coordinate action both locally and across global spaces. So even highly stretched forms of sociality are the accomplishment of everyday life and knowledgeable actors.

In adopting this view, this book is in part a defence of sociology against those who claim that globalization makes redundant all or most previously existing sociological concepts and theories. Understanding social change is what sociology does and was in many ways its original *raison d'être* – to comprehend the changes associated with the emergence of modernity. To suggest, then, as some do, that confronted with the social changes associated with globalization we must abandon all previously existing frameworks and write sociology anew seems bizarre. This book places a discussion of sociality and everyday life in the foreground of the analysis of globalization and attempts to show how the debates about globalization might refashion our thinking about sociology.

My aim is to provide an accessible review of globalization theories and discuss the ways in which globalization is accomplished by social agents in everyday life. In this vast field considerable selection will be necessary to maintain what I hope will be a coherent argument about the relevance of globalization for sociological analysis. The discussion will focus on the extent to which sociological theories of globalization have taken account of the role of agents, social meanings and their reciprocal relations in the ongoing construction and maintenance of globalization. One of the themes of this book will be that globalization refers to multiple processes with diverse effects on everyday life in different parts of the world. It aims to balance examples from the developed world with those from developing countries. It is a paradox of the rise of globalization studies that sociological discussion of the world beyond the focus of Western consumer culture is often relatively muted. There may be widespread recognition of problems of global poverty, for example, but less understanding of the debates about how such problems arose, what processes sustain them and whether globalization exacerbates or alleviates them. This myopia will obscure understanding of the social and political forces operating on the global arena and the ways in which agents and systems act in concert to generate diverse outcomes. This book advocates an approach to globalization that keeps these dimensions in view.

ACKNOWLEDGEMENTS

This book is the product of many debates and discussions over the years. I am grateful to Anthony Elliott for his encouragement to write it, and to many people who have offered advice, debate or other assistance with the issues discussed. These include Farshad Araghi, Joe Asila, Babere Chacha, Michael Hardey, Clarissa Hayward, Stephen Kobrin, John Madely, Barbara Misztal, Jan Pahl, Richard Sakwa, Miri Song, Bryan Turner, John Urry, Andy Weigert and Ian Wilkinson. Finally to Emma, my deep appreciation for support and inspiration over many years.

ABBREVIATIONS

ASEAN	Association of Southeast Asian Nations
BAT	British American Tobacco
BAT(K)	British American Tobacco (Kenya)
CIS	Commonwealth of Independent States
CMC	computer mediated communication
CDRM	Crime and Disorder Reduction Partnerships
CRNM	Caribbean Regional Negotiating Machinery
DNS	Domain Name System
ECJ	European Court of Justice
EMU	Economic and Monetary Union
EU	European Union
FAO	Food and Agricultural Organization (of the UN)
FDI	foreign direct investment
GDP	gross domestic product
GNP	gross national product
ICT	information and communications technology
ILO	International Labour Organization
IP	Internet protocol
IMF	International Monetary Fund
INGO	international non-governmental organization
IPR	intellectual property right
IRA	Irish Republican Army
KWS	Keynesian Welfare State

MTK	Mastermind Tobacco Kenya
MUD	multi-user environment
NAFTA	North American Free Trade Area
NATO	North Atlantic Treaty Organisation
NGO	non-governmental organization
OECD	Organisation for Economic Co-operation and Development
R&D	research and development
SSA	Social Security Administration (US)
TNC	transnational corporation
UN	United Nations
UNCTAD	United Nations Conference on Trade and Development
UNESCO	United Nations Educational, Scientific and Cultural Organization
WELL	Whole Earth Electronic Link
WHO	World Health Organization
WIPO	World Intellectual Property Organization
WTO	World Trade Organization
WTTC	World Travel and Tourism Council

INTRODUCTION
WHAT IS 'GLOBALIZATION'?

There is now an extensive literature on globalization from a wide range of perspectives – sociological, economic, cultural, political and technological. The term has further entered everyday commentary and analysis – featuring in many political, policy, cultural and economic debates. It is a rare example of an academic concept emerging in economics and sociology during the late 1980s and gaining currency in the 1990s that has had wide and deep influence in contemporary thinking in many different spheres. Marshall McLuhan (1992), who coined the term 'global village', envisaged a situation in which information travelling at electronic speeds would replace language with instant non-verbal communication, creating an 'all-at-onceness', although he dreaded this prospect. A globalized world is one of increasing instantaneity, where communication media enable people in disparate locations to experience events simultaneously. This creates a complex range of social interconnections governed by the speed of communications, thereby creating a partial collapse of boundaries within national, cultural and political spaces. However, the meaning and significance of globalization remains far from clear. For Anthony Giddens (1990) the core of globalization is the experience of 'distanciation' as social relations get stretched across time and space and thereby take on an increasingly reflexive quality. Harvey and Mittleman talk of 'compression' and unification of time and space in social, political and cultural life (Harvey 1994: 260) and Castells (1997) of the economy's capacity to work as a unit in real time on a planetary scale. Kobrin (1998) emphasizes the increasing scale of economic activity, inter-firm alliances and information flows, and Gilpin (1987) the interdependence of national economies. While these writers regard globalization as a relatively recent development Robertson (1992) sees earlier historical precedents in the global missions of Christianity, Islam and Marxism in forming a compressed global consciousness. Martin Albrow (1997) emphasizes the impact on people's lives of the global diffusion of practices, values and technology. Urry (2003) sees in globalization a transformation of the world into a complex and chaotic system in which earlier sociological categories and theories collapse. These features are may not be entirely mutually incompatible but together still look more like a series of theorized descriptions of trends than a cohesive basis for research into globalization's effects and trajectory.

Confronted with many theories and definitions globalization begins to look more like a buzzword than an analytical concept, and it has indeed become a metaphor for many contemporary social changes. Nonetheless there is something going on that is worth considering further although we need to raise a number of questions. Is globalization an *outcome* of complex socio-economic developments or an emergent process in its own right? How does globalization theory relate to earlier theories of convergence and world systems? Much globalization literature has become rather tired, with many debates proving difficult to resolve. For example, it is frequently claimed that globalization is destructive of traditional bonds of social solidarity, but little work is done on theorizing the new forms of sociality that emerge within a global order. This book develops two themes in particular. First, unlike earlier theories of convergence, globalization points towards increasing hybridity and differentiation and thus depicts a complex and fluid social world. Second, globalization is an outcome of structural and cultural processes that manifest in different ways in the economy, politics, culture and organizations. Both of these themes have far-reaching consequences for everyday life that will be explored in this book. They will be addressed particularly in Chapters 1 and 2.

Globalization has deep origins in world history and particularly in the creation of a system of international organizations and regulatory bodies after the Second World War – including the United Nations (UN), the General Agreement on Tariffs and Trade (now the World Trade Organization (WTO)), the International Monetary Fund (IMF) and the World Bank.[1] But recent globalization was the outcome of a more specific confluence of factors: what Quah (1996) terms the 'weightless economy' based more on trading information than goods;[2] the end of the Cold War; the growth of 24-hour global news media, digital technologies and their application via the World Wide Web to all areas of communication and commerce; the dominance of neo-liberal strategies of privatization and marketization in the developed capitalist, post-Soviet and developing worlds; and declining international travel costs. A crucial backdrop to these was the crisis in Soviet industrialism since – as I have argued elsewhere (Outhwaite and Ray 2005) – the end of the Cold War was the prelude to the maturity of the concept of globalization. Only after 1989 was it possible to imagine at least a 'borderless' world in which people, goods, ideas and images would flow, since *the* major border dividing East and West had collapsed. Moreover, the world after November 1989 appeared to be one of increasing speed and unpredictability, a view reinforced by the speed and the seemingly unanticipated nature of the changes. The stable order that had been provided by the ritualized confrontation between the US and the USSR was relatively slow-changing and predictable – it had its rules, technologies, ideas and organizational forms. By contrast, the postcommunist order was not only less certain but was changing at an accelerating pace. In the process many certainties and boundaries of social life, too, were undermined. With the collapse of the Soviet system so also fell the belief that state could control and manage all affairs of society for maximum well-being and exclude the rest of the world. There also followed a crisis of alternatives – the end of the great experiment of the twentieth century to create a wholly new kind of society and human being. Moreover, the successive collapses of the socialist regimes were world media spectacles. The rapidity of televisual transmission partly accounted for the speed with which the regimes fell, and the availability of alternative social models to state socialism had been demonstrated by satellite TV.

The impact of the collapses was global, in that the postcommunist world confronts new questions of security, volatility, migration, and so forth. The end of communism ironically fulfilled Marx's 1848 prediction in the *Communist Manifesto* (Marx and Engels 1967) that the whole world would be brought within the capitalist system of production – ironically because communism was supposed to follow, not precede, global capitalist domination.

Globalization became the focus of some key theoretical and conceptual debates in the later twentieth century that brought together a wide range of disciplines in addition to sociology. But it was always surrounded by controversies and uncertainties, and to some extent, in sociology at least, the globalization debate may be showing signs of the kind of exhaustion that set in with postmodernism in the late 1990s. Difficult issues keep recurring in the literature, often without being taken forward, and the core debates need more unravelling and clarity. For example, is globalization an emergent process with effects in its own right (a view advanced by Giddens (1990) and Urry (2002), for example, but rejected by Rosenberg (2000)) or is it the effect of a complex combination of social, economic, cultural and political changes? Does it really depict a novel social condition or simply force already familiar processes into a new language? What does 'globalization' encompass that cannot be analysed through previously existing concepts such as internationalization, imperialism, postmodernity, 'weightless economy', post-Fordism, neo-liberalism and so on? Even if it is a (relatively) novel social condition, to what extent does it require us to rethink existing sociological theory and to what extent did earlier theories anticipate it? Does globalization create a global culture of visual homogeneity in which everywhere looks superficially the 'same' or, on the contrary, does it bring increased differentiation between globalization winners and losers along with eclectic hybrids of local and global cultures? Should globalization be welcomed, simply regarded as inevitable or resisted, and if the latter, how influential is the current wave of anti-globalization social movements? If the juridical role of the nation state has (as some argue) been reduced or 'hollowed out' (as its functions are transferred 'up' to international organizations and 'down' to regional bodies) how effective are international forms of juridical regulation?

Two issues are particularly important and will receive extensive discussion in this book. First, we know that globalization describes the acceleration and compression of spatial and temporal social relations and communications facilitated by new communication and transport technologies. But all these activities (even virtual ones, discussed in Chapter 4) have to take place *somewhere* and require infrastructures located in spaces and places (Perrons 2004: 21). Urry (2002) describes this process as 'mobility/moorings' in that there is no increase in fluidity without extensive corresponding systems of immobilities or mooring structures. Second, this embedding of global flows implies that there are active subjects whose situated interactions, intentions and meanings constitute global forms of sociality and *enable it to happen*. Sociology has often faced the dilemma of theorizing society as an abstract system or structure as opposed to viewing it as the ongoing accomplishment of human subjects. We know that it must be both in that there clearly can be no social life without people, while people often act, as Marx put it, 'in circumstances not of their own choosing'. These 'circumstances' should not refer only to historically given conditions and levels of productive development (which were Marx's main concerns) but also to cultural conditions and forms of socialization that make some responses to external situations more typical than others.

DEBATES ABOUT GLOBALIZATION

There are many views on the nature and impact of globalization. But globalization is not one thing. It can be economic – evidenced, for example, in the global dominance of transnational corporations, global finance, flexible production and assembly and the rise of information and service economies. In the UK more people work in Indian restaurants than in shipbuilding, steel manufacture and coal mining combined and that there are three times as many public relations consultants as coal miners (Foresight 2002: 23). Yet industrial production is expanding in other areas of the world, notably China, so we are really looking at a restructuring and relocalization of global production and consumption relations.[3] Globalization can be political – understood in terms of international organizations, the growth of regional autonomy, the spread of the post-welfare state and the development of global social movements. Again, globalization may be cultural, indicated through the growth of global consumption cultures, media and information flows, migration and identities. Throughout the latter half of the twentieth century we have seen the emergence of global brands that carry both cultural and economic significance. One of the most successful exercises in global branding was the 1971 Coca-Cola global promotion 'I'd like to teach the world to sing' that generated a global image for the product and put the company in a highly competitive position with 300 brands in 200 countries; in 2003 it was still a leading global brand. A related form of cultural globalization occurs with tourism – an industry with a turnover of $7.58 trillion in 2005, employing 212 million people and 10 per cent of the global workforce (CRNM (Caribbean Regional Negotiating Machinery) 2005). As well as the physical movement of vast numbers of people each year, tourism entails the global packaging and selling of culture that has effects on local cultures, economies and industries. This and other aspects of globalization can be viewed as either creating new opportunities or creating threats. Globalization analysis has further been promoted through growing awareness of global risks such as ecological crisis, global pandemics (e.g. AIDS, SARS and the threat of 'Avian influenza'),[4] fears about international crime and trafficking in people and drugs, the growth of ethno-national conflicts and threats of terrorism.

However, just as globalization is not one thing, neither is it 'good' or 'bad', but it is open to multiple evaluations. Nor is it just 'Americanization' – US global political, economic and cultural influence is obviously extensive but many forms of global interconnections and flows operate in the opposite direction (East to West) while many current developments in the US (such as conflicts between secular evolutionary theory and 'intelligent design') have not yet been transported worldwide. Thus globalization does not necessarily involve cultural and economic homogenization although it is often perceived in terms of encroachment and colonization. Many assume that global corporations and technologies will systematically erode local customs and ways of life, and this frequently becomes a point of anti-global resistance.

Globalization is essentially about transnational flows (of people, money, cultures, goods etc.) across borders, but its effects will always be spatially located somewhere, and virtual spaces are downloaded and accessed in particular places. Sassen, for example, has shown how the city has become an important site where processes of globalization are materialized since in order for global markets to function effectively they need to be underpinned by specialized managerial work that is concentrated in cities. In global cities we find a concentration of command functions that serve as production sites for finance and the other leading industries, and provide marketplaces where firms and governments can buy financial services. Cities become strategic sites for the acceleration of capital and information flows and at the same time spaces of increasing socio-economic polarization. There have emerged new 'corridors' and zones around nodal cities with increasingly relative independence from surrounding areas. Networks of global cities densely connected by air have also emerged (Sassen 1996a). But urban landscapes are also sites of global memory, renovation and re-evaluation of the past and ways of readdressing the past, and this view will be developed in a discussion of Auschwitz and Krakow as sites of memory and reappraisal of the past in Chapter 3.

THEORIES OF GLOBALIZATION

There is a wide range of sociological theories of globalization. The following will provide an introduction to some of the important issues. I will consider briefly: Ohmae's 'borderless world'; Friedman, for whom globalization is driven particularly by the communications revolution; Giddens' concept of time–space distanciation and the disembedding of social relations; David Harvey's concept of time–space compression; Robertson's global consciousness; Urry's sociology beyond societies; and Held and McGrew's 'transformationalism'.

Kenichi Ohmae's (1994) concept of a 'borderless world' epitomizes the belief that globalization brings improvement in human conditions. For Ohmae (2000) an invisible continent is a moving, unbounded world in which the primary linkages are now less between nations than between regions (with anything between

5 million and 20 million people) that are able to operate effectively in a global economy without being closely networked with host regions. Increasingly, transnational corporations do not treat countries as single entities and region states make effective points of entry into the global economy. For example, when Nestlé moved into Japan they chose the Kansai region round Osaka and Kobe rather than Tokyo as a regional doorway. This fluidity of capital is creating a borderless world in which capital moves around, chasing the best products and the highest investment returns regardless of national origin. The cyber-world has changed not only the way businesses work but also the way we interact on a personal level. High multiples are awarded to new economy stocks, which are the basis of not only present wealth but also what anyone with a retirement plan hopes will be future comfort. This 'invisible continent' can be dated to 1985, when Microsoft released Windows 1.0, CNN was launched, Cisco Systems began, the first Gateway 2000 computers were shipped, and companies such as Sun Microsystems and Dell were in their infancies. Back then, the economic outlook was gloomy and few saw this embryonic 'continent' forming. Now, of course, it affects virtually every business. Decisions are made on the invisible continent (the 'platforms' that are created by businesses rather than governments) about how money moves around the globe.

Similarly enthusiastic is Friedman (2000: 6–12) in claiming that the communications revolution ushered in a new world that 'began in 1989' with the beginning of the post-Cold War period. With this came a package of shifts: from political spheres of influence to the integration of markets so that 'deal' rather than 'the treaty' has become the defining agreement of international cooperation; from state regulation to de-regulation; from industrialization to digitalization; from the threat of nuclear annihilation to global terrorism as the major global threat. Earlier nineteenth-century 'globalization' was built around falling transportation costs – especially the railroad and steamship – as a result of which the volume of trade and population movement increased rapidly. But now globalization is built around falling telecommunications costs – of microchips, satellites, fibre optics and the Internet – which allow companies to locate different parts of production, research and marketing in different countries but tie them together as though they were in one place. A three-minute call (in 1996 prices) between London and New York cost $300 in 1930 but is now almost free through the Internet (Friedman 2000: 6–12).

For Anthony Giddens, globalization is centrally understood through the concept of time–space distanciation. This is a process in which locales are shaped by events far away, and vice versa, while social relations are disembedded or 'lifted out' from locales. Peasant households in traditional societies, for example, largely produced their own means of subsistence, a tithe was often paid in kind (goods, animals or labour), money was of limited value and economic exchange was local and particularistic. Modernization replaced local exchange with universal exchange of money, which simplified otherwise impossibly complex transitions and enabled the circulation of highly complex forms of information and value in increasingly abstract and symbolic forms. The exchange of money establishes social relations across time and space, which is speeded up under globalization. Similarly, expert cultures arise as a result of scientific revolutions, which bring an increase in technical knowledge and specialization. Specialists claim 'universal' and scientific forms of knowledge that enable the establishing of social relations across vast expanses of time and space. Social distance is created between professionals and their clients as in the modern medical model, which is based upon the universal claims of science. As expert knowledge dominates across the globe, local perspectives become devalued and modern societies are reliant on expert systems. Trust is increasingly the key to the relationship between the individual and the expert systems – it is the 'glue' that holds modern societies together. But where trust is undermined, individuals experience ontological insecurity and a sense of insecurity with regard to their social reality.

Giddens (1999: 19) is less unambiguously enthusiastic than Friedman about globalization since it is a 'runaway world' that 'is not – at least at the moment – a global order driven by collective human will. Instead, it is emerging in an anarchic, haphazard, fashion, carried along by a mixture of economic, technological and cultural imperatives'. Giddens (1990) describes the global order as the result of an intersection of four processes – capitalism (its economic logic), the interstate system (the world order), militarism (world security and threats) and industrialism (the division of labour and lifestyles). However, Giddens does not say what the different weight of these factors is and whether they change historically.

Harvey understands globalization as processes that so revolutionize the objective qualities of space and time that we are forced to alter, sometimes in quite radical ways how we represent the world to ourselves. Thus:

> The time taken to traverse space and the way we commonly represent that fact to ourselves are useful indicators of the kind of phenomena I have in mind. As space appears to shrink to a 'global village' of telecommunications and a 'spaceship earth' of economic and ecological interdependencies – to use just two familiar and everyday images – and as time horizons shorten to the point where the present is all there is . . . so we have to learn how to cope with an overwhelming sense of *compression* of our spatial and temporal worlds.
>
> (Harvey 1994: 240–2)

Time–space compression that 'annihilates' space and creates 'timeless time' is driven by flexible accumulation and new technologies, the production of signs and images (fake it till you make it), just-in-time delivery, reduced turnover times and speeding up, and both de- and re-skilling. Harvey points for support to the ephemerality of fashions, products, production techniques, speed up and vertical disintegration, financial markets and computerized trading, instant-aneity and disposability, and regional competitiveness. For Harvey, the flexibilized computer-based production in Silicon Valley or the 'Third Italy' epitomizes these changes.

Urry (2000) argues that the changes associated with globalization are so far-reaching that we should now talk of a 'sociology beyond societies'. This position is informed by the alleged decline of the nation state in a globalized world, which has led to wider questioning of the idea of 'society' as a territorially bounded entity. This in turn prepares the ground for claims to the effect that since 'society' is the core sociological concept, the very foundations of the discipline have likewise been undermined. The core concepts of the new socialites are space (social topologies), regions (interregional competition), networks (new social morphology), and fluids (global enterprises). Mobility is central to this thesis since globalization is the complex movement of people, images, goods, finances etc. that constitutes a process across regions in faster and unpredictable shapes, all with no clear point of arrival or departure.

As Lechner (2000–2) points out, Robertson was one of the first sociologists to theorize globalization, and central to his approach is the concept of 'global consciousness' that refers to 'the compression of the world and the intensification of consciousness of the world as a whole' (Robertson 1992: 8). Through thought and action global consciousness makes the world a single place. What it means to live in this place and how it must be ordered become universal questions. These questions receive different answers from individuals and societies that define their position in relation to both a system of societies and the shared properties of humankind from very different perspectives. This confrontation of world views means that globalization involves 'comparative interaction of different forms of life' (1992: 27). Unlike theorists who identify globalization with late (capitalist) modernity Robertson sees global interdependence and consciousness preceding the advent of capitalist modernity. However, further, Lechner argues:

> European expansion and state formation has boosted globalization since the seventeenth century, and the contemporary shape of the world owes most to the 'take-off' decades after about 1875, when international communications, transportation and conflict dramatically intensified relationships across societal boundaries. In that period, the main reference points of fully globalized order took shape: nation state, individual self, world system of societies and one humanity. These elements of the global situation became 'relativized' since national societies and individuals, in particular, must interpret their very existence as parts of a larger whole. To some extent, a common framework has guided that interpretive work; for example, states can appeal to a universal doctrine of nationalism to legitimate their particularizing claims to sovereignty and cultural distinction. Such limited common principles do not provide a basis for world order. Global consciousness does not imply global consensus.

Lechner, 2000–1

Further, for Robertson, by the end of the twentieth century,

> if not before, globalization had turned world order into an object of reflection in that everyone must now reflexively respond to the common predicament of living in one world. This provokes the formulation of contending world views. For example, some portray the world as an assembly of distinct communities, highlighting the virtues of particularism, while others view it as developing toward a single overarching organization, representing the presumed interests of humanity as a whole. In a compressed world, the comparison and confrontation of world views are likely to produce new cultural conflict. In such conflict, religious traditions play a special role, since they can be mobilized to provide an ultimate justification for one's view of the globe; the resurgence of fundamentalist groups, innovative traditionalists with a global agenda, is a case in point. A globalized world is thus integrated but not harmonious, a single place but also diverse, a construct of shared consciousness but prone to fragmentation.
>
> Lechner, 2000–2

Held and McGrew (2000) argue that globalization creates profound change as states and societies try to adapt to a more interconnected but uncertain world (Held *et al.* 2000: 2). Organizational interests (of international non-governmental organizations – INGOs – and transnational corporations) along with trading blocs develop into a new system of political globalization. Many others adopt a similar mode of argument. Globalization is defined as the sum of a set of internationalizing socio-temporal processes. This does raise questions about how to measure the extent of social relations that are allegedly so stretched yet tightly integrated as to be permanently shaping global events. Often INGOs have little power to influence outcomes compared with transnational corporations or governments themselves, and this issue is taken up here in different ways in Chapters 5 and 6.

Finally, there are many academic and political critics of globalization who identify with the 'anti-globalization movement'. There is an irony in that many of these internationally organized or linked movements use globalized forms of communication (notably the

Internet) and operate transnationally, mobilizing a global consciousness and solidarities. One example of this is the French movement *La Confédération paysanne*,[5] which was founded by José Bové in 1999 in defence of French agriculture and (especially southern) rural lifestyles but which has become a significant actor in the worldwide anti-globalization scene. Many activists are not necessarily opposed to globalization as such but economic neo-liberal globalization and a corporatist agenda that is intent on constricting individual freedom and local lifestyles in the name of profit. Some further claim that globalization is a new form of imperialism imposing Western (especially US) political and economic dominance over the rest of the world. For anti-globalization critics international bodies such as the World Bank and the IMF are not accountable to the populations on whom their actions have most effects – for example, when loans are made conditional on structural adjustment and privatization of public facilities such as health, water and education. Activists also point out that globalization creates a 'borderless' world for capital and finance but not for labour since strict and increasingly severe immigration controls exist in most developing countries while labour lacks basic rights in many developing countries. The movement (if something so diverse can be called a 'movement') is very broad and includes church groups, nationalist parties, leftist parties, environmentalists, peasant unions, anti-racism groups, anarchists, some charities and others. If we take a broad view of globalization, though, these movements are themselves part of the process by which global solidarities (if in these cases rather weak and transitory ones) come to be formed.

This I hope provides some flavour of the questions raised about the contemporary world by the globalization paradigm. This book will examine the nature of a global sociology that grasps the complexity of post-national formations and transnational networks. In order to understand the nature of globalization and the extent to which it is emerging we will need to take a broader view of social developments and particularly inclusions and exclusions in relation to global systems than one finds from focusing only on Western cultures. Globalization is not simply the spread of 'Western culture' across the world, but this is not always apparent from much globalization theory that draws a generalized picture of what purport to be global trends but are actually trends based largely on the experience of Western societies. There is something of an irony that previous sociological approaches, such as development theories, were rather more in tune with global developments than is often the case with globalization texts in sociology.

1

WHAT'S NEW ABOUT GLOBALIZATION?

Some commentators have denied that globalization is occurring or at any rate have questioned its novelty and inevitability. Others argue that globalization is a chaotic, destructive process, a view that is shared by some sociologists and anti-globalization activists though for different reasons and in different ways. In sociology this stance towards contemporary society is resonant with what I have argued elsewhere (Ray 1999) is a Romantic yearning for a more authentic and secure past. Classical sociology's critique of industrial society often invoked an image of lost past, tradition, customs, folk wisdom, social solidarity, morality and enchantment, a view epitomized by Tönnies' distinction between *Gemeinschaft* 'communal' relations and *Gesellschaft* 'modern' social relations (Tönnies 1971). Some critiques of globalization invoke similar tropes even if (like many sociologists of industrial society in the past) they do regard the process as inevitable. The view to be proposed here is that globalization refers to a complex array of contemporary social changes, some of which were familiar to earlier sociology and some of which are novel. This complexity alone should preclude summative (negative or positive) judgements about globalization.

In terms of the novelty or otherwise of globalization, there is no simple continuity or hiatus – earlier theories did not have to address the new realities of a 24/7 society, global money markets and high technology creating new forms of computer mediated networking and lifestyle niches. But the idea of a globally integrated world is not new to sociology. Nineteenth-century writers such as Saint-Simon, Comte and Marx envisaged an increasingly integrated world in which national identities would be of declining importance. Weber's sociology was world-historical in scope and processes such as rationalization clearly referred to the global spread of systems of rational action and organization. Then later twentieth-century theories of global development (e.g. world systems theory) understood capitalism as a single global system in which events at local levels were structured by the systemic core. On the one hand, world systems theory was heavily dependent on economic analysis rather than the cultural processes that have been emphasized by sociological globalization theories. On the other hand, much sociology of globalization has been highly culturally inflected and has given too little attention to the transnational economic processes that shape a global world. This chapter reviews the key debates surrounding globalization and the challenges these pose to earlier social theories, and goes on to sketch a theory of globalization and everyday life.

COSMOPOLITANISM, SOCIETY AND GLOBALIZATION

The scope, speed and intensity of present global interconnections were largely unanticipated by earlier social theorists, although the idea of imagining the world as a whole and the concept of universal humanity have long histories and point towards later globalization theory. Confronted by dramatic transformations of European society in the nineteenth century, classical social theorists focused in different ways on the dislocation of community and the disembedding of social relations in the modern world (Ray 1999b). Yet it is sometimes claimed that globalization generates a condition so novel that existing social theory, tied to what Beck (2000a: 21) calls the 'container theory of society', cannot comprehend it. The container theory refers to the view that 'society', the object of sociology, is contained within the borders of the nation state that have now been eroded. But I will suggest in this and the following chapters that social theory is amenable to conceptualizing 'the social' on multiple levels of analysis that transcend national boundaries. Here I will suggest that various strands of classical theory placed the increasingly cosmopolitan character of modern societies in the foreground of their theories. This issue is discussed further in Chapter 2 in the context of the problem of social integration.

The classical heritage

To encapsulate 'society' within the nation state was arguably reasonable, of course, given that this was a primary focus of social and political organization and identity for millions of people. But even so, several classical conceptions of 'society' offer multidimensional and fluid conceptions of social relations that acknowledge the internationalization of world connections. There was Saint-Simon's vision of a politically and socially integrated Europe and a system of international governance (his journal was entitled *The Globe*) based on common practices and shared values (Ray 1999b: 36–41). Likewise, Comte's concept of the future was one in which national identifications would be superseded by a commitment to humanity guided by transnational universal values (Ray 1999b: 36–41). Marx, of course, had a grasp of global processes unrivalled by other classical theorists, to the extent that he tended to overlook the ways in which national capitals and interests would counteract internationalization both of capital and the revolutionary proletariat. The historical mission of capitalism was to 'demolish Chinese walls' and bring the world within a single system of production. Hence:

national differences and antagonism between peoples are daily more and more vanishing, owing to the development of the bourgeoisie, to freedom of commerce, to the world market, to uniformity in the mode of production and in the conditions of life corresponding thereto.

(Marx and Engels 1967)

Weber's grasp of social development was historical and global in the sense that he was concerned with world-shaping events – the rise of capitalism, the growth of bureaucratic organizations, rationalization as a world-historical fate, the rise of world religions. For Weber sociology is a cultural science concerned with understanding how different world views are expressed in contrasting institutional forms, which governs the ways in which human existence is experienced as meaningful. Of central concern was the specific and peculiar form of rationalism that gave rise to an uncontrollable spread of bureaucratic and calculable forms of action and depersonalization (Rosenberg 2000: 97). Further, his conceptual focus was on social action rather than 'societies' and the ways in which action was structured through multiple configurations of economic, cultural, institutional and value systems (Weber 1967: 4).

It is important to distinguish the contingent location of social action and structures within the borders of nations from anything essentially 'national' about the concept of 'the social'. Durkheim, for example, used the existence of nationally based data to undertake comparative research, but his concept of the social was not bound to the existence of the nation state. Indeed, he says: 'Every aggregate of individuals who are in continuous contact form a society' (Durkheim 1984: 276). In other words 'society' was any form of ongoing patterned group that could cohere at the level of nations but just as much within local or transnational associations; in contemporary terms they could be e-communities. Contrary to those who accuse him of hypostatizing 'society' Durkheim wished to avoid conceptual generalizations and he grounded analysis of social solidarity in concrete 'social facts' – such as norms, legislative codes, rituals, collective memory, cognitive systems and other forms of mutual intelligibility. Moreover, he argued that social integration in highly differentiated organic societies was possible only though commitment to formal principles of human rights, and his own pioneering involvement in the human rights movement pointed to the possibility of transnational forms of sociality (e.g. Durkheim 1969). He was also aware that the simple and spatially contiguous settings of social integration were undermined by industrialization and social differentiation. Indeed Waters (1996: 5–6) sees Durkheim's 'genuine legacy to globalization' in theories of differentiation and culture. Societies become structurally differentiated as commitment to the state weakens and extra-societal diversity increases.

In the early twentieth century sociologists analysed transnational communities and the effects of migration on concepts of the self. For example, Thomas and Znanieki's classical 1918 study *The Polish Peasant in Europe and America* (Thomas and Znanieki 1996) developed a theory of the trans-cultural self, claiming that people act under habit and continue in this way on a day-to-day basis until a crisis arises. At this point they develop a 'conscious operation' (one could also describe this as a reflexive attitude) that articulates the cultural ambivalence created by tensions between the collectivity and the experience of migration. This ambivalence is resolved through developing a reflexive refashioning of the self, combining (in their case) the values and norms of Polish and American cultural contexts. Thomas and Znanieki chart the emergence of inter-generational divides, with the older migrants retaining their attachment to values of 'home' and the younger migrants showing increasing individualism (and declining familial attachment), hedonism (and decline in restraints on sexual behaviour), instrumentalism and seeking success. Their emphasis on the importance of 'definition of the situation' resonates with Marx's stress that people make their own history but they do not make it as they please; they are constrained by the play of social forces they encounter at their scene of action. This is also picked up in Merton's insistence (1957: 195–206) that social actions need to be explained in terms of individual choices between socially structured alternatives. In this view the self is bounded by space and time and takes the values of the collective as an object of reflection to which they develop attitudes. This is entirely amenable to the idea of the hybrid or transnational self, which actually has a long history in sociology.

The Durkheimian theme of rights-based membership of complex differentiated social orders was developed in Talcott Parsons' later work, in which he developed the concept of 'societal community'. It is true that the notion of societal community presupposed the development of complex patterns of social relations within the framework of national borders. Parsons regarded the processes of adaptation, goal attainment, integration and latency as operating within self-closed societies, although these interact collectively and separately on multiple levels. He rather clumsily defines 'society' as follows: 'It is not essential to the concept of society that it should not be in any way empirically interdependent with other societies, but only that it should contain all the structural and functional fundamentals of an independently subsisting system' (Parsons 1979: 23). If you get the double negative then he is acknowledging that 'society' occupies a bounded space but is also part of an internationally interdependent web of societies. Further, a central theme in Parsons' mature sociology was that societies in the later twentieth century were increasingly internally pluralistic as a result of growing religious and ethnic diversity and specialization of the division of labour. While some contemporary sociologists bemoaned the loss of integrated communities of a (putative) past, Parsons stressed the development of a complex normative order in which common memberships of social orders could be detached from 'national' societal community and grounded in networks integrated through universalistic individual rights – optimistically looking towards strong, open, cosmopolitan and democratic social orders (Parsons 1979).

Nonetheless, it is true that the world of the twenty-first century is very different from that of classical or mid-twentieth-century sociology, even though the relevance of the classical tradition remains both powerful and problematic. It is powerful because the classics constitute a rich source of insights, concepts and analyses that can be deployed and reinterpreted to grasp current problems. But it is problematic because the social world of the classics is largely that of industrial, imperial and high-bourgeois European societies prior to the First World War. In particular, there is a growing hiatus between the civilizational approach that characterized Weber's work and contemporary globalization theories. The civilizational approach was highly influential in founding the school of comparative sociology as well as in Norbert Elias's theory of the civilizing process.[1] There was a tendency in this approach to view civilizations as complexes with symbolic frontiers and internal systems of institutional life, money, myths, language and so forth. As Mandalios (1996) points out these were never generally seen as 'iron walls' but as frontiers rather than borders, across which people, goods and ideas would flow. Mandalios (1996) further points out that prior to the globalization theories Nelson (1973) developed a theory of 'spatio-temporal revolution' that rendered the civilizational approach problematic in an age of the heightened pace, scope and impact of knowledge revolutions and modes of communication, control and transportation. Even so, we should not draw over-general contrasts between national and globalized sociology. There is a danger of assuming that globalization renders the globe a unitary space in ways that occlude the experiences of cultural communities in both core and marginalized regions whose identity and relation to the world is conditioned by disenchantment and exclusion.

Dependency and world systems

Drawing on Weberian and Parsonian sociology, modernization theories of the 1950s and 1960s posed global developmental issues and in sophisticated versions (e.g. Eisenstadt 1987) developed theories of the tradition/modernity transformation in a considerably more nuanced way than do many contemporary accounts (see pp. 58–60). However, modernization theories tended to conceive of relatively autonomous societies engaged in internally driven processes of social development. Global issues were addressed in sociology, particularly through theories of development and the global reproduction of global inequalities. The resurgence of Marxist and neo-Marxist theories in the 1970s addressed global social relations in various ways. 'The single most influential post-Marxist conceptual innovation for the analysis of development within the global system has been dependency theory,' says Sklair (2002: 32). Dependency theory, of which Gunder Frank was one of the best known exponents, conceived of the capitalist world as a system of inequalities reproduced though unequal trading terms between developed and Third World countries, transnational corporations extracting profits based on exploitation of labour and resources to elites in the developed metropolitan countries. This system was sustained by the military power of local elites backed by the US and its allies. Dependency prevented local capital accumulation (except in a few enclaves) and thus obstructed indigenous capitalist development. Dependency theorists were convinced that development was not possible within the global capitalist system, and some (e.g. Amin 1990) argued for 'delinking' the Third World from the metropolitan centre, although attempts to do this (such as the autarkic 'Burmese Way to Socialism' abandoned in 1990) have generally been unsuccessful in generating indigenous development.

A more immediate precursor to globalization theory was world systems theory. The premise of world systems theory is that the world order has a patterned unity in which it is possible to weight the relevance of different components of the system. It proposes that levels in the system are integrated and claims to show how the global system impacts on locales and the reciprocal effects of these on each other. World systems theory claims better (potential) explanatory power than modernization theory since neither its liberal nor Marxist varieties can explain why large regions of the world are not (fully) urbanized, proletarianized or commodified. In particular:

- The concept of 'modernity' was undifferentiated and lacked a focus on capitalism as distinctive and transitory phase of development.
- Dependency and world systems approaches broke with the temporal linearity of evolutionary modernization theories, arguing that the world system contemporaneously generates 'advanced' and 'underdeveloped' sectors.
- Where there are repetitive cycles within the system these are time-bound and the system is undergoing historical transformation. One example of these is the theory of the Kondratieff cycle (K-wave), which identifies a series of long waves of economic activity and is associated with major social upheavals.[2]
- There are no sequences of development, so one cannot say that Europe was the first industrialized region and others 'followed' because the whole system undergoes change at the same time but in different ways at different locations (Chase-Dunn 1983).
- There have been three phases in the development of the world system: (i) world empires such as Ancient Rome; (ii) European colonialism; (iii) post-colonial modern capitalist economies and nation states. Phases should be explicable in terms of a theoretical dynamic that refers to a logic of accumulation and competition among nation states. The theory should further explain differences in the mode of subsumption of peripheral economies to the core (e.g. smallholder production and latifundia).[3]

The international division of labour and dependence of non-capitalist social relations on exchange with capitalism define the spatial boundaries of the world system. The boundaries of the components (core, semi-periphery and periphery) are specified in spatial and logical terms with criteria that link characteristics of the system with outcomes. For example, during the 1980s there was extensive debate among sociologists and economists of development about the persistence of small-scale family farms in much of the developing world. Many Marxist and modernization theories predicted the disappearance of pre-capitalist forms of production with the global spread of transnational agribusiness and more efficient forms of cultivation. However, further research argued that, on the contrary, capitalism encouraged the survival of small-scale agriculture in parts of the world (e.g. Currie and Ray 1986), because global capitalism 'fossilizes and insulates pre-capitalist modes' (Sklair 1991). Thus global capitalism is not universally modernizing but preserves pre-capitalist forms where firms can harness cheaper inputs (such as family labour) by doing so (this is discussed in detail in Chapter 5).

Although world systems theory is not an integrated set of theoretical propositions, it offers an analysis of social change that is sensitive to the global dynamics of capitalism. However, world systems approaches were weakened by a number of developments. First, as for dependency theory, there was the emergence during the 1970s and 1980s of the newly industrialized countries of Singapore, Taiwan, South Korea and Malaysia, whose success in breaking through dependent development appeared to strengthen the model of capitalist rather than socialist development. This further challenged the claim of dependency and world systems theorists that entry into the developed core region of the world was virtually impossible. Second, the theory was heavily economistic (that is, it reduced social life to economic factors) and was eclipsed by more culturally inflected theories of globalization and postmodernity. Third, despite being global in focus, world systems approaches remained within a territorial concept of the social contained within nation states, which were understood to form the relatively unalterable three-tier hierarchy of core, semi-periphery and periphery. Sklair (2002: 42) concludes that there is 'no distinctively global dimension in the world-systems model: it appears locked into the inter-national focus that it has always emphasized'.

Thus far, then, I have argued that various approaches within classical and later sociology were able to theorize world society and to identify levels of sociality that extended within and beyond the container of the nation state. This is a theme to which the following discussion will return from time to time. I have also identified world systems theory as a more direct precursor of globalization theory although I have identified some ways in which this approach is limited. The following section will identify some key debates in globalization theory that will be developed in subsequent chapters.

GLOBALIZATION DEBATES

This section will pose and briefly discuss six key issues in globalization debates. First, one of the central issues around globalization is whether it is happening at all and, second, even if it is, whether it amounts to anything new. Third, there is the question of whether globalization is an emergent process giving rise to social changes in its own right, or whether it is the outcome of other economic, political or cultural processes. Fourth, does globalization generate increasing homogeneity (such as the global spread of consumption styles and brands) or increasing heterogeneity of cultural, economic and political systems? Fifth, what implications does it have for nation states? Are these being hollowed out and made redundant as relevant levels of operation move 'upwards' to international bodies and processes and 'down' to local and regional levels? Finally, even if globalization was operative during the last two decades of the twentieth century, is it now in decline or in reverse drive as global conflicts and economic insecurity prompt disengagement from global networks?

First, one of the central issues around globalization is whether it is happening. There is considerable disagreement as to the pace and significance of globalization. Some theorists – often referred to as 'hyper-globalization' (or 'radical') theorists – predict a 'borderless world' and other utopias of global homogeneity, while sceptics question whether it is happening at all. So-called 'hyper-globalists' suggest that globalization is leading towards an end state in which the whole earth will be criss-crossed by global processes to the extent that individual places will lose significance and there will be a single global society. This will be a space in which disembedded production and consumption chains, placeless capital, homeless subjects, fluid global networks will by-pass and reconfigure locales. For the strong globalization thesis, all socialites are formed within a context of global flows, including resistance to globalization itself (Robertson 1992).[4]

Critics of globalization differ in their approaches. Some argue that such processes are occurring but regard them as undesirable, perhaps representing contemporary forms of imperialism, which are open to resistance (e.g. Petras and Veltmeyer 2001). Others are sceptical that the process is occurring at all and regard the core claims of globalization theory as unfounded. For example, Hirst and Thompson (1996) argue that in the late twentieth century the economy returned to an international mode that it attained between 1870 and 1914 but that remained grounded in national and regional economic and political economic functions. Between 1890 and 1914 trade and investment flows were higher than at present, borders were more open and there were higher levels of transnational migration. Thus they claim that the globalization thesis is overstated and the processes it describes are not unprecedented. There are few truly global transnational corporations (TNCs) but rather nationally based corporations at the centre of networks of subsidiaries. The idea of 'footloose capital' is exaggerated since foreign direct investment (FDI) only contributed to 5.2 per cent of the world's gross fixed capital in 1995 while domestic national savings remain crucial as a source of capital (Thompson 1999). On the other hand, Figure 1.1 shows the very rapid growth in FDI in the later twentieth century, albeit mostly within the developed world, a point made by Figstein (2001) who argues that the bulk of foreign trade and FDI occurs within the triad of North America, the European Union (EU) and Japan, as the world divides into regional trading blocs such as the North American Free Trade Area (NAFTA), the EU and Association of Southeast Asian Nations (ASEAN). Rycroft (2002) points out that by 1994 international trade, as a percentage of gross national product (GNP), had not matched 1913 levels for many countries including the Netherlands, the UK and Japan. On the other hand, world trade as a share of value added[5] had increased and showed that the world economy was more highly integrated than at any other time in the twentieth century. Weiss (1998) argues that although there was internationalization in the later twentieth century there is little evidence of genuinely *global* integration, while the nation state remains the main institution through which economies are organized. Others regard globalization as conceptual imperialism that projects American concerns and viewpoints worldwide, thereby facilitating the very process of globalization (Bourdieu and Wacquant 1999).

One of the counter-arguments to these views is that the critics themselves exaggerate the globalization thesis. The globalization thesis does not claim that the global economy encompasses the earth; it claims only that certain segments locked into particular commodity chains do (Kobrin 1998). Earlier alleged forms of 'globalization' were quite different in scope and intensity from the present. The international economy of the nineteenth century involved discrete links between mutually exclusive, geographically separate national markets whereas twentieth-century globalization *fuses* national markets transnationally (Guillén 2001). Sceptics focus on economic and financial aspects of globalization while evidence exists for extensive political and cultural globalization, some of which

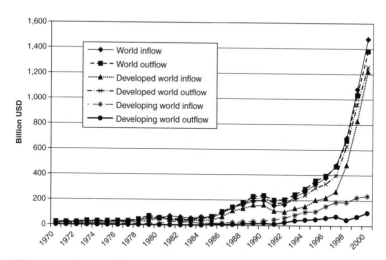

Figure 1.1   Foreign direct investment, inflows and outflows, by region 1970–2001

Source: UNCTAD (United Nations Conference on Trade and Development) 2003: 266–68

has already been referred to and includes 'time–space distanciation', digitalization of communications, facilitating instantaneous inter-action in virtual space, global media and consciousness, global risks, and the flows of people, ideas and commodities across borders.

The second issue here is that even if the processes described as 'globalization' are 'real', do they amount to anything new? Some argue that the antecedents of globalization can be found in the past, sometimes the distant past, where the term can refer to almost any form of international interconnection. Thus early globalization can be located at various points. Following Martin Bernal (1989), ancient Greek civilization developed from a blend of local, Indo-European, Egyptian and Phoenician influences and the ancient Greek notion of *oikoumenê* conceived of the total habitable world as a single realm. Janet Abu-Lughod (1989) describes a 'world system' of the thirteenth century that extended from Flanders to China. A global imagination inspired voyagers in the fifteenth and sixteenth centuries to under-take the first circumnavigations of the earth. On the other hand, Giddens (1990: 63) argues that modernity is 'inherently' globalizing since the two symbolic tokens that facilitate complex highly mediated interactions (money and expert systems) also distantiate time and space. He says, 'The globalizing tendencies of modernity, so apparent in the present day, should be understood in these terms. Modernity globalizes insofar as space is separated from place and reintegrated with the empty dimension of time' (Giddens 1994b: xii).[6] However, Martin Albrow insists that globalization is not a culmination of prior social development, such as the trajectory of modernity, but represents a novel transformation. Modernity was a project of rationalization through the state and the market while globalization represents the boundlessness of culture and promotes endless renewability and cultural diversification. Viewed over the past 200 years it is not obvious that modernity is 'inherently global-izing' but that there have been phases of globalization followed by ones of de-globalization. So, there are three views on globalization: as already mature in human history; as an outcome of modernity; and as a departure even from the recent past. Guillén then concludes:

> there is no agreement as to whether it was with Magellan and Mercator, James Watt and Captain Cook, Keynes and White, Nixon and Kissinger,

> or Thatcher and Reagan that globalization started or, to be more precise, that the narrative of globalization ought to begin.
>
> (Guillén 2001)

To specify the distinctiveness of the concept and reduce confusion as to quite what it refers to, Scholte (2002) identifies several 'cul-de-sacs' that refer to well-established processes that, he says, are *not* specific to globalization. These are political internationalization (the growth of cross-border economic and political activity), economic liberalization ('free market' strategies), Westernization (e.g. the global spread of brands and companies such as McDonald's and CNN) and universalization (global convergence around cultural and institutional forms). These are important in their own right but if we define globalization in these terms, we will 'merely rehash old knowledge'. What Scholte regards as genuinely novel with globalization is the emergence of transplanetory relations and supraterritoriality. The rise of supraterritoriality, he argues, is recent and appears with global jet travel, transworld migrants and economic remittances, satellite communications, transplanetory TV, intercontinental production chains and anthropogenic ecological changes (e.g. global warming). This, of course, is another list of often-reiterated empirical attributes. But what is most important here is that the communications these facilitate do not happen in a specific space nor do they simply link disparate spaces but they presuppose global social relations. 'These global connections,' he says 'have qualities of transworld simultaneity . . . and instantaneity' that brings greater complexity to culture, ecology, economics and politics. These are 'new spaces' where cultures clash and mix both across and within nations (Kennedy and Roudomentof 2001). Yet these in turn presuppose prior offline social knowledge and relations and people's ability to integrate them into their daily lives.

The question of novelty has important theoretical implications because it is central to the question of whether globalization can be accounted for within existing sociological frameworks or requires a complete rethinking of sociology. If global interconnections are the outcome of processes of *longue durée* or if they are the culmination of the modernization process, then the sociological concepts already available should provide the basis for theorizing globalization.

If globalization represents such a qualitative break with the past that pre-existing frameworks have become obsolete, then we need a new sociology to provide the theoretical and conceptual tools to understand it. The view taken here is that globalization is the outcome of recent social and cultural changes that create qualitatively different forms of sociality than in the past but that are organically accomplished in everyday life. By 'recent' I mean particularly the last two decades of the twentieth century, although it is important to locate historically the genesis of these changes.

The third issue here is whether globalization is an emergent process with effects, as for example in the claim that the 'declining viability of the notion that cultures possess a degree of coherence sufficient to guarantee stable identities is due to globalisation' (Kennedy 2002)? Globalization here is an attributed agency – a process that can achieve effects as opposed to seeing it as the outcome of an agglomeration of other processes, such as economic, political or cultural processes. Rosenberg (2005) argues that globalization is a descriptive 'geographical term' that requires another theory of social processes (such as 'capitalism') to explain what is being globalized and where. To attribute to globalization explanatory power is a 'reification of space'. So, is globalization the *explanans* (that which explains) or the *explanandum* (that which is explained)? This may sound like a compromise but in some ways it is both, in that globalization is the outcome of deep cross-border integration, networked interconnectedness in combination with local structures and conditions. But at the same time it could be an outcome of these processes and anyway acts back on its initial conditions, transforming and developing them in various ways.

The fourth issue here is whether globalization generates increasing homogeneity (such as the global spread of consumption styles and brands) or increasing heterogeneity of cultural, economic and political systems. Globalization entails a global culture of consumption and lifestyle, at least among urban elites, and cityscapes become superficially similar in terms of built environment. The city becomes a trans-cultural space shared by a mixture of cultures in various relations of ethnic segregation, integration, assimilation and cultural hybridization. This creates dynamic cultures of technologically supported mobility and, occasionally, conflict. English is the language of global communication and global culture, and one could argue that what is not communicated in English is more local than global. However, there are two issues here. First, global processes are instantiated differently in different places and the specific combinations of global and local will generate different outcomes, so globalism creates patterns of combined and uneven development – new patterns of inclusion and exclusion that harness and select in some local cultural forms while marginalizing others. Second, it engenders resistance and the reflexive appropriation of local cultures and traditions. Thus, for example, English may exercise cultural hegemony in global media but is subject to challenge as a global language since Spanish, Russian, Arabic, French, Kiswahili and Chinese have become the shared languages of certain transnational communities located in specific regions of the world, namely, Latin America, the CIS (Commonwealth of Independent States), the Arab world, sub-Saharan Africa, east Africa, and Southeast Asia, respectively (Guillén 2001).

These considerations relate to a further aspect of global convergence debates. Some accounts of globalization presuppose a globally pacified order within which the institutional framework of the liberal democratic state is replicated. There are accounts of global civil society, global ethics and governance, international law, global social policy and financial regulation (e.g. Eade and O'Byrne 2005). Some argue that a global civil society is developing based on recognition of inalienable human rights detached from membership of specific states (e.g. Turner 1993). Global social movements establish new networks, resources and social capital, providing the infrastructure for global democratization (Smith 1998) and a 'cosmopolitan democracy' (Beck 2000b). But such a view of global order is more an aspiration than an actuality since the framework of international law is weak, many global corporations have the ability to evade regulation, nations have the power of opt out of international agreements such as the Kyoto Treaty, and violent conflicts extend into the home of the developed world. Mennell (1995) further points out that global interdependence and increasing proximity are also likely to produce increased friction, tension and violence as insecurity and fears release aggression and violence. This in turn raises the further question of whether pacified and civil relations are necessary in order to speak of globalization as a form of sociality.

The fifth issue concerns the implications that globalization has for nation states. Are they being hollowed out and made redundant as relevant levels of operation move 'upwards' to international bodies and processes and 'down' to local and regional levels? States are, in important respects, agents of globalization although their function and nature change in the process. States are central to the enactment of treaties and policies that sustain global integration and are key actors in processes of privatization (crucial to global capital flows), border controls (to migration flows), treaty accession (to transnational political flows), establishing regulatory regimes (for investment flows) and welfare reforms (to market convergence). In thinking about the state and globalization we should not be too preoccupied by the *nation* state in the literal form of a territorially bounded state that corresponds to a territorial unit inhabited by nationally homogenous people. This is a very specific, quite rare and recent form of the state. The idea of state sovereignty within a territorially defined area was given shape by the Treaty of Westphalia (1648), but the idea of a nationally and ethnically homogenous state has more recent origins in nineteenth-century nationalism, and only emerged fully formed after the Second World War when the Potsdam Conference[7] of victorious allies drew a new map of Europe made up of national peoples. This process entailed extensive re-drawing of borders and transfer of populations – such as the forcible transfer of 12 million Germans from eastern and central Europe into a newly constituted German state.[8] Even so, for much of the twentieth century political forms that claimed legitimacy from non-national forms of loyalty dominated the world:

- constitutional patriotism, where allegiance is to the republic, the flag and citizenship in the context of a multi-ethnic and multi-national community. The US would be a prime example of this form of the state in which there is, in addition, strong emphasis on privacy and localism and hence rights devolved to local institutions (Turner 1990 and 1993);
- the British Empire, which was a national project on one level but was legitimated in terms of the idea of 'Empire' – loyalty to an idea

of a global community of peoples loyal to the British Crown rather than to Britain per se[9] – an idea that continues in pale form in the British Commonwealth;
• the international union of socialist peoples founded by the USSR that claimed to be the beginning of a future world union based on proletarian internationalism and socialist principles rather than an ethnically or otherwise defined nation as such.

In other words, the *national* state is a highly historically specific form of organization, and even if it is in decline, this is not the same as the demise of the concept of the territorially based state altogether. States will continue to retain crucial characteristics if they are to exercise provenance within territorial areas – monopoly of the means of violence, claims to legitimacy based on shared heritage, internally enforced fiscal, educational and criminal justice regimes of regulation. Further, convergence operates on multiple dimensions and because a territory has undergone a high degree of economic integration into the global economy it does not follow automatically that there will be a similar degree of social or cultural convergence. Cultures may prove more sticky and recalcitrant than flows of capital, goods and technologies. Borders may be open (such as mainland land borders in the EU) but remain markers of cultural and linguistic difference. Further, states may here become particularly important in the management of contradictions and dysfunctions of globalization.

The sixth issue here is to look at the argument that although globalization was occurring during the last two decades of the twentieth century, it is now in decline or in reverse drive as global conflicts and economic insecurity prompt disengagement from global networks. Rosenberg (2005) argues that 'globalization today is yesterday's Zeitgeist' and that the 'global order' is fragmenting as concerns with national security override human rights. James (2002) argues that there may be lessons for the present in the collapse of 'nineteenth century globalization' that, in his view, happened in the 1930s. He cites three reasons for the global shift from free trade and migration to protection, subsidies and migration restrictions – weakness of international regulation, a backlash across the world that mobilized resentments of opponents of international free trade, and self-destruction through the 'Marxist-Keynesian theory of capitalist instability'.[10] This phase of globalization ended because of chronically disordered financial markets, repeated cascades of interrelated financial panics in the 1920s leading to the Great Depression. Political leaders then resorted to palliative efforts of state intervention, protection of national markets and budgetary deficits – there is a similar argument in O'Rourke and Williamson (2001). Nationalism supplanted international capitalism and growing autarky replaced internationalism. The 1930 Hawley-Smoot Tax in the US imposed import duties on 21,000 different goods at an average rate of 50 per cent. But for James a repetition of the collapse of globalization is possible, although not likely, because the essential ingredient for 1930s'-style economic nationalism is missing today: a respectable intellectual package of anti-globalist policy ideas and a successful national model, such as the Soviet Union or Hitler's Germany. Recent experiments in heterodoxy, such as the Mitterrand government's experiment with a French alternative to neo-liberal 'Reaganomics' from 1981 to 1983, have been short-lived.

On the other hand, Saul (2004) argues that 'globalism' as an ideology emerged in the 1970s, reached its heyday in the mid-1990s and is now in decline. By 1995 trade tariffs had fallen considerably, the WTO had been created, hundreds of trade agreements were in place, taxation had fallen, and privatization and deregulation were sweeping the world. But then in 1997 came the Asian financial crisis, which underlined an inherent instability of the system. Malaysia imposed capital controls, and the 1999 WTO conference in Seattle was the scene of huge anti-globalization demonstrations. Talks on the Multilateral Agreement on Investment[11] collapsed, indicating the increasing influence of developing countries working in alliance on the global arena. Globalization, Saul concludes, is now in retreat as neo-conservatives in the US turn away from neo-liberalism towards nationalism.

If Saul is right, then the 1930s' scenario described by James could be replicated in the 2000s. However, both writers understand globalization exclusively in economic rather than socio-cultural terms, a problem noted with others such as Hirst and Thompson. But even within this limited framework there are reasons for thinking that globalization is not about to end. Kobrin (2005) asks 'what

would the end of globalization in the twenty-first century be?'
A 1930s' retreat behind borders is difficult to envisage in an age
of irreversible technological interlinking between economies.
Comparing trade and investment data for 1914 with data for 1994
misses the point, he says: similarities in quantity mask fundamental
differences in the quality of interconnections. Earlier 'globalization'
was facilitated mostly through bilateral transactions between nations
locally producing raw materials and manufactured goods. But now
production itself has been internationalized through a complex web
of foreign direct investment in which over 60,000 multinationals
with close to 800,000 subsidiaries are responsible for 25 per cent
of world output. The line between domestic and international
economies is blurred since many industries are inherently global –
for example, no single market, including that of the US, would be
large enough to allow pharmaceutical firms to recover the costs of
developing a new drug, which could exceed $0.5 billion. Further,
a consequence of the digital revolution is that the global economy
is comprised of networks of technology, production and supplies
that lack a clear centre and national borders. Similarly, though
critical of the term 'globalization' Thompson (1999) also argues
that governments are not likely to allow the international economic system implode into a system of protectionist, inward looking and antagonistically poised blocs. However, while regarding
an end of globalization as unlikely, Kobrin does envisage two
possible outcomes apart from retreat into autarky: continuation
of globalization towards the emergence of a borderless world or
dysfunctional integration. The latter outcome would be marked
by increasing disputes among states and increasing opposition to
globalization from large segments of the population. This outcome
would result in differing modes and intensities of integration into
the global economy across the world.

THE END OF SOCIOLOGY AS WE KNOW IT?

Does globalization entail the end of the social and therefore of
sociology as we know it? The premise of this view is that globalization represents an entirely novel epoch in human history. Urry
(2003: 85) argues that there were simultaneous and partly contingent

transformations in 1990: Soviet communism collapsed; global news reporting took off with CNN (and then other networks) in the 1991 Gulf War; in the late 1980s the financial markets moved online and began the era of global e-trading; and the World Wide Web was launched. Similarly Kenichi Ohmae (2000) talks about the rise of the 'invisible continent' from 1985. This kind of list of attributes is becoming familiarly descriptive in the globalization literature and is largely untheorized.

However, a more systematically theorized challenge to conventional sociology is posed by Urry's 'complexity turn'. He argues that global complexity renders obsolete all classical and much contemporary social theory. 'Since the global is like nothing else, the social sciences have to start more or less from scratch' (Urry 2003: 95). As with Castells, networks are dynamic, open structures effecting communication spread across time and space in ways that other human actions otherwise will not be. However, Castells' network is expected to do too much theoretical work and networks are highly varied (Urry 2003: 20). As an alternative he develops a theoretical metaphor that appropriates complexity and chaos theory in natural systems. For Urry the 'attractor' was glocalization – relationships were drawn in and irreversibly remade.[12] For example, nationality ceased to be based on homogenous and mapped territory, as frontiers became permeable and cultural life interchangeable across the globe. Classical sociology's notion of accounting for a purified social order is past and should be 'relegated to the dustbin of history' (Urry 2003: 106). This issue was addressed above. It is not as clear as this suggests that sociology actually had a concept of a purified social order but even if bounded 'societies' are to go into the dustbin, maybe we can recycle the concept of 'the social' – the adjectival form of 'society' – to refer to all sites of interaction and the accomplishment of shared meaning upon which globalization depends.

Urry says: 'Sociology will not be able to sustain itself as a specific and coherent discourse focussed on the study of given, bounded or organized capitalist systems. It is irreversibly changed' (2003: 3). In a world in which millions of people move across national borders and in which there are uncountable flows of information – a world of inherent disorder in constant motion, terrifying in its uncertainty and disorder – complexity theory provides a metaphor for these processes. For Urry, Giddens' structure–agency 'duality' is better understood as a process of 'iteration' rather than 'recurrence' in which tiny local changes can generate unpredictable outcomes:

> [A]gents may conduct what appear to be the same actions, indeed involving a constant imitation of the actions of others. But because of the tiny modifications that occur in such actions, iteration can result in . . . transformations even in large-scale structures.
>
> (2003: 47)

For example the 'small' event of the collapse of the Berlin Wall in 1989 had the cataclysmic effect of 'overnight implosion of the Soviet system' (Urry 2003: 47).

It is true that social outcomes can be the result of complex iterative changes that produce systemic shifts. For example, I have argued that Weber's Protestant Ethic thesis can be viewed in this way. That an obscure dispute over predestination among Reformation sects could have such cataclysmic consequences as to trigger the growth of capitalism indicates an unpredictability of social outcomes 'slightly akin to what is now described as the "butterfly-effect"' (Ray 1999b: 174–80). However, Urry's metaphor takes no account of the social meanings intersubjectively communicated and interrupted. The social meanings attributed to predestination by Calvinists (rather than a complexity process working *sui generis*) were crucial, and as Weber's *General Economic History* (1984) indicates, worked in a context of *structural* processes of *longue durée*. Similarly the collapse of the Soviet Union did not occur 'overnight' but was the outcome of a long-term process of accumulating dysfunctions and structural crises of which the fall of the Berlin Wall was as much a symptom as a cause (Outhwaite and Ray 2005; Ray 1996).[13] Again, the social meanings attributed to these events by key actors interacted with this structural context. Gorbachev and some close allies had arguably 'talked up' the crisis in the Soviet Union in order to create a political context for change at the 27th Party Congress (1986), admittedly with unanticipated consequences. In his report to the Party Congress Gorbachev claimed that low growth rates due to excessive bureaucracy and conservatism had created a 'pre-crisis situation'. Combined with an increasingly open and critical approach to Soviet history a legitimation crisis began to ensue, the results of which are well known. This illustrates that crises do not necessarily emerge autonomously from systems contexts but are embedded in the construction and interpretation of communications. Outcomes are dependent on the social meanings people give to their situation and the ways in which social actions are mobilized, along with the unintended consequences of these and the reflexive procedures that follow.

At the same time powerful corporate actors are instrumental in enacting forms of exclusion and localization in the global system that perpetuate inequalities. While Urry refers to multiple interdependent organizations that are collectively performing 'the global' he pays little attention to multinationals in spheres other than the media. Perhaps, Spencer suggests, 'the sweatshops of Indonesia are altogether less fluid and cosmopolitan than images, exchanges of flows and football teams' (Spencer 2004). Further, one can say much of this without the heavily laboured theory of complexity and strange attractors. How do these work exactly? TNCs are organized through globally integrated networks to counter the 'extraordinary turbulent environment' in which they operate (Urry 2003: 57). But TNCs have global reach and extensively condition the flows of power in the periphery where, in combination with many local social, political and cultural structures, patterns of life and inequality are reproduced. Sociology needs to get a better grasp of how the everyday world of work, labour, communication and inequality is reproduced, with local and global impacts.

There are four further problems with the claim that sociology must begin again (a view shared by Beck and Lau 2005 and Giddens 1990: 142). First, it is epistemologically problematic because knowledge never begins anew but always and inevitably draws on existing accumulated ideas, data and frames of meaning. A new sociology would do this in practice even if in unacknowledged ways (and, anyway, it was argued above that sociology has a wide repertoire of frames for viewing increasingly cosmopolitan societies). Second, it is inadequately argued because the claim posits globalization as something new and therefore beyond sociology's capacity to understand it rather than showing systematically why existing approaches fail to explain contemporary processes. Third, it is ahistorical because globalization has historical origins and precursors that are amenable to sociological investigation, and to reconstruct sociology around the purportedly new age of globalization would exacerbate the current tendency to ignore the relevance of history for the present. Because somewhere has McDonald's and MTV and takes Amex does not mean it is exactly the same as everywhere else – and one differentiating factor here is the particular path of historical development followed. For example, the post-Cold War world in which globalization has been intensified has seen sporadic but violent nationalist conflicts that need to be understood in historical terms. Again, the diversity of emergent forms of capitalism and private property in postcommunist countries relate to local configurations of ownership and legal rights. Where property and other right-based forms of institutional life have weak historical presence (e.g. Russia) capitalism will tend to be organized through clientelism and informally rather than through open and fluid systems. This kind of institutional diversity can only be explained with reference to particular national contexts and trajectories. Fourth, the argument makes the mistake noted above of assuming that globalization is the *explanans* whereas if it is also the *explanandum*, then we need to refer back to social processes of the kind with which sociology is already familiar, such as class, structures, bureaucracies, capital, social solidarities and so forth.

EVERYDAY LIFE AND THE GLOBAL SELF

Having reviewed several theories of and debates around globalization, an outline of an approach to globalization and everyday life can now be sketched. Many globalization theorists suggest that a core feature of globalization is the movement of abstract systems such as Giddens' symbolic tokens that collapse, condense or distantiate time and space. On the other hand, it has been noted that in addition to these steering processes that act 'behind the backs' of knowledgeable social actors, globalization is also the accomplishment of multiple social actors and the ways in which they invest these processes with meaning. This will be developed in the following chapters. Globalization is further the outcome of multiple situated social relations through which people communicate in settings structured by power, social capital, locality, organically embedded cultural forms and so forth. David Ley (2004) makes the important point that with a few exceptions (e.g. Hannerz 1996) globalization theory is a discourse largely 'devoid of knowledgeable human agents', which he sees as an inherent consequence of the privileging of global political economy. This creates the impression that globalization is an inevitable destiny that is fixed and unalterable. Of course, this is the age-old problem in sociology between systemic and action centric approaches that has yet to be adequately resolved.

One approach to this issue is Habermas's distinction between system and lifeworld. 'System' refers to steering media such as money and power that are transmitted in highly abstract symbolic forms that mean they can be measured, stored and permit formalized action responses – for example, the way markets respond to price fluctuations or the performance of routine bureaucratic tasks. 'Lifeworld' refers to intersubjective linguistically mediated communications that deploy culturally specific values and beliefs, non-verbal understanding, ambiguity and background knowledge essential to the conduct of conversations (Habermas 1989: 328). This in part invokes Husserl's notion of a pre-reflective background consensus and Gadamer's 'infinity of the unsaid' (Gadamer 1975: 443–4). However extensively lifeworld background knowledge is explicated and subject to reflection it always draws upon reserves of cultural meaning that remain inaccessible to conscious reflection (Schutz and Luckmann 1974: 169). Michael Polanyi similarly made an influential distinction between tacit and codifiable knowledge. Unlike codified and easily transmissible knowledge (such as that in manuals and textbooks) tacit knowledge is based in the observation that 'we know more than we can tell' (Polanyi 1967: 4) since the meaning of words and knowledge of social practices are communicated through participation in a shared social context. This social background knowledge can be appropriated as a topic for reflection, but only piecemeal – one cannot call all our tacit knowledge into question at once.

This distinction is often accompanied by the claim that modern societies undergo a 'crisis of meaning' as modern pluralism undermines common-sense 'knowledge' and the world, society, life and

personal identity are called ever more into question. No interpretation, no range of possible actions can be accepted any longer as
the only true and unquestionably right one. Luckmann, for example,
claims that individuals are thus faced with the question:

> whether they should not have lived their lives in a completely different
> manner than they actually did. This is experienced on the one hand as a
> great liberation, as an opening of new horizons and possibilities of life,
> leading out of the confines of the old, unquestioned mode of existence.
> The same process is, however, often experienced as oppressive (often
> by the same people) – as a pressure on the individual to repeatedly make
> sense of the new and unfamiliar in their reality.
>
> (Luckmann 1996)

Some may relish this uncertainly while others may 'feel insecure and
lost in a confusing world full of possibilities'. Thus it is claimed,
that the range of taken-for-granted assumptions shrinks to a relatively small core, a process driven particularly by technological-
economic forces. Similarly, Habermas argues that the illegitimate
intrusion of system into lifeworld contexts, where systems of money
and power take over steering of communicative and ethical life gives
rise to resistances (for example social movements) and 'pathologies'
(see Ray 1993).

Globalized transactions presuppose extensive knowledge of the
social and change the ways in which social knowledge is deployed and
transmitted. Lifeworld and system are *not* simply or even primarily
a distinction between the local (lifeworld) and global (system),
because global communications can be guided by intersubjective
norms (for example, in email or chat-room communications where
the actors may be spatially disparate) while everyday interactions are
clearly mediated by money and power. But it is through an attempt
to conceptualize the processes that indirect systemic processes
and everyday life intersect. However, the distinction is open to question. Urry (2003: 123) claims that he has shown how 'systematic
non-linear relationships of global complexity . . . transcend most
conventional divides in social science', including that of system-
lifeworld. But this point of view is itself problematic in at least two
ways. First, it mistakes an analytical distinction (system-lifeworld)

for concrete sociality – that in social practice the two processes will operate together does not in itself mean that it is illegitimate to make a conceptual differentiation between them. A unitary theory will not begin to evaluate claims about the effects of systemic intrusion or the accomplishment of global sociality. Second, it is open to Ley's (2004) objection to much globalization theory of leaving out the active subjects and seeing the whole of social life only through (in this case, complexity) systems analysis. This point will be elaborated in the following chapters.

Nonetheless the system/lifeworld distinction is open to critique. Calhoun (1991) argues that human sociality is coordinated on multiple levels of internalized cultural norms, sanctions, oral traditions, communications technologies, bureaucracies and markets. Therefore the system-lifeworld distinction needs to be unpacked into several dimensions of directly interpersonal relations of face-to-face interaction, imagined personal connections (e.g. on television but also through tradition), the one-directional world of active relationships (e.g. surveillance) and system integration through impersonal steering media. Television is particularly important here because by simulating direct communication it creates a fantasy and an illusion of personal contact such that it has been claimed that people trust television more than print media because 'you could tell if people are lying' (Meyrowitz 1985). This is discussed further in Chapter 4.

Globalization has intensified the transition that occurred between pre-modern and modern societies. In the former, almost all forms of social organization depended on direct interpersonal relationships while modernity was the growth of more indirect relations of bureaucracies and markets. Even so, these distinctions should not be viewed as rigid. As Calhoun argues, 'behind the impersonal patterns of the market and the mediation of bureaucratic organizations . . . a chain of concrete interactions exists'. As Marx attempted to show through his critique of the fetishism of commodities, the apparent objectivity of social processes such as the market is an illusory form of social labour that takes on the appearance of a relation between things (1977: 436). Beneath the apparent autonomous life of things (or systems) there is the substratum of human action. The ways in which market processes are organically embedded in social and cultural action and values has been one of the central insights of sociology (e.g. Granovetter 1992). This is not just true of labour in Marx's sense but in the world of daily interaction, especially primary relations, where people actively invest social life with affectively charged meanings.

To what extent does globalization impact on these processes? Meaningful action clearly can spread across geographically distant places, the remote may be invested with memories of home, and both local and long-distance social relations may be integrated into the routines of daily life. But analysis of tacit knowledge in everyday life might point to some limitations to notions of 'frictionless space'. Everyday life is the site of reproduction of global relations and and the space where a recognizable social order is rendered meaningful through social practices. Social actors sustain globalization through patterns of interaction and construction of social orders even where these are enmeshed in networks whose nature and consequences will not be fully known. Extensive tacit knowledge and trust that social actions are meaningful are essential to enable transactions to occur at all but also to repair, as ethnomethodologists put it, breaches in communications. The more complex the interactions in which we engage over greater distance and variety, the more work needs to be done to maintain meaningful orders and the higher is our dependence on explicitly codifiable knowledge in maintaining normative and cognitive expectations. Using a credit card in an Internet transition, for example, is a form of mediatized interaction in that it is monetary, highly abstract and brings into play multiple financial, commercial, social and political systems. The normative expectation of success is tempered by awareness of the existence of credit card fraud and 'identity theft' so the e-consumer will develop detailed and systematic knowledge of Internet transactions and will probably know about various security options such as stored-value cards, smart cards (that include a processor not magnetic strip), digital cash (cash credits), e-wallets and encryption devices. The smart e-consumer also knows that they should use one card for all online transactions (to reduce the risks of fraud) and should never give out passwords or user ID information unless they are sure they know who they are dealing with. They should also keep a record of transactions and expect email confirmation of purchases and details of their order. Now there is a lot of explicit codified knowledge involved in these transactions that can be communicated independently of a specific social context, as I just have done.

However, in everyday interactions we also retain an extensive reliance on tacit knowledge, which is true, to an extent, of both proximate and long-distance interactions. We switch seamlessly from conversation in a coffee room to email exchange with someone who could be down the same corridor or thousands of miles away. This is not to say that the quality of these interactions is the same, however. Face-to-face interactions embedded in local settings generally have higher quality of tacit knowledge and there are questions about the extent to which tacit knowledge can be shared over long distances via impersonal forms of communication. Proximity, for example, seems to be an important factor in the speed of knowledge dissemination despite the existence of instantaneous electronic communications (Mattsson 2003). Gertler (2003) argues that one effect of globalization is that previously localized capacities become ubiquitous. But what is not ubiquitous is non-tradable non-codified knowledge that is a key determinant of geography and place and arises in 'doing' social interaction. It is grounded in shared norms, conventions, values expectations and routines arising from commonly experienced frameworks of institutions. Not all tacit knowledge is localized – one could be in email correspondence with someone one has never met but would share tacit knowledge of conventions of email use as well as wider knowledge about culture, expected behaviour, appropriate topics of conversation that would point towards aspects of globally extended culture and experience. However, it is rare that a body of tacit knowledge can be completely transformed into codified form without losing some of its original characteristics. Most forms of relevant knowledge are mixed in these respects – knowledge codification requires tacit knowledge in order to do it while the conversion between tacit to explicit knowledge also happens but unconsciously. The less proximate our interactions then the less easily they will be able to trade on tacit knowledge, although as globalized sociality takes shape so new forms of solitary relations can take shape. This will be explored in the next chapter.

CONCLUSION

This chapter began by posing the question of whether globalization renders 'society' an inappropriate unit of analysis. This is discussed further in the next chapter. But surely the central issue here is not only a matter of where the boundaries of 'society' might be drawn but also one of understanding the dynamics of social solidarity in cosmopolitan, globalized societies. If solidarity was once tied to shared cultural and value systems based on common 'nationality', this becomes less tenable in societies with multiple forms of membership and identity. One solution to this is the formation of rights-based solidarities as the foundation for pluralistic societies constituted by multiplicity of memberships – of religious, political, cultural, occupational and ethnic groups. As people are less bound together by common values or ways of life the importance of formal procedures (such as liberal democracy and guarantees of rights) have become crucial to the articulation of substantive differences. These changes have been described as 'rooted cosmopolitanism' (Tarrow 2003), that is, 'individuals and groups who are equally at home in their own societies, in other societies, and in transnational spaces'. With the unprecedented population mobility of the twentieth century and the emergence of global economies, media and communications, new forms of cultural hybridity and transnational identities have emerged in which many people have overlapping memberships of national, religious and ethnic communities. Cosmopolitanism becomes rooted in the fabric of modern societies, which calls for new strategies of regulation and integration.

2

GLOBALIZATION AND THE SOCIAL

Society is merely the name for a number of individuals, connected by interaction.

(Georg Simmel 1971: 10)

This chapter will focus on theories of globalization and social solidarity. It has been seen in Chapter 1 that according to some social theorists globalization transforms our understanding of 'the social' in ways unanticipated by earlier theory. Urry for example argues that in order to address globalization as an emergent reality, sociology must renounce outmoded conceptual systems (including the 'concept' of society) and develop new rules of method. A similar theme is present, if less dramatically, in theorists such as Giddens, Robertson, Beck and Held who have pointed to the far-reaching impact of globalization on understanding social interaction and institutions. This chapter will review some of these claims, with particular reference to Beck's theory of globalization, in order to argue for the continuing salience of 'the social'. In this chapter Beck will be taken as an example of a theorist who outlines in general terms the destructive power of globalization (Giddens' notion of the 'runaway world' would be another), arguing that it undermines existing forms of solidarity without obviously generating any new modes. In this sense he restates the core problem of classical sociology, which was how, if at all, the dynamic destructiveness of capitalism was consistent with the possibility of social cohesion and integration.

Social solidarity is the core problem in sociology and major theoretical schools have developed around the variety of available answers to this problem. This issue needs to be addressed again in relation to globalization. This is not to say that sociology should be concerned only with the 'problem of order'; nor should we assume that societies *are* necessarily ordered places. On the contrary, I think that there has been a widespread bias in sociology towards focusing on social peace rather than violence and disorder (with the exception of theorists such as Norbert Elias, Stephen Mennell and Thomas Scheff). It would be naive to suggest that social *harmony* is possible (or necessarily desirable), but it is nonetheless a central sociological question to address the bases and extent of social solidarity in the face of deep conflicts of interest, values, politics, class, identities and all the other lines of difference between people. It was suggested in the last chapter that sociology has regarded this as a problem that arises especially with the emergence of complex forms of modern social differentiation. Durkheim's analysis, despite its many limitations is an important statement of the problem, that is, what forms of solidarity are possible in a complex society based on high degrees of interdependence where common values and beliefs have been undermined? He rejected the view shared by Spencer and liberal political economists that functional integration generated through the market and division of labour would create social integration. Writing against the background of a political doctrine known as solidarism, which dominated French political thinking in the second half of the nineteenth century, Durkheim sought new forms of social solidarity based on reconciliation and moral mediation between capital and labour and market regulation.[1] Further, he did not regard the market as self-equilibrating but rather pointed to its dependence on supportive moral and institutional moorings, arguing that a contract 'is not sufficient unto itself, but is possible only thanks to a regulation of the contract which is originally social' (Durkheim 1984: 196). Developing an argument that resonated with later discussions of economy and society (e.g. Granovetter 1992), Durkheim saw economic forms and individual agreements as embedded in morally guided cultural and institutional arrangements. Society cannot therefore be reduced to the competitions and agreements of individuals since these can be sustained only through shared, regulatory moral frameworks. Contracts depend on trust, which is implicit in any agreement; thus, in the labour contract the parties agree not only to exchange labour for wages but also to uphold the agreement, the latter being implicit and presupposing the existence of pre-contractual solidarity. Altruism, not competition, is the fundamental basis of sociality. Moreover, affect mobilized through public rituals and symbolic representations are means by which the social bond is re-affirmed in non-instrumental ways.

Marx, in contrast, regarded capitalism as a transitory epoch in the historical movement towards communism. Its historical mission was to destroy all pre-capitalist, archaic and traditional forms of life but was itself in continual revolution and thus too dynamically unstable to construct a 'halo' comparable to the elaborate belief systems of the Middle Ages. This, indeed, would be its undoing. In his early writing on alienation he counterpoised the division, misery and objectification of capitalist society to a non-alienated communist future. Whereas in capitalism producers are separated from other producers, the products of their labour and indeed their very humanness (species being), a communist society will represent a return of humanity to its social being (Marx 1977: 89) and hence to solidaristic social relations impossible under capitalism. In *Capital* Marx does suggest that the division of labour creates mutual interdependencies that give rise to harmony: 'the co-operative character of the labour process is . . . a technical necessity dictated by the instrument of labour itself', i.e. the machine (1976: 365). But in due course, Marx and Engels assumed that the global triumph of the 'cash nexus' would hasten capitalism's demise by destroying all old solidarities while being incapable of creating new ones. The formation of working-class solidarity was clearly crucial for Marx and Engels, but they also acknowledged that class solidarity was not an inevitable outcome of people having class interests in common. As Crow (2002: 25) argues, this 'highlighted the need to explore what precisely solidarity is founded upon and what sustains it'. Durkheim similarly regarded nineteenth-century capitalism as 'anomic' – unstable and divided by conflict, lacking stable forms of cultural integration – but sought to identify the possible ways in which new integration might arise while recognizing that modern societies place a high value on individual autonomy (the 'cult of the individual'). But Durkheim further understood the affective nature of social bonds expressed through ritual and veneration for symbols even when these necessarily take the modern forms of declarations of human rights.[2]

This will be relevant in the following discussion when we examine contemporary theories of globalization that emphasize both the destructive and the individualizing power of modernity at the expense of social solidarity. Three views of social integration have been presented here. First, interdependencies arising from symbiosis in the division of labour give rise to cooperation and functional integration. Second, shared values and norms (rather than simple co-dependencies) create shared identities and solidarity. Third, procedural norms (such as universal human rights and democratic processes) coordinate action among people with substantive differences of values and belief. Procedural norms are central to Habermas's concept of social integration in post-traditional societies and provide an alternative to the 'crisis of meaning' view noted in the last chapter. Forms of solidarity link with concepts of trust and legitimate authority, the traditional focus of which has been the territorial state, where loyalty was be generated through traditions, social memories and public rituals as well as formal rational procedures. If globalization is undermining territorially based notions of the social, then there will be a corresponding decline or at least a restructuring of forms of social bonding. These issues will be considered in the following discussion, which will address ways in which a globalized world is accomplished in everyday life, where the focus will be on the importance of agency in the constitution of the global social.

BEYOND 'SOCIETY'?

There is a growing interdisciplinary consensus that a major consequence of globalization is the end of the 'social' in the sense of territorially bounded 'societies' that have previously been at the centre of sociological analysis. Urry invokes former British prime minister Margaret Thatcher's much publicized comment that 'there is no such thing as society'[3] to argue that 'Thatcher might have been right to claim that "there is no such thing as society" or at least the riposte from the sociological community was not fully justified' (Urry 2000). There is talk of a 'post-Westphalian' politics in which 'society' as the traditional object of sociology has disappeared or been transformed. There are many examples of the end of the nation state position, such as Ohmae's (1994) theory of the borderless world and rise of the region state in which the primary linkages in the global economy are regions not states since the former make better points of entry into local markets than the latter. A less optimistic view of this is found in Guéhenno's (1996) neo-Spenglerian prophecy that traditional precepts rooted in belief in a shared territory and destiny become obsolete and the power formerly claimed by the state is shifting to a new medium of influence and authority in an implacable but pervasive network of networks. Guéhenno further warns that postcommunist Europe with no eastern boundary will lose cohesion and internal bonds of identity – having no 'Other' against which to define itself, it will lose its self-identity.

A number of social theorists have, in recent years, aimed to replace an outmoded concept of the social based on a concept of territorial containment with a more fluid, globalized concept. The claim here is that emerging social relations take shape on multiple levels that transcend territorial borders – for example, global flows of capital and trade, commodities, production systems, cultural images, migration and conflicts and terrorism. Each of these in different ways challenges the received sociological idea of society as contained within national borders, which was allegedly shared by all classical sociologists and many since. In particular, it is claimed that international migration and transnational communities dissolve the idea of the culturally homogenous *nation* state by creating multiple linkages and allegiances (Spoonley 2000).[4]

Ulrich Beck, for example, says:

> With multidimensional globalization, it is not only a new set of connec-
> tions and cross-connections which comes into being. Much more far-
> reaching is the breakdown of our basic assumptions whereby societies
> and states have been conceived, organized and experienced as a *terri-*
> *torial unity separated from one another.* Globality means that the unity
> of national state and national society comes unstuck; new relations of

power and competition conflict and intersect, take shape between on the one hand, national states and actors, and on the other hand, transnational actors, identities social spaces, situations and processes.

(Beck 2000a: 21)

As we saw in Chapter 1 the 'container theory of society' presupposed state control of space through which the concept of the political is identified with the (nation) state. Classical sociology, it is claimed, shared a territorial definition of society that should be replaced by a concept of transnational social spaces – new social landscapes that combine places of departure and arrival (for example for diasporic migrant communities). We now live in a world of 'place polygamy' (2000a: 72) and globalization of biography through, for example, multicultural marriages and families. One's own life is no longer tied to a particular place, which is 'further reason why national sovereignty is being undermined and a nationally based sociology is becoming obsolete' (2000a: 74).

Similarly, Urry's argument rests on the claim that 'sociological discourse has . . . been premised upon "society" as its object of study' (2000a: 6) but with the demise of the nation state has now been surpassed. Urry acknowledges that there are various senses of 'society' in different sociological perspectives but claims that these formulations neglect 'how the notion of society connects to the system of nations and nation-states' (2000a: 7). Societies came to be understood as sovereign entities organizing the rights and duties of each societal member, while the spheres of economy, politics, culture etc. constitute territorially bounded 'social structure'. Again, for Scholte: 'Methodological territorialism lies at the heart of currently prevailing identities and society. Thus the vast majority of social and political geographers have conceived of the world in terms of bordered territorial units' (Scholte 2002). However, he does not claim that we have witnessed the end of territoriality per se, since production, governance, ecology and identities remain highly significant and borders still exert strong influences. Social space is *both* territorial and super-territorial, creating greater complexity than in earlier periods.

Beck writes of an 'epochal break' from the society-state concept such that concepts of nation and class are 'zombie categories' because 'they are dead but somehow go on living, making us blind to the realities of our lives' (Beck 2000b). This catchy phrase 'zombie categories' is often quoted but avoids the difficult task of working through what really has been transformed and what purchase existing analysis might still have on social life. I will argue that the constitution of the globalized social in everyday life requires more multi-dimensional forms of analysis.

GLOBALIZATION AS CREATIVE DESTRUCTION

Central to Beck's theory is the idea of the 'risk society' – a state in which (principally ecological) risks generated by industrial society rebound as a defensive attempt to transform hazards into calculable risks. The hazards of pre-industrial society (famines, plagues, natural disasters) were experienced as pre-given, whereas risk awareness and monitoring aims to render calculable what was incalculable and this in turn brings into play new forms of agency, choice, calculation and responsibility. Industrial societies were organized within national territorial spaces within which risks were managed in part collectively (for example, through welfare systems) and in part through public and private insurance. But risks today threaten irreparable global damage (such as a nuclear accident or global warming) that cannot be limited either individually or collectively and against which financial compensation is obsolete. Moreover global risks have arisen from processes of industrialization itself and entail a reflexive stance on progress, science and technology. For Beck, reflexive modernization denotes a new form of society that is contrasted with the 'simple modernization' of industrialism. Reflexive modernization opens 'the possibility of a creative (self-) destruction for the entire epoch of industrial society'. Changes throw established forms into crisis – towards a self-critical appropriation of traditions; the generation of egalitarian forms of solidarity and the acquisition of expertise in the independent shaping of one's life (Beck and Lau 2005). This undercuts 'its formations of class, stratum occupation, sex roles nuclear family, plant, business sectors and of course also the prerequisites and continuing forms of natural techno-economic progress' (Beck 1994: 2). Echoing Marx, Beck says that the dynamism of industrial society undercuts its own foundations, except that now it is the victories of capitalism that produce a new social form – not class struggle but 'modernization' dissolving the contours of industrial society (Beck 1994: 2). This is breaking a 'taboo' because the transition to another society is happening without revolution or political decisions through small measures with large cumulative effects.

Whether this is breaking a 'taboo', in the sense of our expectations based on previously experienced social change, is doubtful since, it could be argued, that is how most social transformation occurs – incrementally rather than through revolutions. Anyway, Beck's concept pulls together in a fairly undifferentiated way most contemporary developments under the banner of 'reflexive modernization', which encompasses 'nationalism, mass poverty, religious fundamentalism . . . economic crises, ecological crises, possibly wars and revolutions, not forgetting the states of emergency produced by great catastrophic accidents' (Beck 1994: 4) to which list he has subsequently added 'terrorism' (Beck 2003; Beck and Lau 2005). Indeed, ecological risks are central in his account and to his view that risks arise globally from unforeseen consequences of modernity's attempts to control nature. Thus what 'the early sociologists and large parts of current sociology understood as "decay", "anomie" and "crisis" within the frame of reference of first modernity is the dominant normality in the theoretical perspective of reflexive modernization' (Beck and Lau 2005). This is not to be approached only pessimistically, though, but seen as a 'providential gift for the universal self-reformation of a previously fatalistic industrial modernity' that can gain from them the impetus to assure viability in the future (Beck 1994: 51–2). Beck offers a vision of a new modernity of novel personal experimentation and cultural innovation, not least because new technologies themselves create new risks and ethical dilemmas – such as those that surround genetic engineering.

Beck claims that reflexive modernization involves individualization and the possibility of new politics based on demonopolization of expertise, open participation and decision making, public dialogue between agents and public and norms of self-legislation and self-obligation. The old nature-like structures and boundaries are seen to be fluid and insubstantial. Beck *et al.* develop a more systematic model of transition from:

> *a first modernity* that was largely synonymous with the nation-state to a *second modernity*, the shape of which is still being negotiated, [in which] modernization ends up stripping away the nation- and welfare state, which at one time supported it but later restrained it.
>
> (Beck *et al.* 2003)

Table 2.1 summarizes the main contrasts between 'first modern' and the 'second modernity'.

Table 2.1 First modern societies and second modernity

First modern societies	Second modernity
Nation states defined by territorial boundaries	Globalization undermines the nation state. Rise of supranational entities
Individualization bounded by collective life still rooted in pre-modern structures such as the sexual division of labour. Nuclear families	Erosion of collective life and more intense individualization Transformation of gender roles and sexuality as part of a 'denatura-lization' of social divisions. Flexible families
Work societies (for adult men) in which unemployment is so low it can be considered fictional	Flexible employment and consumption 'progressively independent of income'. Increased insecurity
Nature is conceived of as outside society and an object of exploitation for endless growth	Global ecological crisis and incorporation of 'nature' in 'society'
Belief in progress through rationality and instrumental control	Recognition of extra-scientific justification, debate through ad hoc institutional means of reaching a decision
Functional differentiation into sub-systems. Either/or logic	Dissolving fundamental distinctions and fluidity of boundaries. Both/and logic

Source: summarized from Beck *at al.* (2003)

Beck and Lau claim to provide the thesis with empirical foundation. But the contrast offered is essentially a familiar one between Fordist industrialism and post-Fordist informationalism:

> [The] 'high modernity' of industrial society was . . . characterized by a configuration of institutions that mutually confirmed and supported one another, such as the nation-state, the Fordist company, the nuclear family, the system of industrial relations, the welfare state and unquestioned science.
>
> (Beck and Lau 2005)

The either/or distinctions of the first modernity (knowledge *or* not knowledge, nature *or* society, the organization *or* the market) are replaced by hybridity (knowledge *and* not knowledge, nature *and* society, organization *and* the market, war *and* peace) and so forth. This is experienced as crisis of meaning – how are decisions to be made if it is no longer clear whether climate change is a human-made or a natural phenomenon? How do authorities deal with migrants who belong to several societies and cultures at the same time? Where are the boundaries of 'patchwork families' to be drawn? Radicalized individualization, they say, not only leads to the erosion of the nuclear family as a standard way of life but also exerts an impact on the increasing flexibility of conditions of work and on structures of social co-existence. Any evidence of the continuation of 'first modern' structures is explained in terms of 'boundary taboos' –attempts to recreate the old stable associations of the nation state, the family, class or a normal biography. Whether these attempts will succeed in the long term is hard to predict, as it depends on the interests that would be adversely or positively affected by a boundary shift, and on their potential to assert themselves strategically. This suggests a rather open-ended model of possible outcomes and seems to build in an 'escape clause' for dealing with any data that appears to contradict the putative trends associated with the 'second modernity'.

In summary, it is claimed that the impact of globalization and reflexive modernization is to weaken forms of cohesion around the nation state and dislocate the traditional flow of community. The flexibilization of work results in a decline of occupation-based solidarities and blocks attempts to form a new social contract. Thus 'the global does not lurk and threaten out there . . . it noisily fills the innermost space of our own lives' (Beck 2000a: 74). This combines with a decline in welfare-based solidarities and increasing geographic mobility, which have a detrimental effect on social capital. Residential mobility breaks up social networks and lessens social contacts between friends and family. Systems of money and expertise are disembedded from locales and structure interactions on a global scale. But important questions remain unanswered – how are new forms of sociality constructed? How is the tension between constraint (power) and reflexive individualization structured? To what extent do these observations apply globally and to what extent are they the reflection of a privileged developed world perspective?

While the trends Beck and others identify in general terms may be valid for some aspects of developed societies, there are problems with their level of generalization. Beck *et al.* (2003) concede that their model is Eurocentric and that the paths of non-European societies still have to be described, but this does not inhibit them from claiming this as a global trend. Further, several of the claims made in Table 2.1 (admittedly, this is my summary of their argument) are problematic in various ways, some of which will be briefly listed. Nation states continue to exist within a context of globalization (see more detailed discussion of this in Chapter 3) and individualization is still structured by collective identities to a considerable extent, often in nationalist and ethno-religious forms underpinned by collective memories and institutions. The transformation of gender roles has involved sustained mobilization of women as collective actors rather that the product of some quasi-evolutionary movement of reflexive modernization. Beck's thesis does not deal well with the social structuring of risk (Elliott 2003: 24ff.), and individualization is part and parcel of the global and local restructuring of capital. Further, it might be possible to find examples of dedifferentiation (the increasingly cultural inflection of economic action, for example), but modern societies remain dependent on complex systems of differentiation and specialization. Differentiation between and within social systems is a development crucial to reducing complexity and transforming risks. The disengagement of the state from economy in postcommunist societies, for example, has involved increased differentiation between polity, economy and public and private life. It is difficult to sustain the view that a 'second modernity' has 'dissolved' fundamental divisions, which are often reproduced within new patterns of work and family life. From a global standpoint the argument looks rather parochial, and outcomes of globalization are vastly more complex and differentiated than this simple conceptual schema suggests.

Even within the Western world, the empirical basis for the global trends identified is open to question. To take one example – reviewing employment trends in the UK, Doogan (2005) takes issue with the argument that the allegedly ubiquitous pursuit of flexible labour markets is said to have engendered a sense of precariousness in the word of work and undermined the notion of the career and heralded the end of 'jobs for life'. The 'traditional industries' in decline have latterly become associated with stable employment while new service industries in the ascendant are linked, in many accounts, with the flexible labour market and temporary, part-time and casual employment. Thus the individualization that attends the arrival of 'risk society' emerges from the meltdown of labour market structures, yet Doogan argues that 'the audacity of this vision is matched only by its implausibility'. Contrary to the anticipated decline in long-term employment, he shows that there has been a significant and widespread increase in long-term employment in the UK between 1992 and 1999: from 34.6 to 36.7 per cent for men and from 21.2 to 28.5 per cent for women (Doogan 2005). Some industries experiencing shrinkage, such as manufacturing and public administration, nonetheless saw an increase in rates of long-term employment for remaining employees. The rate of long-term employment in financial intermediaries increased from 31 to 37 per cent and in business services employment has increased by some 917,000 accompanied by large increases in long-term employment of 336,000, which raised the rate of long-term employment from 19 to 24 per cent. There is an association between skill level and length of service such that long-term employment is higher in skilled, managerial and professional groups and lower in unskilled manual and service occupations. Doogan concludes that despite these trends people do display increasing anxiety about employment security, which he explains in terms of 'manufactured uncertainty' that accompanies the introduction of market forces in the public sector, which is more significant than the impact of technological change or the knowledge economy. But this insecurity is best understood in its institutional and ideological contexts as the greater exposure of the state sector to market forces, corporate restructuring in the private sector in terms of mergers, acquisitions and sell-offs and the diminution of social protection systems. The implication of this is that the employment related trends identified by Beck and others as global phenomena are highly locally varied and the result more of ideological and cultural shifts than fundamental structural transformations. This further points to the importance of agency and organizational strategies in managing global transformations.

POST-TRADITIONAL MODERNITY?

For Giddens, reflexive modernization is again essentially destructive of past forms of sociality and especially our relationship with 'tradition'. The decline of 'tradition', one can say, forces us from a naturalistic attitude (in Schutzian terms) to a reflexive one where, as Habermas says, people are thrown onto their own resources to accomplish 'risky self-steering by means of abstract ego-identity' (1989: 146). With the decline of traditional and fixed forms of identity there appear more fluid or 'plastic' forms of individuality (Beck and Beck-Gernsheim 2001). Reflexive modernization is a 'radicalizing of modernity – an evacuation, disinterring, and problematizing of tradition', which entails a new concept of the self. Tradition was to do with the control of time, which involved organizing the medium of collective memory (Giddens 1994a: 63–4). This was accomplished through ritual that enmeshed tradition in practices that had, however, to be interpreted by guardians, who possessed 'formulaic truth' (1994a: 65). Unlike modern 'experts', guardians' truths were not communicable to others and their authority derived from status in the traditional order rather than from expertise. Although the advent of modernity involved a clash with tradition, this confrontation was only partial. The capitalist spirit of accumulation was a new form of motivation but became an 'endless treadmill', an end in itself and a drive to repetition. It was 'tradition without traditionalism' (1994a: 70).

The new era of 'reflexive modernization' overcomes earlier partial modernization and brings into being a new self and relationship with tradition. Reflexive modernization entails the excavation of most traditional contexts of action, a process that is closely linked to both risk and globalization. For Giddens 'Few people anywhere in the world can any longer be unaware of the fact that their local activities are influenced, and sometimes even determined, by remote events or agencies' (1994a: 57). Similarly, individual actions – such as purchasing a particular item of clothing – affect the livelihood of someone living on the other side of the world and may contribute to ecological decay. Life becomes increasingly experimental and the global experiment of modernity intersects with the penetration of modern institutions into the tissue of day-to-day life. We are all caught in everyday experiments whose outcomes are open. This awareness and the institutional changes associated with it entail a process of 'detraditionalization' in which the reflexive project of the self depends upon a significant measure of emotional autonomy and new forms of intimacy. Freed from the constraints of collective habit, we have no choice but to choose, although Giddens concedes that many areas of life are governed by *decisions*, and who takes these and how are matters of *power* (1994a: 76). One could add that the crucial question then becomes how this tension between choice and constraint is structured in different socio-spatial locations. Globalization necessarily involves the disembedding of tradition because in a world where no one is 'outside', pre-existing traditions cannot avoid contact with others. Traditions may be discursively articulated and defended *only* through dialogue with others. In modern societies tradition is called into dialogue with alternatives – for example gender divisions were once segmented but now gendering of identities is placed in question. Giddens suggests that the alternative is fundamentalism, which he calls 'tradition in its traditional sense' (1994a: 100), which protects tradition against radical doubt through the assertion of formulaic truth without regard to consequences.

I will make only a few brief comments on this. First, a digression on the question of when was tradition: this is significant because there is currently some rather loose and ahistorical periodization in this literature. Giddens makes the distinction between modernity and tradition central to his thesis (as do many others, such as Bauman 2001), although the distinction is often stereotyped and generalized. The notion of 'tradition' needs more careful delineation and the simple dichotomy of traditional/modern lapses back into the over-generalized categories of modernization theory. While it may be true, as Habermas argues, that the decline of sacred forms of authority increases public reflection on norms and values, reflexive appropriation (and construction) of tradition long predates modernity. Indeed the very concepts of the traditional and modern have a long history, the Latin *modernus* from the fifth century referring to the Christian present as opposed to the Roman pagan past. The idea of unreflective traditional authority hardly fits with the religious wars and conflicts between temporal sovereignty and Rome that continued during the Middle Ages through to the Reformation. Eisenstadt (1973: 99) argues that even if 'tradition' was typographically different from modernity, there were different degrees to which traditions impeded modernity and anyway these require *enacting* rather than exercising blind constraints on people's action and beliefs. The idea that traditions are enacted, summoned up, rather than just 'being there', is important for understanding contemporary traditional revivals such as Islamicism. Thus loose and generalized concepts of 'tradition' and 'modernity' risk losing sight of the complexity and ambiguity of social orders.

Second, the claim that post-traditional subjects make lifestyle choices – while true – is hardly new (see, for example, Simmel's essay on 'Fashion'), and the idea of the reflexive feedback of unintended consequences was central to both Marx's theory of the crisis of capitalism and Weber's theory of its origin. Further, I have argued elsewhere (Ray 1999a) that Giddens' account of 'fundamentalism' is insufficient since this movement is itself detraditionalizing in many respects, and indeed emulates aspects of the modernist Jacobin revolutionary mode of organization. Global Islamist identities are post-traditional in that they involve the selective appropriation and hybridization of Islamic thought and Western politics – including fascism and anti-colonialism. A crucial question here is what factors structure the 'choices' between civilizational dialogue on the one hand and an assertion of moral and cultural absolutism on the other. In the event, reflexive modernization is vague about the drivers of the changes identified and provides next to nothing by way of empirical support for the claims that they are occurring at all. It implies that there are inescapable trends brought by globalization that (like earlier modernization theories) is insensitive to the possibility that actors in the global system undermine 'traditional' relations and cultures in some places while preserving them in others. In Chapter 5, I argue that this is indeed what happens.

NEW MODES OF SOCIAL COHESION

The emphasis given to globalization by Beck and Giddens is not at issue here. When Beck (2002a), for example, writes of the permeability of national boundaries and the hybridization of local cultures and of the city as a 'grid of cross-boundary processes', he is depicting key global transformations. But social orders are rendered intelligible through everyday practices by which sociality is sustained. So what forms of post-national or globalized solidarities does Beck identify? On the one hand, there are generalized descriptions and normative projections of a global civil society, transnational state and cosmopolitan democracy. On the other, there is the idea of a 'world society . . . the horizon within which capital, culture, technology and politics merrily come together to roam *beyond* the regulatory power of the national state' (2000a: 107). But what actually emerges here is a depiction of a pre-social individual. If he is serious in his claim that modernity has emancipated people from all forms of social ties, then the globalized world takes a novel form of post-solidarity, which he does imply – the second modernity as an 'age of flows . . . disembedding without re-embedding' where individualism takes the new radical form of 'enforcing individualism and biographies full of risk and precarious freedom' (Beck 2001). The suggestion of social ties that might hold this together seems to take the following forms.

There are 'transnational social spaces' (Beck 2000a: 36) that cancel local associations of community contained within national concept of 'society' and are based on networks of informal supports and organizations in migrant neighbourhoods. These transnational communities are formed around religion, knowledge, lifestyles, kinship and political movements. There are in addition transnational structures of work, production, cooperation and financial flows across distances. We participate in these more generally through new contestations between cultures, supermarket foods, people, culinary hybrids etc. Again, in the latter point Beck shows a predilection for running together within one conceptual breath very different experiences – contestation between cultures can be a deadly serious business and is at any rate of more weight than buying imported supermarket goods.

There is no theory here of how these interactions are (or are not) sustained over time and space yet in order to develop a sociological understanding of globalization this is surely the central issue. He then (echoing Virillio) talks about something else entirely – the 'inner mobility of an individual's own life' (Beck 2001a: 75) such that it is possible to be *immobile* according to official registration statistics yet live a non-settled existence in several places at once. But these are quite different claims – actual mobility and transnationalism as opposed to static location in space from where one can communicate globally. They presuppose quite different forms of social life and solidarity.

Global processes require embedding in locales. Indeed, as Jessop (2000) argues, economic flows are global while social reproduction is always territorially embedded. This tension within globalization opens a way of addressing some of the uncertainties and confusions mentioned above. Capital flows globally in fast and sophisticated ways. The central issue is that while the economy operates on a global scale social reproduction takes place within definable territorial units – the household, cities, regions and the nation state (Perrons 2004: 239). Similarly, Jessop (2000) argues that capital flows into concrete moments where it is materialized in specific types of spatio-temporal locations, which 'justifies the analysis of comparative capitalisms and of their embedding in specific institutional and spatio-temporal complexes'. Capital remains dependent on fixed place-bound ensembles and configurations of technology, means of production, industrial organization and labour process combined. Post-Fordist economic restructuring in Western societies has created new dynamics of inclusion and exclusion. These arise in part from Veltz's (1996: 12) paradox: that capital depends upon increasing interdependence between the economic and extra-economic factors making for structural competitiveness. This generates new con-tradictions that affect the spatial and temporal organization of accumulation. Temporally, there is a contradiction between short-term economic calculation (especially in financial flows) and the long-term dynamic of 'real competition' rooted in resources such as skills, trust, collective mastery of techniques and economies of agglomera-tion and size. The latter take years to create, stabilize and reproduce. Spatially, there is a contradiction between the economy considered as a pure space of flows and the economy as a territorially and socially embedded system of extra-economic as well as economic resources and competencies (Jessop 2000).

This sketches out the structural context within which every-day interactions are located. If we follow this line of argument, then place becomes a significant factor in economic competitiveness and connectivity, and in social life more widely. However, spatial locations are also a site at which the crises and failures of neo-liberalism are manifest. Social reproduction in locales becomes increasingly problematic, as life is insecure and individualized as Beck (2000a) argues. Capital defines costs in terms of lowest global costs, for example, through subcontracting. In contrast to employers of the previous industrial era, which frequently provided social wages and a focus for social network formation, few Information Age firms provide such benefits. Changes in the workplace also affect the family: as workers compete as economic actors, they are required to be flexible and to spend long hours on the job or engaged in activities not compatible with family life. These changes, and related changes in family structure, make it difficult for the family to fulfil its role as the primary institution facilitating the inter-generational transmission of knowledge. Ironically, this is occur-ring precisely at a time when national economic success will depend on knowledge transmission (Carnoy 2000: 143). Thus the problem of social cohesion becomes central in a world of chain networks, irregular working patterns, migration and mobility, and global sociality. This is an issue that is largely neglected by globalization theories that assume that somehow this complex social interaction just gets done or is accomplished through the existence of complex interdependencies (a position implicit, I think, in Urry 2003).

More than this, though, theories of reflexive individualization construct an excessively individualized subject. Giddens noted in passing that individualization is constrained by power, and the global and local spatio-complexes will constrain the kinds of social relations that emerge between people both virtually and in immediate environments. Not only this but many of these social ties will be *affective* ties of reciprocation and obligation that will operate on multiple levels. Thomas Scheff has critiqued the 'myth that the isolated individual is the only conceivable unit of human existence' (Scheff and Retzinger 1991: 15). This, indeed, entails the danger that social bonds become 'unmentionable and unthinkable secrets'. The basis of social solidarity then is 'attunement' or mutual understanding grounded in secure identities and shared pride rather than denied shame. Reflexive individualization depicts an asocial world, in which social bonds and the affective processes sustaining them become unacknowledged. By-passed shame for Scheff is the source of alienation and violence. This threatens the bonds themselves and generates what Habermas calls 'pathologies' where people seek pseudo-bonds in nations and sects that create a semblance of community. If we follow Scheff's argument, then the global world of Beck is one of by-passed shame and unacknowledged bonds that risk the search for fantasy communities based on humiliated fury and murderous rage. This view is probably an exaggeration but one might say that what Beck has inadvertently depicted is an alienated state of everyday life.

Transnational social networks and affective bonds

The movement of people across space requires stretching the social bonds and the sustaining of meaningful connections on multiple levels. In addition to sociality that is based in spatial proximity, Hess (2004) identifies various 'non-local forms of embeddedness' where people are connected by culture and networks. These may be both territorially localized but also translocal networks of actors. David Ley (2004) argues that globalization is made by knowledgeable actors and subjects, yet their voices are strangely absent in the inevitability of destiny that appears to arise 'before the global space of flows, [which is] an interpretation that has been internalised all too often by policymakers and politicians in their pursuit of the place marketing strategies of business elites' (Ley 2004). Emotional sites may be in geographically distant places so people live with 'polycentredness' that requires multiple site ethnographies.

Transnational social bonds are located in places; they have situatedness somewhere. The global is also local, and in fact it is *only* local in that it is always an abstraction from the experiencing self attempting to make sense of myriad relations of information, imagery, culture, networks and effects within which lives are enmeshed. At the same time our knowledge of the world can be highly localized – Ley uses Tom Wolf's *Bonfire of the Vanities* to illustrate how a global individual such as Sherman McCoy may be at home in Wall Street and international locations, while simultaneously finding the backyard of the Bronx a fearful world that he scarcely understands, the consequences of which he is ill-prepared for. This contrast of excess and poverty epitomizes the situation of the global bourgeois lifestyle in which social connections are built around globalized work, bars and 'astronaut families'. However, the extension of social connections across space is dependent on sustained emotional and financial bonds. Further, the nature of these relationships is structured by particular patterns of culture and economy.

Research on 'astronaut families' illustrates this. The term 'astronaut families' was coined by the Hong Kong mass media to describe contemporary dispersed, middle-class, nuclear families (Ho and Farmer 1994). Astronaut families often begin with one spouse and the children settling in a host country while the other spouse, usually the husband, continues with business in Hong Kong, periodically shuttling between the two places. An associated concept, 'parachute kids', refers to children left in the new host country without one or both of their parents. Some work on this developed a consensus that this spatial detachment was psychologically and socially damaging. Initially temporary, the 'astronaut family' arrangement is one that can over time place strain on families and marital relationships – especially for women in the country of migration who report homesickness, frustration, boredom, and depression (Aye 2001). But other research suggests that the experience is affected by the circumstances of migration and the extent to which astronaut family members become linked with local social networks.

Spatial ruptures need not signal family disintegration and may reflect a social reconfiguration that enables family members to maintain a sense of multiple and multi-localized belonging (Herrera-Lima 2001). The migration of economically active members of the family unit might be an effective strategy for diversifying income sources by placing family members in different labour markets. Multi-local transnational families cannot simply be regarded as irregularities destined to result in family collapse or as necessarily temporary arrangements. Landolt and Da (2005) compare the experiences of migrants from San Salvador to the US and from China to Australia and suggest that people are positioned within interconnected power hierarchies that confer varying degrees of advantage and disadvantage through 'power geometry', which refers to the types and degrees of agency people exert, given their social location. Migrants from China were able to draw on resources in social networks, and their migration was often planned, documented, regulated and enveloped by a discourse of Chinese patriotism and national pride. But in the Salvadoran case, immigration was born of necessity – survival during the civil war and, in the post-war era, the need to supplement the family income to ensure livelihood. Movement across borders and the search for work and long-term settlement were unregulated, precarious and undocumented and therefore fraught with risk for individuals and their families. While the Salvadoran state espouses a discourse of diasporic nationalism and takes strategic measures to regulate the situation of unauthorized Salvadorans living and working in the US, its initiatives are largely symbolic and do little to ensure migrant families' citizenship rights either at home or abroad. Again, studying Taiwanese migrants in Vancouver, Canada, Waters (2003) found that while for many migration was planned around 'flexible' citizenship and spatial separation of the family, these arrangements were highly dependent on women developing cultural capital and social networks in Vancouver – for example through English classes, voluntary associations or other local networks.

In some ways these studies highlight the importance of considering the new spatiality of family relations and family practices. The definition of the family as a network of spatially distant individuals breaks with the notion of the family as a geographically intact household. The circulation of family members within this transnational network prompts a redefinition of notions of home and away, as well as of presence and absence. Phone calls, emails, letters, remittances, care packages and air travel enable families to maintain relationships and make decisions together across borders, allowing migrant members of the family to remain present. Increasingly, the idea of being 'present' is tied not to face-to-face interactions between loved ones but rather to remittances and other kinds of resource contributions by migrants and non-migrant caregivers alike. However, there is not only one type of transnational family but rather a continuum of familial arrangements. Some families can shrink and successfully bridge long distances or their multi-local transnational practices may be ruptured, fragmented and even interrupted for substantial periods of time. In this way society and space are reconstituted from below (Ley 2004) through the social and emotional ties people sustain as they move across borders.

Global money and everyday life

The practices of everyday life underpin and interact with techno-social changes at a global level, and the growth of global exchanges does not necessarily undermine existing social divisions. Money is depicted by Habermas as a steering medium and by Giddens as a symbolic token driving the impersonal coordination of action and the distanciation of space and time. It should be noted, though, that although money facilitates coordination of action across space and time, it is not simply an impersonal medium but presupposes wider social processes of trust, legitimacy and social differentiation. There is a view of money in banking and economic policy as wholly a phenomenon of the market and of economic value, but money shapes and is shaped by social relations and cultural values. Money requires social networks of trust and especially so with e-money where lack of physicality has the important effect of becoming *information* for individuals and households (Zelizer 1994).[5] Simmel

(1990) described money as a 'profound cultural trend' towards greater symbolization – from substance (measured against the gold standard for example) to symbolic paper value, a process intensified by ICTs and ATMs (Singh 2004). The circulation of money pre-supposes temporal boundaries – the possibility of deferring decisions about satisfaction of needs while providing guarantees that they will be satisfied in time thus acquired. It then becomes possible to believe in a contingent future and conceive of the present as the moment when decisions are made about the future (Luhmann 1992: 36). If these boundaries disintegrate, with a collapse in the value of a currency, for example, the present moment becomes crucial, since money cannot then store value for use in the future. This leads to the de-differentiation of other social relations, such as a return to barter and dependence on face-to-face encounters. On the other hand, the more complex and abstract the money exchanges are, the greater the flexibility and potential for rapid global exchanges. Globalized financial systems required the digitalization of money but also a changed relationship between government and the economy.

The impact on everyday life of myriad changes brought about by globalization – and in particular global financial transactions – can be illustrated by contrasting it with the recent past. In July 1966 the British government announced a £50 per person limit on money taken out of the UK by travellers, in sterling or other currency. Sterling had been under pressure for the previous two weeks, as the UK's gold and foreign currency reserves were falling. A previous seven-month National Union of Seamen's strike had reduced the UK's exports, the balance of payments deficit was increasing, and this was expected to further exacerbate demand on foreign currency reserves (*The Times* 1966). The £50 limit was part of a package of measures of austerity designed to reduce domestic demand (especially for imported goods) and stem the flow of trading against the pound. This was an event in an era of national governmental control over the economy and flows of exchange that harked back to the tight currency regulations imposed following the end of the Second World War (see, for example, *The Times* 1951). That it was possible to introduce and strictly enforce this kind of restriction through a tightly controlled banking and exchange system reflected an era in which flows of money involved the physical movement of notes and

change and in which people going on foreign holidays (itself relatively new for many) did not have access to telegraphic forms of
transfer. Banks kept track of the physical movement of money by
private individuals across borders, and transactions were recorded
in passports and other paper records. The exchange control and its
policing were possible in a society prior to the explosion of credit
card ownership, e-money and the globalization of electronic financial exchanges that would escape many of the restrictive controls
of national governments. However, these controls were imposed
at a time when the financial facilities available in everyday life
were beginning to change. A month before the £50 limit was imposed Barclays Bank had launched the first UK credit card – the
Barclaycard credit scheme. This was to become a separate company, Barclaycard Company, in 1977 as the credit card became a
routine personal possession, and it was followed in the next decade
by the 'Big Bang' and by digital money (Pahl 1999).[6]

There is a close interaction between technologies of transfer
and (especially of resources) individualization and the limits of
governmentality. In 1970 the £50 limit was removed and the
country entered a new phase of extra-territorial financial transactions
with the UK's entry into the European Economic Community
(subsequently the EU) in January 1973. The 1979 Conservative
government, opening the way for an explosion in global currency
dealing, finally abolished exchange controls in the UK and in 1986
liberalized share dealing in the 'Big Bang'.[7] The everyday world
of credit cards, e-money, Internet transactions, and click and purchase commodities worldwide entails a considerable reduction in
governmental controls over what can be traded between individuals
across borders. One example of this is the global trade in unlicensed
pharmaceuticals and counterfeits (especially lifestyle drugs such as
Viagra) that has been valued at $32 billion per annum (Yar n.d.).
This trade is the unintended consequence of freedom of commodity
supply that escapes the regulation of national states and international bodies.

However, although the global circulation of e-money and un-
limited currency exchange created new regulatory problems, this
does not necessarily imply a weakened or de-regulating state. On
the contrary, the levels of trust that are involved in complex everyday

transactions and the principle of confidence in currency at all are dependent on state legitimacy. Exchange controls remained in place in many countries through the following decades – especially the state socialist and many developing countries where governments attempted (with decreasing success in the face of uncontrollable illicit markets in foreign currency) to retain economic and political autarky. The crisis of political legitimacy of socialist states and the collapse of governmental systems in the late 1980s meant that the illicit street market in foreign currencies had become largely open and increasingly tolerated to the point that many countries of central and eastern Europe offered 'tourist rates' that were several times the official published exchange rates, in an attempt to circumvent illegal trading and the consequent loss of state revenue. As these states entered terminal crisis, so confidence in local currencies collapsed and everyday transactions were routinely conducted in US dollars. During the early 1990s, Russia and other post-socialist countries re-stabilized local currencies, established more realistic exchange rates, liberalized currency exchanges and prohibited the use of US dollars for everyday transactions.[8] In other words, the *re-assertion* of state power and restoration of confidence in local currency was a partial condition for beginning to be integrated into the global economy. Effective states, societal trust, stable social differentiation and embeddedness of market transitions within cultural restraints are conditions that facilitate monetary globalization.

New flows and technologies clearly have an effect on social relations but are at the same time constrained and shaped within them. The £50 limit presupposed a world very different from that of the early twenty-first century, and the globalized world of e-money presupposes and facilitates new kinds of social solidarities and exclusions. But although Beck argues that in the second modernity traditional social divisions of class and gender are superseded, the evidence available suggests that these are actually often *reproduced* through digital transactions. There is evidence of increasing polarization between those who use new forms of money and those who do not. Those who are affluent and technologically confident may experience a 'thrill' of on-line banking and management of personal investment portfolio but these will also be people who are relatively privileged. For those with lower incomes credit cards may be a source of anxiety (making it difficult to budget), while others may be carefree about credit (Pahl 1999). Again, the use of e-money is structured by existing patterns of exclusion based on income, gender, employment and age. The credit rich are also often information rich and vice versa (Pahl 1999). At the same time cash remains important especially in working-class communities, and many customers still seek personal attention when arranging high-risk activities such as mortgages (Singh 2004).

The Financial Services Authority (2000) found marked social differentiation in the use of digital money and the creation of vicious circles. While only 7 per cent (1.5 million) of households in the UK have no mainstream financial products (such as credit cards, bank accounts, mortgages, insurance, pensions), 20 per cent (4.4 million) use them only marginally and have only one or two products. In the US (in 1998) 9.5 per cent of families (10 million) made no account-based transactions At the same time the withdrawal of physically based services in favour of online facilities often occurs in locales already adversely affected by deterioration in the built environment, limited economic growth and multiple social problems. The financial system discriminates between people and communities on the basis of risk and credit rating, so the financially excluded will also be geographically excluded and typically live in deprived neighbourhoods.

Although studies of money and globalization have focused on its economic significance there are important social dimensions. For example, money is not *socially* a universal commodity – rather, different kinds of money (e.g. wages, inheritance, bonuses, gambling winnings etc.) have different uses and significance for people (Singh 2004). Further, the growth of e-money is changing ways finances are controlled and managed within families. Money as information appearing as figures on a bank statement rather than cash in hand may facilitate more 'jointness' in family finances and change traditional arrangements (Pahl 1999; Singh 2004). On the other hand, it may give more control to whoever controls the flow of information in households, who will often be men. E-commerce does not float freely but is organically integrated into relations of social power and solidarity.

There are also important social dimensions to the phenomenon of global remittances, which facilitate global families and emotional ties (Singh 2004). Much research is on the economic impact of remittances, which are the second largest financial flow to developing counties after FDI – more than double the size of official finance and greater than the combined money given by the international foundations, NGOs and corporate philanthropy. There is a strong multiplier effect, with each $1 spending generating $2–$3 in local activity if spent on locally produced goods. But there are also significant social and emotional dimensions to remittances. For example, the Indian family is a single tax unit (which means there is a lack of clear enforceable rights for woman to marital property) governed by a code of familial care. Among transnational Indian communities, sending money home has considerable emotional and well as economic significance (Singh 2004). Globalization in this context has become 'domesticated', since the idea of self is rooted in a mix of homeland and identity through family, work and friends. The reference points and tensions are social as the cultural concept of the trans-generational transnational family contests with the new individualism among younger migrant communities.

CONCLUSIONS

Globalization is an accomplishment of everyday life involving human agents engaged in the active construction of global forms of sociality. A great deal of globalization literature based in political economy and abstract systems theory emphasizes the ways in which globalization undermines pre-existing social bonds but has relatively little to say about how social life 'gets done' in a globalized epoch. I do not want to dispute that the nature of the social has undergone fundamental change and that the idea of societies as territorially bounded entities is less appropriate now than it might have been, say, in the mid-twentieth century. As I have argued elsewhere (Ray 2002) the degree to which sociology ever actually *was* wedded to such a view is open to question. In particular classical sociology, it seems to me, was more centrally organized around concepts such as capitalism, civil society, industrialism, bureaucracy, world religions and so forth that are not particularly 'territorial' and anticipate post-national forms of society (a prediction that Marx made in the *Communist Manifesto*, probably to excess). Classical sociologists were generally aware, too, that apparently free-flowing and disembodied forms of exchange (especially the market) were grounded in embedded forms of social reproduction – see, for example, Marx's critique of the fetishism of commodities and Durkheim's attention to the non-contractual bases of contract. This, indeed, points to a difficulty with *some* versions of globalization theory that construe the process as disembedded and disembodied, offering no – or only sketchy – theories of how these global flows and processes are instantiated and sustained through situated interactions in specific places. Similarly, theories of individualization and reflexivity (associated particularly with Beck and Giddens) risk becoming pre-social since they lack any account of how everyday life is sustained or any critique of how the ideology of individualism might belie a reality of more complex social bonds and inter-dependencies. The individualization thesis is exaggerated and essentially asocial in its depiction of the self in 'second modernity'. Embedded and disembedded social relationships can be identified across the dimensions of both the local and global, which is sketched out diagrammatically in Figure 2.1. Socially affective bonds may be either local or global while the steering media of money and power have both local and global effects – in the former case, for example, where a factory relocates to lower wage costs and in the latter the operation of global finance markets. However, no real world social transactions will be entirely disembedded from the cultural constraints of face-to-face interactions nor will any situated interaction be divorced from systemic steering. Social coordination may be accomplished in various ways, in particular:

- symbiosis (system integration, which is a largely impersonal intermeshing of action responses), although this will always be situated spatio-temporally within contexts of shared values, in particular, fiduciary and institutional relations;
- institutional bonds of solidarity provided by common language, culture, collective memory and rituals – precisely the forms that Beck and others regard as having given way to cosmopolitanism;

- meaningful inter-subjective face-to-face encounters in shared space and direct communications that occur across space.

These issues will be pursued in relation to globalization and everyday life.

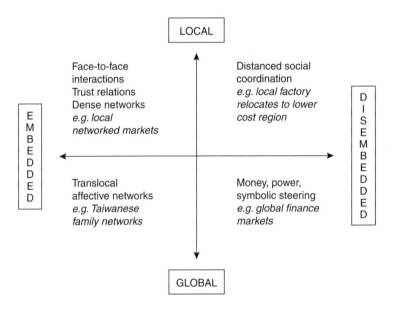

Figure 2.1   Dimensions of embeddedness

Source: the author

3

BEYOND THE
NATION STATE?

One of the central tasks to be resolved by all complex societies is the management of infinitely possible connections between people, the vast majority of whom remain anonymous to one another. The nation state as a territorially bounded community of people who identify with each other as common members of a 'national' civic culture has become one of the ways modern societies have organized a binary divide of inclusion/exclusion and established a space within which to organize social, cultural, communicative, administrative and economic life. Some nations achieved this more successfully than others, of course, and these organizational principles were never based on the exclusion of multiple exchanges (both peaceful and violent) with other nations. In the modern period there have always been possible bases of commonality that called into question loyalty to the nation state, such as those that appealed to solidarities across national borders – notably the international socialist movements of the nineteenth and twentieth centuries – and those that appealed to alternative national communities. The latter could aim at transcending existing divisions (e.g. pan-Arab nationalism) or ceding from an existing state as with Québécois nationalism. Nonetheless the nation state became one of the major forms of social solidarity in national communities and the aspiration of 'peoples' mobilized around sentiments of common ethnic, cultural, linguistic, religious or other belonging. We have seen how some globalization theorists suggest that nation states are imploding under the dual pulls of devolution of functions to local or sub-national levels and the transfer of sovereignty 'upwards' to international institutions and processes. According to this view, if there is a role left for the territorially based state, it is one of regulation of flows of capital, people, images commodities and risks across its borders. It is suggested that the global begins to replace the nation state as the 'decisive framework for social life' (Featherstone and Lash 1995: 2). But 'replace' in what sense? Mostly people continue to live within nationally bounded governmental systems, taxation regimes, educational and welfare systems, banking and finance regulations, planning and development regulations and so forth. They live in communities of shared language and history and participate in national public festivals and banal rituals, among which sporting allegiance, in particular, tends to play an important part.

This chapter reviews evidence for the changing role of capital and the state and suggests that national states remain key actors in the global economy and society, although alternative outcomes and forms of state capacity are clearly possible (Berger and Dore 1996; Dore 1996). It is true that enlargement of the EU raises questions about the extent to which regional-bloc integration is possible within state-like structures or, indeed, the emergence of post-state cosmopolitanism. Territoriality may not be essential to state-like structures such as the EU, which is constituted by its organizational ability rather than territorial boundaries, in that these are periodically revised by enlargement. However, it is unclear to what extent the European Union will continue along the path of closer integration of state structures since the proposed constitution has run aground.[1] Beck and Giddens suggest that this is attributable to uncertainty about globalization that has stimulated 'emotional return to the apparent safe haven of the nation' (Beck and Giddens 2005). But this might reflect a more fundamental problem with the European project – that 'Europe is an uncertain nation, born of confusion, with vague borders, a shifting geometry and subject to slippage, breaks and metamorphosis' (Morin 2002: 126).

This discussion will develop a differentiated model of state organization opposed to Beck and others' uniform model of globalized structures. It will further emphasize how the territorially based state has not rendered the notion of 'society' redundant but has, on the contrary, initiated projects of societal formation in response to consequences of global economic and social restructuring. It has been argued above that globalization creates diversity rather than homogeneity, so we would expect there to be a range of various modes of state formation within the global system. Further, a distinction needs to be made between the concept of a 'nation state' referring to a territorial entity encompassing a mostly nationally homogenous people and the territorial state per se that may encompass cosmopolitan populations with multiple national identities. National belonging was understood in the former sense at the Potsdam Conference that drew the map of post-Second World War Europe and may have in some respects become weaker in the early twenty-first century, although we should not ignore the continuing force of nationalism. But this does not necessarily mean that territorially based state forms become unimportant. States may remain territorially embedded and organize governance within bordered spaces yet appeal to loyalty less in terms of national identity and more in terms of what Habermas calls 'constitutional patriotism'. 'Multicultural societies,' he says, 'require a "politics of recognition" because the identity of each individual citizen is woven together with collective identities, and must be stabilized in a network of mutual recognition' (Habermas 2001: 74). For Habermas the individual's right to culture stems from the fact that every person has an overriding interest in personal identity and the solidarity of citizens is based less on 'substantial commonalities' of the nation as a community of shared descent and increasingly on the abstract foundation of 'constitutional patriotism'. This essentially means that (similarly to Parsons' notion of the societal community discussed in Chapter 1) people can be bound together by principles and values of cultural rights and mutual respect, that is, a territorial community that is also a post-national one.

GLOBALIZATION AND THE NATION STATE

A significant theme in globalization literature is that the nation state is declining, having become, as Daniel Bell famously put it, 'too small for the big problems of life and too big for small problems' (Bell

1987). Similarly, Castells (1997: 261) claims that globalization 'undermines the autonomy and decision-making power of the nation-state'. I will argue that although there are some grounds for this view it has been overstated (so to speak), and the territorial state remains a key actor in the global system and, crucially for the arguments in this book, a significant form of social solidarity. In this sense the position advanced is similar to what Held and McGrew describe as 'transformationist' – the view that the internationalization of government activity and transnationalization of society mean that the state has been reconfigured but not eliminated. They see the state as a 'space of flows' through which pass money, migrants, cultures, pollution, trade and investment etc. (McGrew 2004: 149). They stress the importance of political agents in shaping global governance, although this most often refers to NGOs and social movements. Sassen, similarly, argues that 'sovereignty and territory remain key features of the international system' although they have been reconstituted (1996b: 29). The argument here emphasizes that state actors themselves, or agencies and policy makers within them, also exercise crucial influence over the nature of globalization.

End of the nation state?

First, let us look at the arguments for the end of the nation state. One standard argument for the end or decline of the nation state is some version of the transition from national Fordist to post-Fordist modes of capital regulation. After the Second World War capitalism was organized within national territorial spaces that were regulated through a corporatist alliance of national capital, trade unions and state interventionism. The state was extensively engaged in management and often ownership of the economy (through nationalized industries and public utility monopolies)[2] and maintained a post-war class compromise between capital and labour through Keynesian interventionism, high progressive tax and social welfare. Post-war Fordist economies were predominantly based in industrial manufacturing, and national economies competed with each other in international markets for manufactured goods within which system the state provided protection (for example, through subsidies and import controls) for national companies. There was a broad political consensus between left (Labour and Social Democratic) and right (Conservative and Christian Democrat) political parties that the parameters of this system should be maintained. However, during the 1970s and 1980s global Fordism and the Keynesian Welfare State (KWS) underwent crisis as productivity levels fell, energy prices rose and the industrial basis of the economy declined in the midst of rapidly growing finance and service sectors. Following the collapse of fixed exchange rates with the end of the Bretton Woods agreement in 1971, international competition between different currencies increasingly structured the internal economic policies of the capitalist countries. Then world financial markets regulated the global trading system largely beyond the control of any one national government while pressures to be internationally competitive ended the political consensus over the KWS.

The effect of globalization on states' welfare expenditure is a matter of debate. Pierson (1998) argues that reduced welfare spend is not caused by globalization but by political choices made by conservative governments that have reduced the revenue base of the state and attacked organized labour. Fligstein (2001) and Gilpin (2000: 312–15) argue similarly. Garrett (2001) reviews data from 100 countries between 1985 and 1995 and argues that globalization is not accompanied by a reduction in government spending, concluding that there is no necessary trade-off between globalization and competitiveness. However, Beck insists that the KWS entailed a gendered division of labour between the male 'breadwinner' and the non-economically active wife – 'Anyone who wishes to restore the good old solidarity must turn back the wheel of modernization . . . push women out of the labour market' (Beck 1998: 34). But Ananiadis (2003) argues that globalization is not incompatible with plural welfare policies that address diversity of home and work lives, although this is not the same as a return to the KWS. In any event spending on welfare has increased in OECD (Organisation for Economic Co-operation and Development) countries in recent years. The average percentage of GDP (gross domestic product) spent on welfare in OECD countries between 1980 and 1992 increased from 8.6 to 10.2 (Michael 2003). Different types of welfare state have proven relatively resilient in the face of globalization, though there may be economic costs to maintaining particular programmes or social priorities (Huber and Stephens 2001; Scharpf 1999). So when governments downsize social programmes, it might not be because global forces pull them but because they are pushed by certain political coalitions at home.

Even so, the French experience suggests that the classical KWS option has become unviable. Nowhere was this national option pursued as enthusiastically as in France, and its defeat there in the early 1980s removed it from the agenda in the rest of Europe. After the Socialist victory in the Presidential elections of 1981 and Assembly elections of 1982, the French government nationalized a dozen industrial groups and 36 banks and pursued a Keynesian policy of demand stimulation through wage increases, enlarged social security benefits, increased government spending, and higher taxation of wealth and profit. But by late 1982 unemployment was rising rapidly, inflation was at 14 per cent per annum, and the national budget and trade balance deficits were increasing. The Socialist Party was split over the appropriate reaction to the crisis, with the left wing wanting to radicalize economic policy behind protectionist walls and the right wing arguing for a reversal to a monetarist policy that emphasized budget austerity, low inflation and industrial restructuring to encourage export-led growth. While the former wanted to insulate the French economy from global pressures – including potential withdrawal from the European Union – the latter maintained that French industry should become more competitive abroad, particularly by expanding trade in the European Union. By early 1983, the latter had won the argument and by the 1990s European social democrats had largely abandoned the KWS model (Hooghe 2003).

So, whether driven by global or local political logic, in the 1980s Conservative governments pursued large-scale privatization of state assets as part of a broad programme of neo-liberal economic and political restructuring. They withdrew from direct economic management, allowed unemployment to rise to what would have previously been regarded as politically unacceptable levels, while reducing welfare provision and driving a cultural shift from collective to individual notions of risk and responsibility. These policies, combined with the increasing global fluidity of capital, meant that national economies escaped the control of governments and became subject to transnational economic flows of finance, commodities and production regimes. The post-Fordist world, then, is more fluid, uncertain, individualistic and above all globalized to the extent that national governments have little control over socio-economic processes that are driven by combinations of local and global forces. Production has been internationalized (Kobrin 1998 and 2003) and the line between domestic and international has therefore been erased; in the electronic global economy there is no clear centre.

This argument can be developed to suggest that the end of the Cold War and autarkic communist systems in Europe in 1989–91 further weakened the territorial state structure by opening the flow of competitive capitalism worldwide. Thus according to Giddens: 'What happened in 1989 was not just a crisis for Marxism. It was also, and continues to be, a crisis for Western socialism too' (Giddens: 1999). So the upshot of these profound political and economic processes was the eclipse of national state projects such as social democratic welfare and the end of the era of the nation state as such.

Further, there is the argument that states cannot provide solutions to issues of pollution, terrorism, the drug trade, currency crises, and global pandemics such as AIDS (Krasner 2001) and latterly, perhaps, Avian flu. Power has multiple loci and the state shares power with international organizations and bodies such as the World Bank and the IMF, such that political space (the areas in which political action is situated) are no longer determined by politically defined territories. States cannot necessarily control monetary policies because of open international capital markets; international crisis can overwhelm national policies, for example, tax rates are limited by the possibility of flight of capital to more favourable regimes; and states cannot control illegal trade because of the volume of traffic and its transnational organization (Krasner 2001, although he goes on to argue that these claims are exaggerated). Similarly Kobrin (1998 and 2003) argues that globalization increases the cost, risk and complexity of technology and that many national markets are too small to sustain product development. No national market for semiconductors, aerospace, pharmaceuticals, biotechnology and telecommunications, for example, can sustain the very high research and development (R&D) and production costs of new products. In the process the structures of assembly and distribution become flexible transnational networks rather than organizational hierarchies organized in single countries alongside national state bureaucracies. This has political implications too since there is a blurring of distinctions between public and private with very large banks becoming public actors where failure or default would have catastrophic international economic implications while INGOs such as Greenpeace are public bodies that influence opinion and policy. Even so, Kobrin concludes that

> I see no evidence that the nation state will become obsolete, that other sources of allegiance and identity will replace it. However, globalization is weakening territorial sovereignty to the point where economic and political governance based primarily on geographic jurisdiction may no longer be viable.

(Kobrin 2003)

However, the debates about the national state project are not limited to political economy. Global flows of finance, media images, risks, consumption patterns, populations and power destabilize multiple notions of national spatial boundaries. The classical state aimed to create internal cultural homogeneity and unity within a bordered territory and was intolerant of difference (Bauman 1992). The nation state, therefore, imposed official languages on a mosaic of speech patterns, which can be illustrated by attempts to suppress vernacular languages as significant means of establishing unified states. Along with this went common currency, national laws, loyalty to the state, clearly demarcated boundaries, shared (imagined) history and fate. With globalization there have been large-scale migrations of people, images, capital and goods across boundaries but above all a complex and deep interlocking of territorial spaces with abstract flows of money and culture. States are increasingly integrated into international systems of transnational regulation and networks of INGOs, the number of which rose from 6,000 in 1990 to 26,000 in 1996; some 1,500 are registered observers at the UN (McGann and Johnstone 2005).[3] At the same time, the internal cultural homogeneity characteristic of the nation state has been eroded by increased internal heterogeneity of cultural identity, lifestyles, loyalties and memberships combined with increasing homogeneity in the international commercial culture drive by brands such as McDonald's and Coca-Cola, TV globalism and multiple forms of cross-cultural consumption. Thus the nationally imagined image of a unified people is diminishing in favour of lifestyle consumers but also the emergence of separatist fragmentary nationalism. In this detachment, however, some see depthlessness and loss of deep emotional attachments in a pastiche of superficial identities. There are a 'multiphrenia' of selves where people are saturated with information and relationships but lack a secure sense of self (Gergen 1991). Melucci (1984) wrote of nomads wandering between un-connected places. In this state of homelessness people are driven to seek secure identities in myths of religion, so alongside the disenchanted self there is the passionate intensity of fragmentary ethno-nationalism (Billig 1997: 140). Two divergent cultures then emerge – on the one hand, passionate intensity of commitment to the sacred land and culture of the 'nation' and, on the other, a cosmo-politan culture of global consumption and identity and detached secular cool in which nationalism is of little concern. Both, however, are manifestations of globalization and the eclipse of exclusively national communities.

A number of social theorists have aimed to replace an outmoded concept of the social based on a concept of territorial containment with a more fluid, globalized concept. Some writers therefore refer to the emergence of a 'post-Westphalian national system in which the state's jurisdictions become problematic (Kobrin 1998 and 2003). Guéhenno (1996) writes of the 'death of politics' in post-national forms of fragmentation where religion divides rather than unites and violence that was previously the monopoly of the state is privatized. According to these writers, emerging social relations take shape on multiple levels that transcend territorial borders – for example, global flows of capital and trade, commodities, production systems, cultural images, migration and conflicts and terrorism. Thus with global economic and political changes there is a weakening of the state:

> The things most important for the well-being and life-prospects of its citizens are largely beyond the government's control: they are in the hands of the so called 'market forces' – that enigmatic entity reminiscent

of primeval elements, natural disasters or blind fate, rather than of well considered, purposeful and rational human decisions. Governments can do less and less to influence the course of events which affect directly the livelihood of their subjects.

(Bauman 1998a)

This has implications for social solidarity. It was noted above that in the post-war period the Western welfare state was an integral element of the Fordist circle of growth based on mass production and mass consumption, which offset tendencies to social polarization and class conflict. The Western social democratic concept of welfare was one in which risks were pooled and individuals no longer faced uncertainty alone but as part of a group (Baldwin 1990: 2). With the decline in shared perceptions of risk and a culture and practice of individuation social solidarities weaken and the role of the state in relation to ensuring the basis of cohesion changes, in ways illustrated below. One example of this is the global dominance of more individualized and targeted systems of state welfare combined with a rapid expansion of private pensions and health care plans. This trend is reflected and to some extent extolled in sociological theories of reflexive individualization in which life is a project and where identities are constructed and subject to experimentation. In some ways these theories take at face value neo-liberal claims that the state has an inevitably limited role in everyday life that is now organized through informal networks of civil society.

The claim is then that the core of the social is thus undermined by on the one hand post-national formations, global mobilities of people and commodities, and on the other, new forms of individualization. However, it was argued above (pp. 61–2) that while many economic flows are global, social reproduction always takes place in territorial space. This is one of the central tensions within globalization but also a way of beginning to address some of the uncertainties and confusions mentioned above. While the economy operates on a global scale social reproduction takes place within definable territorial units – the household, cities, regions and the nation state (Perrons 2004: 239). Thus place becomes a significant factor in economic competitiveness and connectivity. However, spatial locations are also sites at which the crises and failures of

neo-liberalism are manifest. Beck (2000a) argues that social reproduction in locales becomes increasingly problematic, as life is insecure and individualized. In contrast with employers of the previous
industrial era, who frequently provided lifetime employment, social
wages and a focus for social network formation, few Information Age
firms provide such benefits. Changes in the workplace also affect the
family. As workers compete as economic actors, they are required to
be flexible and to spend long hours on the job or engaged in activities
not compatible with family life. These changes, and related changes
in family structure, make it difficult for the family to fulfil its role
as the primary institution facilitating the inter-generational
transmission of knowledge. Ironically, this is occurring precisely
at a time when national economic success will depend on knowledge transmission (Carnoy 2000: 143). Thus the problem of social
cohesion becomes central in a world of chain networks, irregular
working patterns, migration and mobility, and global sociality.
This is an issue that is largely neglected by globalization theories
that assume that somehow this complex social interaction just
gets done or is accomplished through the existence of complex
interdependencies, which is a position that would seem implicit in
Urry (2003).

End of the nation state? Not quite

Many of the above claims accurately depict the changing relationship between the territorial state and the global system, but the
arguments have some limitations. There are actually a series of
claims being made in these arguments. Sovereignty refers to different things – to state institutions, appeals to nationhood and national
identity, and democratic sovereignty and legitimacy (Houlton
2005). There are claims about the limitations to national sovereignty
both within national territories and externally in relation to a world
system of states. Sovereignty is no longer indivisible and absolute,
but of course it never was either in historical or modern periods.
The capacity of states to act was always conditional on treaties,
balances of power, resource limitations and home and international
social movements (Krasner 2001). Yet many key policy areas of
the national state – taxation, infrastructural planning, immigration,

education, research, development and training, social policy – all remain essentially national even if conditioned by international bodies and agreements. Robertson (1992) writes of the 'heyday of the nation-state' having been between 1880 and 1920, a period that was associated with the zenith of European modernism. But it could be argued that at that time most of the world's population did not live in nation states, and it was only in the latter part of the twentieth century, with the end of European colonialism and then the break-up of the Soviet Union, that the nation state became the standard political unit (Fulcher 2000). While there were only 51 UN members in 1945, there were 127 by 1970 and 189 by 2000 so, paradoxically, the age of globalization has also been the age of the proliferation of the territorial state.

Then again there is the question of economic processes loosening moorings from state controls to the extent that it may be difficult any longer to speak of the 'Japanese' economy, 'British' economy etc. Fulcher argues that globalization has strengthened rather than weakened the nation state and that although the global system of financial regulation has been dismantled national policy differences still affect capital flows. Boyer (1996) argues that global capital flows are affected by nationally endogenous factors such as the pace of technological change (which is structured by past investment in R&D, education policy and patterns of product differentiation) and labour market factors such as wage rates and skill levels, along with the stability and nature of the local political environment. Wade (1996) argues that companies are not in the main 'footloose' but rooted in home bases that render them susceptible to pressure from the home government. In fact:

- OECD countries show big differences in the level and sectoral pattern of technology and specialization.
- Most large firm technology is done in the home country.
- There is a close correlation between firm technological development and that of the home countries.

He concludes that 'national boundaries still demarcate the nationally specific systems of education, finance, corporate management and government that generate social conventions, norms and laws and therefore pervasively influence investment in technology and entre-preneurship' (Wade 1996: 73).

Further, territory is still core to state structures, hence 'the issue of immigration, more than any other shows that the state has not withered away in an age of late capitalism' (Billig 1997: 141). The state has reconfigured itself as a surveillance-informatic state such that the claim that it as 'hollowed out' obscures the reality that 'big government continues' (Luke 2002). The power relations of the state have been altered by a redistribution of functions, which is not a reduction in state power but rather a deepening of the state's grasp over facets of the social process and everyday life. Privatization, for example, does not mean the reduction of state power but reflects policies that facilitate the movement of capital (Luke 2002). One example of this, Simon (2005) argues, is the rise of post-panoptic surveillance in the form of dataveillance – the collection, organization and storage of information about people. Biometrics, the use of the body as a measure of identity, becomes a regular feature of everyday lives and positions subjects within identities, especially as citizens of a polity whose regulatory gaze is embodied in ubiquitous urban phenomena such as CCTV and enclosure within the observed discipline of the highway and the aeroplane terminal – each recording a passage from one spatial and cultural zone to the next. Behind this there are administrators, bureaucrats and scientists whose actions are integral to the whole operation. Again, with the census the state uses observational and data categories to generate profiles of various populations, guide the development of government policies, and organize everyday life within juridically bound territories. The citizen of the polity is thus increasingly the subject of state and private surveillance and data logs. Data-life generates new subjects and biographies that 'live' in data archives where they have an exist-ence independent of the embodied subjects they purportedly repre-sent. But these are globalized forms of the instantiation of state power through surveillance rather than its demise.

Agency, global context and consequences

Globalization is sustained by actors orientating their behaviour towards a concept of the 'global', which reflexively constitutes and reshapes globalization. Global processes are instantiated differently in different places, but this process is affected by local responses and strategies, which in turn can alter the pattern of globalization. A good illustration of this is the development of the European Union as a form of regional globalization that also demonstrates the importance of actors' responses even though these may have unintended consequences. As Hooghe (2003) argues, the European Union has become a battleground for opponents and proponents of globalization. Some want the EU to be a bulwark against global pressures, and others want it to accelerate the pace of increasing global, as opposed to national or European, interdependence. There is extensive anti-globalization resistance in Europe – such as José Bové's protests, the destruction of GM crops and the campaign against the 2005 constitution. Yet at the same time Eurobarometer surveys regularly indicate strong support for the EU as a means of combining its benefits with protection from its negative effects (Gordon 2004). This protection takes the form of structural funds (aid to poorest regions), the social chapter of the Maastricht Treaty, higher state expenditure in the EU (average 48 per cent GDP) than in the US (36 per cent) and protection of traditional farming through the Common Agricultural Policy. The development of the EU in its present form was the outcome of agents' responses to globalization that at the same time affected its nature.

In response to the global crisis of the KWS two models of national response emerged in the 1980s. On the one hand, Anglo-American neo-liberalism argued for a global shift to laissez faire and, on the other, the German model advocated protecting national economies within the European region though consolidating the internal market and strengthening political integration within the EU (Hooghe 2003). Many multinational corporations preferred the global option because the benefits of specialization through free trade were potentially greater between European and non-European firms than within Europe (Sandholtz and Zysman 1989). What became the preferred regional path was a result of a combination of the convergence of diverse political actors and an element of path dependence[4] in that deeper market integration had been on the European Commission agenda for some years and by 1985 more than half of the internal market legislation was already in draft form

(Hooghe 2003). Various economic studies were produced that argued that an integrated European market would yield a cumulative benefit of between 4.3 and 6.4 per cent of aggregate GDP. At the same time, the Uruguay Round[5] had reached an impasse amid conflicts of interests between Europeans and the US over issues such as agriculture and intellectual property rights. By contrast the idea of deeper European regional integration appeared to offer plausible solutions to coordination problems and a clear edge over global integration (Hooghe 2003).

The element of path dependence in this process was evident in the way the nature of pre-existing institutions at the European level made it likely that agreements would be implemented. The internal market programme was preceded by the empowerment of the European Commission and establishment of the supremacy of EU law through the European Court of Justice. By the mid-1980s, these supranational institutions had the authority to enforce EU regulations (Garrett 1992; Pierson 1998) while equivalent global institutions for monitoring national commitments were lacking or less authoritative than EU institutions. The WTO is in principle a weaker body since it does not require a *de jure* surrender of national sovereignty and a member state can refuse to comply with a ruling, although *de facto*, smaller or economically more dependent countries may find it difficult to exercise that sovereign right (Hooghe 2003). In contrast, EU Commission fines and European Court of Justice (ECJ) rules are binding for both small and large members.

However, as well as this institutional logic, one of the most important lessons from this process is that outcomes, in terms of transnational institutional structures, are often unintended rather than led by an inexorable process of globalization. One of the main reasons for the political success of the internal market programme was precisely its ambiguity, which enabled it to appear to be all things to all actors. For neo-liberal groups and parties market liberalization would limit European integration to an economic enterprise administered by government elites. But other parties conceived of the Single European Act as a first step towards capital regulation at the European level in line with European Social Democratic and Christian Democratic traditions. Economic and monetary union, decided at Maastricht in 1991, was to replay a similar convergence between divergent interests. Neo-liberals saw the EMU (Economic and Monetary Union) as a means of insulating economic activity from political regulation and forcing national governments to compete for investment by reducing taxes and shifting the tax burden from mobile capital to less mobile factors of production. Opponents of neo-liberalism, on the other hand, saw the EMU as a signal of deeper political regulation at the European level and that national governments would be pushed toward redistributive measures and some form of European fiscal policy. Hooghe (2003) concludes: 'The implications of EMU are no less ambiguous than those of the internal market program, which is why EMU has been able to attract support on the left as on the right.' Thus the development of closer integration, which is also subject to challenge and contestation by local political actors, could be understood as both a producer *and* regulator of globalization.

REMAKING 'SOCIETY'

States, then, remain significant actors in complex fields of action and unintended consequences in which concepts of the global are reflexively appropriated. Rather than view 'society' or indeed 'sociality' as pre-given objects of social inquiry (whether these are housed within the nation state or not) they should be seen as constituted and given particular character by processes of governmentality. The state is not only transformed by globalization but is also an active agent in the spread and nature of globalization. State agencies further have a role as mediators of the effects of globalization and in the process can be engaged in remaking 'society'. If one role of the state is to maximize the conditions for national competitiveness and profitability of locally based capital, the state will need to address issues of social cohesion and social capital, which fix the global into place and underwrite private risk (Leys 2001). Drawing on concepts of social capital and social cohesion state agencies reflexively reconstitute the social as an object of intervention. Concerns about a lack or reduction in social cohesion currently lead the policy agenda in many governmental and non-governmental institutions (Jenson 1998). Social cohesion, she says, 'involves building shared values and communities of interpretation, reducing disparities in wealth and income, and generally enabling people to have a sense that they are engaged in a common enterprise'. This agenda is advanced specifically in response to the belief that 'the cohesiveness of societies is being affected by globalization, technological and demographic pressures, the implications of which we are only beginning to understand' (Jenson 1998). This process occurred in many parts of the European Union and in Canada in the 1990s with the return to power of social democratic parties with a 'realistic agenda' of redressing some social consequences of global neo-liberalism (especially rising inequalities) while acknowledging that there was no possibility of a return to Keynesian welfarism.

In some ways these debates hark back to similar concerns expressed by Durkheim in late nineteenth-century France and Talcott Parsons in mid-twentieth-century America. In the face of class conflict and social disorganization brought by classical market liberalism Durkheim developed an approach similar to the Solidarism movement, and Parsons was also aware of the limitations of capitalism's ability to create the necessary conditions for social stability. Social cohesion is defined as a 'set of social processes that help instil in individuals the sense of belonging to the same community and feeling that they are recognized as members of that community' (Plan – Commissariat Général du Plan 1997). The social cohesion agenda directly addresses the social dislocation that is perceived to be a consequence of globalization and neo-liberal restructuring and, ironically, is often pursued by the very bodies such as the OECD that also drive neo-liberal policies. Thus the OECD (1997) identified a group of social problems within nations, consequent on neo-liberal global restructuring. These included the fear of social deterioration, instability, rising inequality and homelessness, rising crime and the politics of intolerance and exclusion.

A crucial issue here is that the social cohesion agenda is a state project that is dependent on maintaining the legitimacy of public institutions that act as mediators and maintain spaces within which mediation can occur (Jenson 1998). Kymlicka and Norman (1995) argue that the stability of modern democracies (i.e. states) depends not only on their basic structure but also on the ability of people to negotiate competing forms of national, regional, ethnic and religious identity – abilities that neo-liberal policies have undermined by weakening ties of belonging. Since the 1990s there have been international movements to develop the concept of the social economy, and to address 'social exclusion' through governmental and non-governmental initiatives. The social economy invokes cooperative and mutual associations founded on principles of service to the community, democratic decision making and empowerment of communities (Lipietz 2000). But these 'economies of reciprocity', though grounded in community initiatives, require extensive state involvement and support – to facilitate recreating local commerce, renovation of the built environment, cultural spaces for youth, neighbourhood transport, local services such as crèches, bringing artisans together etc. (Garmadi 2001).

The consequences of globalization may increase the need for governments to provide welfare services because of economic dislocation. As the government manages social risk without bearing it, it allocates risk between individuals, markets and states, while developing social investment decisions and balanced portfolio strategies (Mitchell 2000). These strategies in turn require legitimacy of government institutions and processes within wider national culture and public opinion. In other words, they entail a relatively successful embedding of the state within a wider but bounded national community.

In the 1980s Skocpol (1985) wrote about an upsurge of interest in the state in social science after a period of neglect and something similar seems to be happening today around the issues of the state and globalization, especially regarding the *role* of the state in the globalization process. Far from being hollowed out or relegated to a residual role in globally integrated societies the state has a crucial position both as agent of globalization and in regulating and policing the failures of neo-liberal restructuring. The former role is evident in, for example, the state's role in privatization (an essential condition for global capital flows), border controls (regulating and facilitating migration flows) strategic decisions and entering into treaties (permitting political integration and jurisdiction) creating a regulatory regime (essential for investment flows) and instigating and winning political support for welfare reforms (increasing competitiveness and convergence).

Not only this but state agents are actively attempting to re-constitute the 'social' in a new mode of societal governmentality reflecting the debates outlined in the previous section. An example of this, while also regulating the effects of neo-liberalization failures, can be seen in the UK government's reaction to violence in northern English towns in 2001 and its aftermath. During the spring and summer of 2001 there were violent conflicts between South Asian and White young men (mostly) in Bradford (in April and July), Burnley (in June) and Oldham (in May). There were around 1,500 incidents of violent disorder, 476 people were injured and around £10 million worth of damage was done (UK Home Office 2002). The background is complex (see Ray and Smith 2004) but the conflicts were related in various ways to outcomes of global restruc-turing. During the 1960s, the mill towns such as Oldham and Roch-dale invested in new technologies, which were operated twenty-four hours a day to maximize profit. The night shifts, which were unpopular with the existing workforce, soon became the domain of Pakistani and Bangladeshi workers. Global restructuring in the 1980s then had particularly dramatic effects in these industrial towns since the collapse of the regional manufacturing base gener-ated high levels of social inequality and structural unemployment, and intensified racial and ethnic divisions. One of the defining characters of these areas was a very high degree of residential segrega-tion and the deep fracturing of communities on racial, generational and religious lines. The break in class alignments and social networks that was a general feature of these changes, along with the globalization of cultural as well as economic ties, transformed the locale in ways that crystallized oppositional identities among local White and Asian youths.

In the aftermath of the conflicts the UK government initiated a wide range of interventions with the intention of reducing com-munity conflicts and building community cohesion. These combine community interventions and supports with a tough judicial stance on crime and disorder. One example of these state interventions is crime reduction and enforcement – for example through Crime and Disorder Reduction Partnerships (CDRPs) made up of the local authority, the police and other agencies such as Primary Care Trusts, and the probation and fire authorities. Recent criminal justice legislation allows for the distribution of Anti-Social Behaviour Orders that can be issued to an individual in response to complaints of anti-social behaviour even if they have not committed a crime. There is a range of local community initiatives, including:

- neighbourhood renewal, which is a UK government strategy that aims to tackle social exclusion in areas of high social deprivation. It aims to encourage economic prosperity, safe communities, high-quality education, decent housing and better health, while encouraging communities to be at the centre of decision-making processes;
- community cohesion promoted by the Community Cohesion Unit at the Home Office that funds a number of community pathfinders to provide examples of how the idea of community cohesion can be implemented;
- Civil Renewal – a UK government initiative that aims to promote civil renewal by strengthening communities in which people work together to find solutions to problems and through partnership in meeting public needs;
- challenging attitudes of offenders, for example, through anti-bullying initiatives that incorporate procedures for preventing and responding to bullying, improving playground supervision, encouraging victims to report incidents. Schools must file reports to the local authority for any racist incidents, with a follow-through plan to show what steps have been taken to prevent recurrence;
- crime prevention (reducing levels of crime, anti-social behaviour and fear of crime) through environmental improvements – tackling litter, graffiti, working on the general state of repair of properties and public areas.

These and other 'social cohesion' initiatives explicitly attempt to reflexively reconstitute the social – to recreate social capital and community cohesion – that is seen as having been undermined by global neo-liberal economics. This is itself a global strategy, and this form of governmentality is premised on the Third Way view that state socialism was unable to generate economic growth while neo-liberalism destroyed social cohesion. It also exemplifies the process

Habermas as described as 'juridification' (*Verrechtlichung*) whereby formal law increasingly regulates processes of social integration, representing an intrusion of system into lifeworld (Habermas 1996). Thus new strategies of governmentality restructure the social in ways that attest to the continuing potency of the state but question traditional notions of the state–society dichotomy. New forms of managed sociality and community action are constituted by the regulatory agency of the state in responding to the consequences of global economic restructuring.

Further, increased state regulation can itself constitute new forms of sociality and social subjects and have globalization effects. The linkage between immigration policy, border controls and migration illustrate this. All developed countries have tightened border security in response to new global migrations, the global rise of anti-migrant politics and, since September 11th 2001, additional security concerns. New forms of sociality take shape at the intersections and borderlands of regulatory controls. 'What common people have done in response to the process of globalization,' says Portes (1997), 'is to create communities that sit astride political borders and that, in a very real sense, are "neither here nor there" but in both places simultaneously'. One could add though that the economic activities that sustain these communities are grounded precisely on the differentials of advantage created by state boundaries. Further, there is a symbiotic relation between controls and global mobility. As borders are more policed and migration more regulated, migrants, especially those without documentation, are forced into higher dependence on locally embedded networks and flows of knowledge. At the same time, the tighter the border controls the higher the risks involved in trafficking people, so the more lucrative and competitive the business becomes. Obokata (2001) concludes that: 'One of the ironies is that tight immigration and border control policies are among the causes of trafficking and smuggling . . . stringent immigration laws and policies are actually aggravating the situation.' The upshot of this is that would-be migrants are increasingly locked into global criminal networks and the transmission of knowledge through transnational communities and informal market exchanges.

Sassen (1996b) argues that immigration renationalizes politics at the same time that economic integration denationalizes it. The state border is at the heart of regulatory efforts, but these will have unintended consequences. She cites the US sugar price support provision in the 1980s in which taxpayers paid $3 billion annually to support the price of sugar for US producers. This kept Caribbean Basin countries out of the competition and resulted in the loss of 400,000 jobs there between 1982 and1988. Predictably, then, the 1980s was also an era of large increases in migration to the US from that region (Sassen 1996b: 78–9). Indeed, the process of economic globalization has an effect on migration. Increased competitive pressures, on the one hand, favour off-shore production and FDI linked to export-led growth and preference for low wage as opposed to unionized workers at home. The latter fuels a demand for low-wage migrant labour while the establishment of production overseas increases cultural links between metropolitan and developing countries, which in turn increase both documented and undocu-mented transnational migration.

The formation of transnational networks and links are thus caught in complex and often unintended consequences of state strategies. Migrants will often seek solidarity and refuge in communities of shared language and identity. By contrast with Beck's superficial notion of cosmopolitanism, Hannerz points out that while cosmo-politans can afford to experiment with an uprooted sense of self, migrants, asylum seekers and exiles too acutely experience dislocation and displacement (Hannerz 1990). The most frequent reasons for migrants' choice of destination are the transmission of ideas, stories told by migrants and returnees, rumours of opportunities and recruit-ment agencies (Papastergiadis 2000). These social networks create chain migration effects that stretch from destination countries back to locales, villages and families. This attests to the importance of closely bound networks, powerful webs of identity and sociality, and face-to-face transactions that underpin the existence of global net-works. In the UK migrants have concentrated in London because of the size of the labour market, the unmet labour demand, links to others via networks, including networks for undocumented migrants providing work, forged papers, accommodation etc. (Glover *et al.* 2001). In these transactions, local knowledge is crucial – such as the 'Wailing Wall' side window of a London newsagent that advertises jobs in a variety of languages (Gibney 2001). Migration (especially 'asylum seeking') exemplifies contemporary mobility but also the embedding of these in complex networks and solidarities structured by inter-relations between states and economies.

There are four consequences of this discussion. First, the role and structure of the state has been transformed by globalization. Second, however, the state retains a crucial regulatory (and in some ways enhanced) role in relation to global processes. Third, rather than being redundant or surpassed, the concept of the social is constituted by the intersection of global/local effects and state strategies for management of the consequences of a neo-liberal globalizing strategy. State regulation positions new subjects of regulatory interventions in ways that are both intended and unintended. Fourth, to understand how global sociality is accomplished we need a detailed understanding of the face-to-face or at least interpersonal linkages that operate across space. This argument is developed in Chapter 5.

COSMOPOLITAN VERSUS NATIONAL SOCIETY

The territorial state has become in many cases a state of cosmopolitan nationalities. Beck writes of:

> [the] transcendence of boundaries around national spaces . . . [that] . . . makes is clear that society in second modernity can no longer be conceptualised using the concepts and categories of the nation state, but that a new perspective of 'methodological cosmopolitanism' must be developed for this task.
>
> (Beck and Lau 2005)

Cosmopolitan society brings 'the otherness of the other' in a negotiation of contradictory cultural experiences into the centre of activities. With the pluralization of borders there is an implosion of the dualism between national and international that points towards the need for cosmopolitan governance and global norms within 'a new space of globality' (Beck 2002b). The national is 'no longer the national' but an internalization of the global within the local. In other words, the interpenetration of local and global and the fusion of place and globality means that the local and national spaces are simply sites in which the global and transnational are instantiated.

The processes that once took place within national borders are now organized globally – so production is *influenced* (a rather weaker claim, surely?) by global possibilities and competition, the concept of social class 'obscures the collapse of the nation-state class ontology' and we experience in everyday life a clash of cultures, globally shared collective futures, a growing responsibility for a 'world risk society' and self-reflexivity towards divergent and entangled cosmopolitan identities (Beck 2002b).

In support of the concept of cosmopolitan society Beck sites Levy and Sznaider's (2002) thesis of cosmopolitan memory cultures. While this has validity, I will examine it in order to highlight some difficulties with Beck's argument. Levy and Sznaider argue that globalization and, in particular, the emergence of common European identity has generated a 'new form of memory' (cosmopolitan memory) that transcends national boundaries. They argue that in a Europe no longer divided by the Cold War and freed from nationally based historical and moral narratives, the Holocaust takes on the role of a common moral touchstone. They chart the emergence of the Holocaust as an iconic representation of evil, racism and genocide in the 1960s–1980s in the process of which it not just came to signify the destruction of European Jewry but also became a symbol of transnational solidarity and acquired the status of a point of reference of unquestioned moral value. This transnational status for the Holocaust as a universal moral touchstone was disseminated through mass media (from the 1970s' TV series *The Holocaust* through to *Schindler's List*) and the proliferation of public commemoration – such as the Washington Holocaust Museum and the international observance of 27 January as Holocaust Memorial Day. In this way the Holocaust took on the status of a cosmopolitan memory of suffering and the motto 'Never Again' could be transferred to contemporary conflicts such as the conflicts in the former Yugoslavia – the campaign for NATO (North Atlantic Treaty Organisation) intervention in Bosnia and Kosovo invoked images of the death camps and portrayed the Serbs as Nazis. Thus, 'after the Cold War the Holocaust is officially part of European memory and becomes a new founding moment for the idea of European civilization' (Levy and Sznaider 2002).

The Holocaust has become a symbol of suffering and genocide, and Auschwitz in particular has come to represent the enormity of the event and human capacity for inhumanity. However, examining the disputes over the Auschwitz and they way in which they become embroiled within national and international narratives of memory and justification reveals the complexity of the interaction of global and national processes. The national in this process has clearly not been transcended but rather joined by other layers of meaning and memory. The camp has been an object of contestation of competing claims to rhetorical ownership (Kapralski 2001). First, it should be noted that in 1947 the Polish parliament determined that Auschwitz was to be 'forever preserved as a memorial to the martyrdom of the Polish nation and other people' and would be an international site of commemoration of victims of fascism. In fact for much of the communist period (1948–89) in Poland the camp museum did not acknowledge that 1 million of the 1.1 million murdered at Auschwitz were Jewish.[6] It was with the relaxation of ideological control over historical commemoration that the particularity of Jewish suffering was asserted within the international frame of meaning. Second, for the Poles, Kapralski claims, Auschwitz symbolizes the Polish tragedy during the Second World War, which was a condensed history of German attempts to subordinate and eventually destroy the Polish nation. Polish nationalists, denied a chance to express national identity freely outside state-designed channels, redefine identity via the memory of Auschwitz as a solely 'Polish' place and a national–religious symbol. These conflicts came to a head in the early 1990s with the dispute over the Carmelite nuns at the site, who had appropriated a camp building and erected more than 100 crosses (Misztal 2003: 121–2). This resulted in a fifteen-year conflict amidst accusations of the Christianization of Auschwitz and ended when the convent was moved outside the camp's boundary, and a large wooden cross that had been erected at the height of the convent crisis in 1989 was allowed to remain at the site (Klein 2001).[7] However, struggles for national appropriation of Auschwitz symbolism continue. In 2006 the Polish government requested that UNESCO (United Nations Educational, Scientific and Cultural Organization) re-name the site of the camp to the 'Former Nazi German Concentration Camp Auschwitz-Birkenau'. This followed references in the European Parliament and British press in 2005 (the sixtieth anniversary of the liberation of the camp) to 'Polish camps' that provoked public resentment in Poland. Not only this but the museum at Auschwitz 1 is ordered on national lines with separate displays in former barracks commemorating the suffering of different nationalities – one of the largest and newest sections is devoted to Polish resistance to the German occupation.

Cosmopolitan memory thus contests with multiple national narratives for appropriation of Holocaust symbolism. This can be identified further in the resurgence of Jewish sites of commemoration across Europe. Restitution and memory has become central to postcommunist politics and *dual* movements towards national and European identities. This is illustrated by the regeneration of 'Jewish quarters', for example in Kazimierz (Krakow), Spandauer Vorstadt (Berlin) and Josefov (Prague). The (UK) Institute for Jewish Policy Research charted cultural events in 2000–01 in countries with small Jewish populations – Italy, Sweden, Belgium and Poland. They counted over 450 individual events, and another 280 that were component parts of festivals, of which 27 were in Poland (Schischa and Berenstein 2002). Reassessing the past is ongoing and is having an impact on built spaces, but the contested nature of memory politics also illustrates the tenuousness of national narratives and coming to terms with the past is a multi-layered process. These disputes are not primarily about physically present Jews (whose numbers are very small) but rather about ways in which European countries now integrate Jewish memory and history and the Holocaust into an understanding of their own national history (Pinto 1996). These 'memories' and memorials are polyvalent. To some extent they signify the re-incorporation of local Jewry (in absentia) into national heritage – which also thereby magnifies the devastation of the entire country. This regeneration of 'Jewish' urban spaces is also linked to the growth of tourism and the presentation of the national culture as 'exotic' and multicultural. This can also be a displacement mourning (Remmler 1997) in which Germans, unable to mourn 'their own', have found common reference since unification in the Holocaust as a symbol of loss and suffering. At the same time Jewish culture can symbolize the 'good old days' of pre-communist national life expressed through nostalgia and stereotypes as a stage set shtetl,

Fiddler on the Roof. Finally, rather than become a cosmopolitan memory for a global Europe there is a risk of trivializing the past by forcing it into the lens of the present (Todorov 2003: 161). The re-enactment of ritual commemoration may be a retreat from the present in which one adopts the mantle of a stalwart fighter from the past but will not risk facing the present (Todorov 2003: 175).

There is a crucial 'dialogue', then, between cosmopolitan and national forms of memory and identity that will be resolved differently at different times and places. This brings us back to the issue of constitutional patriotism mentioned at the beginning of the chapter. There is a well-established theme in sociology that appears in different ways in Durkheim and Weber to the effect that societies with multiple memberships based on diverse cultural values and occupational specialisms will develop modes of integration that are increasingly formal and rights-based. For Durkheim this would require quasi-sacred commitment to the value of human rights that, if defiled (as happened in the Dreyfus Affair), 'inspires us with a feeling of horror in every way analogous to that which the believer experiences when he sees his idol profaned' (Durkheim 1969). Weber's more disenchanted view of modern forms of integration pointed towards the expanding role of formal rational and universalistic procedures that were rule-following and blind to the particular characteristics of individuals. Beck's notions of cosmopolitan democracy and Habermas's constitutional patriotism in many ways echo these traditions. Habermas's concept of post-national forms of solidarity is grounded in his theory of communicative competence. Whereas bureaucracies and capitalism are founded on instrumental rationality, which highlights efficiency and results, the lifeworld is the site of communicative rationality, which highlights the interpersonally based requirement to provide compelling reasons for one's actions. Rights are intersubjective in character and are 'based on the reciprocal recognition of cooperating legal persons'. Thus Habermas (2001: 74) links individual rights to the notion of individual autonomy and places particular emphasis on the vital link between democracy as popular sovereignty and the constitutional state. Constitutional patriotism posits a post-national form of solidarity in which citizens can be bound together by democratic procedures themselves. However, he is clear that constitutional principles *alone* are not sufficient to produce a cohesive civic identity. On the contrary, in order to experience themselves as co-members of a particular community they need particular ethno-cultural norms and values that define 'sub-political' identity-communities within pluralistic societies (Habermas 2001: 74). However, constitutional patriotism is 'neutral' vis-à-vis the particular values that underscore collective identities. While this in some way answers critics who regard constitutionalism as too universal and insufficiently 'thick' to generate collective solidarities (see discussion in Kumm 2005), it leaves another problem unresolved. In particular, neutrality works so long as all particular ethno-cultural and religious groups accept liberal principles, but it gets into difficulties once these values clash – as they did, for example, over the Danish cartoons incident in 2005, when the publication of cartoons of the Prophet Mohamed by the *Jyllands-Posten* newspaper was met by violent protests organized by Muslim groups across the world. There may be no a priori way of resolving this tension and Hayward (2004) is probably right to argue that: 'The tension between democratic principles and civic ideals is a chronic tension. Yet it . . . can be productive of democratic contestation.' What this discussion has aimed to establish, though, is that there are post-national forms of social integration that operate on both territorial and supraterritorial levels and one does not preclude the other, nor should one take analytical priority over the other.

CONCLUSIONS

Several contemporary sociologists including Beck, Bauman and Giddens write of the end of the 'container theory of society', a claim that is based largely on the putative end of the national state. Beck refers to the nation as a 'zombie concept' derived from nineteenth-century sociology that is dead but lives on, despite having lost all meaning in a globalized age. This chapter has taken a different view. Underlying the debate about the nation state are wider sociological principles about the management of complexity and social solidarity. Global sociality entails multiple levels of action that are complementary, although to be sure – like all complex social relations – they may give rise to tensions. People manage multiple identities and points of reference – so they may in rapid succession buy in local markets, order goods via the Internet, attend meetings of a local pressure group concerned with environmental issues of waste disposal, vote in national elections, follow the fortunes of the local as well as the national football team, chat to neighbours and send instant messages to friends several thousand miles away. People manage hybrid identities with overlapping historical, national and global reference – such as African-American, Asian-American, British-Asian, Chinese-British, British-Jewish, Christian-Arab etc., although at times these hyphenated identities may give rise to conflicts of loyalty both within the self and with others. At the same time people's lives are enacted within particular spaces that are both invested with memory and meaning and also spaces of governance. With relatively few exceptions global space is organized in terms of territorially bounded civic communities, political parties, definitions of citizenship, borders, institutions, official language(s), political, educational, cultural systems etc. The *nation* state as an ethnically homogenous realm is relatively new and has co-existed with other forms of state organization throughout the modern period. But because populations are now diverse, and economic, cultural and political life is complex, it does not follow that the state and territoriality are no longer significant. On the contrary, the state has arguably become more significant as an actor in the global area than it was previously.

A theme of this book is that global processes are also necessarily spatially embedded processes, and within this general frame of understanding the tension between (relatively) mobile capital and (relatively) immobile labour is an important constraint on unfettered market integration. Far from being undermined by increasing global integration, then, the state has a crucial role in restructuring the capitalist project of 'development' (Radice 2000). Social reproduction takes place in territorial settings that are at the intersection of global flows but where crises of neo-liberal restructuring are experienced. Among the consequences of global economic restructuring have been (as, indeed, Beck and others claim) a weakening of social solidarity and institutional supports (notably welfare), uncertainty and fluidity of work experience, and – partly as a consequence of the undermining of some traditional forms of masculinity – high levels of mobility along with an increased perception of global risks. However, it is equally important to note that the responses of state agencies in many parts of the developed world have been aimed at reconstructions of sociality in a reflexive appropriation of globalization as an object of intervention. In the process state actors have given rise to a complex mixture of intended and unintended consequences, some of which have had the effect of creating novel forms of social networks and action (such as the contradictory effects of migration controls on migration).

It is the case that the nature of sovereignty has changed, and many problems exceed the capacity of the territorial state to respond effectively in isolation from other nations. Certain options for social policy may not be viable in that nations may be bound by treaty (e.g. regulations on levels of public sector borrowing for countries that use the euro as their currency) or because costs are judged to be unacceptable (a return to the KWS for example). However, states will only be effective insofar as they have legitimacy among locally definable civic cultures. Legitimacy can in part be procedural, based in the democratic process itself but also in complex forms of national memory and culture.

4

VIRTUAL SOCIALITY

The unity of nearness and remoteness involved in every human relation
is organized, in the phenomenon of the stranger, in a way which may be
most briefly formulated by saying that in the relationship to him, distance
means that he, who is close by, is far, and strangeness means that he,
who also is far, is actually near.

(Simmel 1971: 143)

The development of digital technologies has been a major factor in
increasing the speed and extent of social communications, and in
many ways it epitomizes the process of globalization itself. The ICT
revolution is sometimes seen as a 'fifth K-wave' – following cotton,
steam power, engineering and electrification – increasing the speed
and ease of communications between institutions, governments,
firms and citizens, with immense implications for social life (Perrons
2004: 169).[1] As with new technologies in the past, the Internet has
been invested with utopian hopes for a radically new communicative
age as well as dystopic warnings of an electronic anomic 'lonely
crowd'. Again, as with globalization itself, there are many who regard
ICTs as ushering in a qualitative break with the past. But the
circulation, development and effects of new forms of cultural and
technological learning will be organized within social relations.
A theme of this chapter will be that, as with extreme reactions to
globalization in general, both these responses are flawed. Some
similar dynamics apply in online as in offline interactions as – like

earlier technologies – the Internet is being integrated into the rhythms of everyday life.

One theme that will be pursued here is the play of personal against impersonal interactions and the differing kinds of sociality they entail. In his famous essay on the Stranger, Simmel (1971) depicted a person who is 'not passing through' but 'comes today and stays tomorrow' within a particular spatial group but without belonging or rootedness. The stranger is someone who is potentially in transit but within a group and who confronts the dispositions of the group with an 'objective attitude' of both remoteness and nearness. This affords the stranger the privileged position of receiving 'the most surprising revelations and confidences, at times reminiscent of a confessional, about matters which are kept carefully hidden from everybody to whom one is close' (Simmel 1971: 145). In modern social settings of high lifetime geographical mobility the stranger in this sense becomes a more typical figure of the 'rooted cosmopolitan' who is 'equally at home in their own societies, in other societies, and in transnational spaces' (Tarrow 2003). These relations become even more apparent with the Internet user, who is a stranger, both spatially distant and also near through a combination of distance and proximity characteristic of global sociality where space is both stretched and compressed. The Internet affords closeness without intimacy and the blasé attitude of detachment that for Simmel epitomized life in the modern metropolis (Simmel 1971). Although the Internet is, or is seen as, a place of atomization and impersonality, like Simmel's stranger the Internet participant could be privy to details people would withhold from more intimate others since the Internet offers the possibility of relatively risk-free disclosure with fleeting or at least transient interlocutors.

Digital representation could, moreover, be seen as part of the process whereby social transactions acquire an increasingly symbolic and abstract quality, which Simmel regarded as a deep and long-term tendency of human culture (Simmel 1990). This was part of an evolution from purely instrumental to symbolic and increasingly visual communications, which is illustrated by the development of money. As barter transactions became increasingly complex, money appeared as a symbolic token of value that had the advantage of moving fluidly, storing value over time (so permitting the stretching of transactions over time) and simplifying complex exchanges. Throughout much of the Ancient World and the European Middle Ages money required the solidity of precious metal that had value in its own right. But gradually in China and then in Europe symbolic forms of paper and credit replaced hard value in metals as money acquired value that was increasingly disembodied, abstract and uncoupled from external measures such as the gold standard. Money is an example of how social interaction becomes increasingly abstract and in the process becomes more abstract itself. Once tied to a guarantee of value in gold, it now floats freely and expands into more abstract forms such as credit and trading on future prices. These are imaginary and symbolic worlds that Simmel did not directly anticipate but are suggested by his analysis. Money became iconic for the modern age, bringing flexibility and freedom but also depersonalization, proximity and distance in paradoxical unity.

Further, Simmel noted that individuals are at the node of an 'intersection of social circles' through which they move (Simmel 1971: 95–110) thereby anticipating the analysis of networks that is central to studies of the informational society.[2] The modern individual is inserted within unique personal networks where social solidarity is a product of coordination of activities through the network rather than shared commitments in a traditional sense (Barbesino 1997). The Internet intensifies this process since virtual communities offer windows for multiple selves – a 'distributed self' that exists in many worlds and plays many roles at the same time (Turkle 1999). In this way the general feature of complex modern life – to present oneself in different ways in different situations – to be a 'different person' at work, socializing and at home – is intensified.

However, the novelty of ICTs is the way they appear to collapse distance while hugely proliferating the social contacts and networks available. Societies in the past have existed in socially organized space, which is being changed though telecommuting, teleshopping, computer dating, electronic job markets, automatic tellers and desktop publishing – all of which mediate between the local and the global in complex ways. This raises questions such as whether the 'friction of distance' becomes irrelevant as people and organizations become 'footloose' at least in virtual if not actual space. Does this mean an advance of impersonality as the 'warm joys of intimate sociability are forever replaced by cooler pleasures of technologically mediated communication' (Boden and Molotch 1994: 257)? Has Weber's iron cage of bureaucratic rationality been replaced by the electronic trace? Or, on the contrary, are these dystopian visions exaggerated since modern systems inevitably rest on micro-orders of interaction and communication? Will digitally globalized processes facilitate and enhance social life, creating new forms of sociation? To begin to answer these, let us review debates about social solidarities.

SOCIAL SOLIDARITIES

A central theme in this book is the question of how globalized forms of sociality are sustained through the techniques of everyday life. Contrary to claims that globalization is destructive of previously existing forms of social solidarity, I am suggesting that many social bonds and relations are reaffirmed through globalized communications and that the process is only sustainable through the knowledgeable active participation of people in everyday life. I am further arguing that globalized forms of communication are rooted in social meanings and networks in which they often take their place within shared and routinely accomplished forms of behaviour. Although globalized and technologically mediated interactions are often impersonal there is a significant body of research suggesting that people and organizations have a preference for face-to-face interaction and that the growth of globalized communication has not necessarily been at the expense of direct relations. Further, online interactions can themselves be the medium of new forms of sociality.

A familiar contrast underlies many of these debates. Human society is dependent on its capacity to coordinate action in different ways. This occurs through direct (face-to-face) interactions and reciprocal bonds but also along complex chains of indirect mediation through communication technologies, bureaucracies and markets. Direct (primary) relationships exist with people with whom we have regular face-to-face and often intimate relations – such as family, friends, neighbours and work associates. These will tend to be diffuse in that multiple aspects of our lives and personality will be brought into play in interactions, involving affective bonds (based on love, trust, close personal involvement and so forth) rather than instrumental ones (based on what people can do for us in any given situation) and be particularistic in that people act differently towards intimates based on the nature of their relationship. These patterns are complex and culturally variable. A gift of money may be a token of friendship in one culture but a bribe in another. Western cultures tend to separate business and friendship whereas the Chinese concept of *Guanxi* intertwines friendship and business networks of mutual obligation (Luo 1997). Modern social life depends upon combining informal and impersonal affective and instrumental social relations and new communication networks generate new types of strangeness and intimacy.

By way of ideal–typical contrast (real life relationships will never be this clearly defined) indirect relationships will operate at the other end of a continuum of decreasing closeness, multiplicity and completeness. They will tend to be impersonal (often involving 'interaction' with non-human agents such as computer programs and automated voice activated responses), highly specific (when you actually get to speak to a real person in a call centre you are both focused on the specific matter in hand (buying insurance, paying or querying a bill, etc.) and instrumental (the interaction ends at the point the specific business has been completed).[3] 'Indirect' here refers to two different species of relations. One is where actions are undertaken directly by agents such as bureaucrats acting 'without regard for persons' as Weber put it, that is, following rules that require judgements to be made impersonally to create standardized effects.[4] The other kind of indirect relationship is where actions of many individuals have aggregated effects that are unintended but follow from the logic of their mutual interaction and cannot then be explained with reference to the behaviour of any particular individual. The classical case for this is the market that moves between disequilibrium and equilibrium through the operation of the price mechanism. The latter kind of indirect action (which Habermas and others call 'systemic') is facilitated through mediatized exchanges in which highly complex forms of value and social relations are crystallized within the symbolic form (money) that is highly fluid and transportable. Clearly direct relationships are no longer solely constitutive of modern society and everyday life involves complex claims of highly impersonal mediatized indirect relations. However, the argument here is that globalization, as the culmination of indirect forms of communication, remains the accomplishment of actors' shared meanings and tacit knowledge of the social.

That the modern world has involved a proliferation of indirect relationships is something that was noted often with dismay or foreboding by classical sociologists. For Marx the dominance of the commodity form and market exchange produced inequalities, alienation, exploitation and conflict, although these conditions would be overcome through the socialist revolution. For Durkheim industrialization had destroyed the communal regulatory systems of medieval society and created an anomic and anarchic division of labour although this could be overcome through moral education and regulation in a guild-like system of professional associations. For Weber the dominance of rationalized and bureaucratic systems of action was a world historical movement that offered little possibility of escape except through occasional revolutionary periods of charismatic leadership. Again, for Simmel modernity represented the dominance of 'objective' (impersonal and formal) over 'subjective' (authentic and meaningful) culture, which he regarded as a tragedy in the classical sense – like the character whose otherwise noble qualities are fatally flawed, the destruction of the unified subject is the necessary result of the very nature of social life. When Giddens writes about globalization as a 'runaway world' he is expressing again this sense of a world experienced as beyond subjective human control (Giddens 1999).

Globalized modernity appears to represent the triumph of systemic and objective social relations in which direct relationships are increasingly supplanted by indirect relations embedded in communication technologies, bureaucracies and markets. However, objectified impersonal systems are not self-steering or autonomous from human action. Calhoun (1991), for example, argues that concrete (or direct) relationships form a sort of scaffolding for all forms of social integration including apparently indirect relationships and 'we do recognize that behind the impersonal patterns of the market and the mediation of bureaucratic organizations (wholesalers, department stores and the like) a chain of concrete interactions exists'. However, ICTs take us beyond these binary divides by simulating a play of immediacy. Television already creates an illusion of primary relations in which soap stars and politicians are attributed with the characteristics of personal acquaintances and viewers imagine themselves members of communities defined by common identity, tastes, habits and concerns. This potential was exploited early on by political leaders who realized that they could appear as if they were in people's living rooms and build trust. An early exponent of this technique was Richard Nixon who, when running for Vice-President in 1952, bought time on TV to defend himself against allegations of financial impropriety. This came to be known as the infamous 'Checkers speech' in which he attempted to demonstrate his political integrity by broadcasting intimate details of family life, including a sentimental story about his daughter's dog, 'Checkers'. He created a false sense of intimacy in order to project an image of simple honesty and invited the nation to judge him not as a politician but a private person, a technique many politicians were to deploy in the following decades (Gallagher 2004). In the process, images of the political system were reshaped into proportions appropriate to the emerging world of televisual communication immediately which entered into private spaces. Internet communications facilitate powerful mechanisms of coordination of action through indirect relationships that simulate directness. But at the same time they can become media through which direct personal relations can be created and sustained.

DEBATES ABOUT THE INTERNET

The Internet began as a US military communications system but acquired its contemporary potential around 1990 when Tim Berners-Lee developed a way of linking documents to each other in a large web and launched a graphical browser, Mosaic. But the desire for – or at least the social practice of – communicating across distance faster than the speed of human messengers over land appears to be archaic. Table 4.1 provides a brief summary of the stages in the development of interpersonal communication across distance. Although this is a rough and inevitably selective sketch it is notable that the speed of innovation accelerates during the nineteenth and twentieth centuries facilitating increasing intensity space–time compression. This accelerated speed was epitomized by Moore's Law in the 1960s that the number of transistors on a chip doubles about every two years while the cost per component is inversely proportionate to the number of components, which meant that computers became smaller, cheaper and more powerful over the following decades (Moore 1965).[5]

Although the Internet is but the latest in a series of technological advances that have been interwoven with social changes, like earlier developments it has been met with a mixture of enthusiasm and concerns about its potential to weaken communities. The nineteenth-century telegraph eliminated physical distance in communication and through the Morse telegraph people could learn of events in remote parts of the world within hours of them happening. Among telegraph operators 'online' communities of thousands of people developed who spent their working time communicating with each other though they rarely met face to face. During low-traffic periods operators would communicate socially, and some of these relationships developed into 'offline' intimacy – for example, Thomas Edison, who began his career as a telegraph operator, proposed to his (future) wife Mina over the telegraph (Bargh and McKenna 2004). However, these 'online' communities were limited to specialist operators and the medium was not used in everyday life to generate multiple transworld linkages and access to millions of resources as the Internet does.

ICTs constitute nodal selves within simultaneous but routinized complex networks of social interaction. Urry (2003: 63) argues that the Internet can be 'seen as a metaphor for social life that is fluid, involving thousands of networks, of people, machines, programmes, texts and images in which quasi-subjects and quasi-objects mix together in new hybrid forms'. Nonetheless the Internet remains embedded in and shaped by socially facilitating cultures and structures. Something that illustrates this clearly is the persistence of 'digital divides'.

Digital divides

As with other areas of globalization we need to be cautious about overestimating its transformative effects. 'In the 1990s,' says Castells (1999), 'the entire planet is organized around telecommunicated

Table 4.1   Sketch of the development of human communication across space

776 BC	First recorded use of homing pigeons used to send message – the winner of the Olympic Games to the Athenians.
200–100 BC	Human messengers on foot or horseback common in Egypt and China with messenger relay stations built. Sometimes fire messages used from relay station to station instead of humans.
AD 37	Heliographs – first recorded use of mirrors to send messages by Roman Emperor Tiberius.
1455	Johannes Gutenberg invented a printing press with metal movable type.
1560	Camera obscura invented – primitive image making.
1714	Henry Mill received the first patent for a typewriter (but not commercially developed).
1793	Claude Chappe invented the first long-distance semaphore (visual or optical) telegraph line.
1814	Joseph Niépce achieved the first photographic image.
1821	Charles Wheatstone reproduced sound in a primitive sound box – the first microphone.
1835	Samuel Morse invented Morse code.
1843	Samuel Morse invented the first long-distance electric telegraph line. Alexander Bain patented the first fax machine.
1861	Coleman Sellers invented the kinematoscope – a machine that flashed a series of still photographs onto a screen.
1876	Thomas Edison patented the mimeograph – an office copying machine. Alexander Graham Bell patented the electric telephone.
1889	Almon Strowger patented the direct dial telephone or automatic telephone exchange.
1894	Guglielmo Marconi improved wireless telegraphy.
1899	Vladimir Poulsen invented the first magnetic recordings – using magnetized steel tape as the recording medium – the foundation for both mass data storage on disk and tape and the music recording industry. Loudspeakers invented.
1902	Marconi transmitted radio signals from Cornwall to Newfoundland – the first radio signal across the Atlantic Ocean.

1906	Lee Deforest invented the electronic amplifying tube or triode – this allowed all electronic signals to be amplified, improving all electronic communications i.e. telephones and radios.
1914	First cross-continental telephone call made.
1925	John Logie Baird transmitted the first experimental television signal.
1944	Computers such as Harvard's Mark 1 was put into public service – government owned – beginning the Information Science age.
1958	Integrated circuit invented – enabling the further miniaturization of electronic devices and computers.
1969	ARPANET – the first Internet – started.
1971	The computer floppy disk was invented. The microprocessor was invented – considered to be a computer on a chip.
1979	First cellular phone communication network started in Japan.
1994	American government released control of the Internet, and the World Wide Web permitted communication at the speed of light.

Source: information adapted from 'The History of Communication' at http://inventors.
about.com/library/inventors/bl_history_of_communication.htm

networks of computers . . . The entire realm of human activity depends on the power of information.' Actually, this is something of an exaggeration because access to Web networks, as with global-ized networks in general, is highly uneven. 'At the turn of the millen-nium,' say Keohane and Nye (2000) 'more than a quarter of the American population used the World Wide Web compared with one hundredth of 1 percent of the population of South Asia.' Although the number of Internet users globally increased from 16 million in 1995 to 360 million by 2000 the latter represents only 5 per cent of the world's population. As with other communication media, use is concentrated in the developed world where 97 per cent of Internet host computers are located (DiMaggio et al. 2001).[6] The global pattern of Internet use by region is shown in Table 4.2. Of the world's total online community 84 per cent live in developed countries and the 35 countries with lowest levels of development have around 1 per cent of the world's online population (Norris 2001: 45). Only 20 per cent of the world's population have access to telephones although access to mobile phones is expanding rapidly, but illiteracy in many parts of the world is an obstacle to Internet use (Misztal 2000: 175). Most e-commerce is within the OECD countries and between 75 and 80 per cent of e-transactions are between businesses rather than with private customers (Perrons 2004: 172). Access to the Internet is expanding, but this growth is not uniform and is patterned by global and local inequalities, which among other things illustrates the way embedded social relationships structure global technology use. There are reasons to believe that the uneven spatial and social development of the Internet (the 'digital divide') is perpetuating existing social divisions. The Internet facilitates global production chains – fruit boxes can be tagged and traced throughout a journey from the field to supermarket shelf, for example – but the Internet 'does not suspend [the] social relations' that promote uneven development (Perrons 2004: 180). There are parallel communications systems – one for those with income, education and connections and another for those blocked by high barriers of time, cost and uncertainty. There is a fairly uniform rate of growth of Internet take-up but from highly different starting places, so if this trend continues, the global digital divide in relative terms will remain constant. In a rank order of 50 nations based on Internet use as a share of the population there was a high correlation between Internet use and GDP (.78 Pearson according to Houston 2003). So the most affluent countries have on average the highest numbers of people with regular access to the Internet.

Within the developed world there are marked divisions of use, too. In the US between 1995 and 2001 the number of online Americans grew from 25 million (3 per cent of adults) to 106 million Americans (56 per cent of adults) a figure that rises to 76 per cent among the 12–17 year olds (DiMaggio *et al.* 2001; Pew/Internet 2004). The online population is weighted towards the young; those with college education in households with incomes over $75,000 per annum are twenty times more likely to have Internet access than those with low incomes (Perrons 2004: 196). However, the digital divide does not signify a clear single gap that divides a society into

Table 4.2   Internet usage 2004

	Population (millions)	Internet users 2004 (millions)	Growth 2002–04 (%)	Penetration of population
Asia	3,590,196	114,303	84.50	5.90
Middle East	259,318	12,019	128.00	4.60
Africa	879,855	8,073	78.00	0.90
Central America	141,640	5,799	85.80	4.20
North America	323,488	201,339	86.30	62.20
South America	359,595	28,075	96.40	7.80
Caribbean	40,130	1,411	152.30	3.50
European Union*	378,002	171,199	97.20	45.30
Non-EU members	344,506	18,335	84.60	6.80
Oceania	31,528	13,058	71.30	41.40

* EU prior to the accession of new states in 2004

Source: World Internet Stats – www.internetworldstats.com/stats.htm

two groups; rather, it signals disadvantages that can take such forms as access only to lower-performance computers, lower-quality or high-priced connections (e.g. narrowband or dialup connections), difficulty in obtaining technical assistance, and less access to subscription-based contents. There is a new urban dualism between the space of flows based on market value and the isolation of people on low incomes and lack of connections (Perrons 2004: 188).

Further, regions and firms that have the most advanced production technologies generate both inclusion in and exclusion from global networks. Those with the most advanced production and management systems are able to attract global skilled migrants while excluding a significant fraction of the local population whose skills and education do not fit the requirements of the new production system. For example, in Bangalore, Mumbai or Seoul engineers and scientists work with high-technology hubs connected with 'Silicon Valleys' around the world while a large proportion of the population remains in low-status, low-skill jobs when they are lucky enough to be employed at all (Castells 1999). Indeed only 4 per cent of those who work in Silicon Valley's high-tech companies are Black, and only 7 per cent are Hispanic – about half of what the figures would be if they were proportional to the local population. Although many California computer firms are government contractors, most do not meet federally mandated goals for minority hiring. In the past decade, more than a dozen have been cited for affirmative action violations, and several, including Apple, have paid hefty fines (Jacoby 1999).

To what extent is this pattern changing? There is a debate here that parallels wider debates about globalization. There are cyber-optimists who argue that inequalities of access to ICT and, indeed, wider inequalities of economic productivity will gradually fade as the take-up of ITC spreads globally. Some nations such as emerging South-east Asian economies are emulating successful models of ICT diffusion and so may leapfrog stages of development and innovation that earlier economies had to pass through (Norris 2001: 41). Others are more sceptical and point to the persistence of the digital divide both within and between nations and regions. Poorer countries have multiple problems of indebtedness, disease and poor infrastructure, so they may not join the global digital world for many decades (Norris 2001: 5). According to this analysis the Internet is not going to eradicate problems of differential development nor will it (any more than globalization) be an agent of global convergence around new forms of individualization and reflexivity but will by and large reflect existing global disparities of income and life chances. This observation is reinforced by the association between the availability of existing forms of electronic communication and the availability of the Internet – where there are already many radios, telephones and TVs there is most likely also to be access to networked computers. The online population expands exponentially once countries rise above \$9000 per capita GNP.[7]

Whether Internet use in itself can increase economic productivity will depend in part on how it interacts with existing and technological and cultural patterns. More conservative and authoritarian governments and societies regard the Internet as threatening and therefore attempt to protect existing culture while more open and flexible societies may see wider diffusion of ITCs. Even so, it is possible that the Internet will have less impact than previous technologies such as electricity, the telephone and the internal combustion engine because of the 'stickiness' of geographically embedded cultures. Cultural learning will be slower and less embedded via electronic as opposed to face-to-face communications. On balance, then, its effect may be more to reinforce than to overturn existing patterns of economic advantage although this will be a complex and far from uniform relationship. For some at any rate, far from creating a 'borderless world' or the 'death of distance', the current uneven access to ITC suggests that existing social and spatial inequalities will be intensified within and between countries. While stages of development may be leapfrogged, uneven development will remain (Perrons 2004: 185).

Cyber-optimists and pessimists

Globalization enthusiasts extol the potential of the Internet, for example for the democratization of information. For some the technology becomes detached from constraining social and cultural embedding, establishing its own logic and effects.[8] Friedman (2000: 61) argues that with the Internet we can see through almost 'every conceivable wall' since restrictions on broadcasting have gone and global audiences have been created. The Internet, he says, is the 'pinnacle of democratization of information' since no one owns the Internet, it is totally decentralized, no one can turn it off, and it can potentially reach into every home in the world. Never before in human history have so many people been able to learn about so many other peoples' lives, for example, through millions of blogs, and web pages to which millions more have access. Friedman sees here the emergence of a parallel and self-governed society and points to free and interactive facilities such as Wikipedia, the online encyclopaedia to which readers can contribute and edit[9] and OhmyNews International, a Korean newspaper written by readers.[10] Police states, he concludes, cannot afford not to have the Internet but cannot then control the information, thus opening the way for the spread of democratization (Friedman 2001: 70). Similarly, for Poster (2001: 109) access to the Internet has frustrated governments' attempts to regulated or ban it – indeed, 'terrorism' signifies forces that are trans-territorial and cannot be contained within the space of the nation. There are again analyses of the fall of the Soviet Union that refer to the inability of the centrally planned economy and authoritarian state to develop decentralized, open and democratic forms of computer mediated networks (e.g. Shane 1995).

However, this optimism is exaggerated since forces of centralization and commercialization are finding ways to slow or prohibit access as the development of the Internet in China illustrates. It would be better to say that the Internet has become a central site for contest over control and autonomy in communications. In terms of world usage of the Internet what happened in China is significant since between 1995 and 2005 users grew to over 100 million, the second largest online population in the world after the US with 185 million in 2005. Since this represents only 8 per cent of the Chinese population, in a few years the single largest national group of users will be there. However, recognizing the subversive potential of Internet communications, the Chinese authorities have built the so-called the 'Great Firewall of China', a project also known as 'Golden Shield'. The system blocks content by preventing IP addresses (an identification specific to each device on a computer network) from being routed through it, and it consists of standard firewall and proxy servers at the Internet gateways. The system also selectively engages in 'DNS cache poisoning' – a technique that tricks a DNS (Domain Name System) into believing it has received authentic information when, in reality, it has not. The government has been able to block searches with certain key words such as 'democracy', 'Tibet', 'BBC News', 'Google', sex sites and many blogs.[11] In 2004 47,000 Internet cafes were shut down (*People's Daily Online* 2005). China has 2,800 surveillance centres to monitor text message traffic and in July 2004 installed a system that allows authorities to filter messages for 'false political rumours' and 'reactionary remarks', as well as references to Amnesty International, the BBC, Tibet, the Tiananmen Square massacre in 1989 and Falun Gong, a religious movement. The system generates automatic alerts to the 30,000 police officers monitoring online messages. Of 107,000 illegal messages tracked since during November 2005 alone, 14,000 were sent by illegal lotteries; 7,062 were related to prostitution or pornography, and 11,000 came from groups soliciting fake receipts or other financial information.[12]

However, the Chinese government does not appear to be systematically examining Internet content, as this appears to be technically impractical and the firewall is not infallible. Yahoo!, Microsoft and, in 2006, Google assisted Chinese censorship by setting local servers to block politically unacceptable content. But Net users in China know how to get round some restrictions – addresses of proxies are well known and users who log on to hosts outside China may still access prohibited sites at the risk of detection. Further, China's needs to attract capital to fund communications expansion may exert pressure to liberalize Internet access and in due course it is possible that, as Friedman and others expect, the democratic decentralized potential of the medium will be realized. It is fairly clear, though, that efforts by governments to regulate Internet use will intensify, as will efforts by individuals seeking alternatives to oppressive societies and governments.

Of course, attempts to control the Internet are not limited to authoritarian regimes but are evident in the commercial world, too, as businesses lobby for global copyright enforcement and media corporations such as News Corp take possession of the web search tools on which all but hardened geeks depend and rent them out. The Internet is used extensively for commerce, generating around $300 billion of consumer trade in 2004, and with 95 per cent of the world's computers running Microsoft software the Internet could be seen as becoming a major commercial machine (Technology News 2007).[13] More commercial investment and ownership could have consequences for regulation, as illustrated by the Intellectual Property Rights' Initiative. A small number of global corporations and few dozen national corporations control the majority of film, photographic, writing, music and research archives, and this control is being tightened. For example, the World Intellectual Property Organization (WIPO) is proposing an international treaty that would extend the power that broadcasters have to control how images and sounds are recorded and used including material in the public domain. Once material (even that not subject to copyright) has been broadcast, broadcasters would receive intellectual property rights (IPRs) for 50 years. This has been prompted particularly by file swapping and illegal downloading of music. While this may appear reasonable, campaigners against the WIPO claim that it is in the interests of music companies, since 40 per cent of revenue from US live concerts gets to performers as opposed to only 4 per cent from CD sales revenues. According to one performer, musicians are not being abused by Internet users swapping files but by the industry that is 'robbing them blind'.[14] Whatever the truth of these claims they illustrate how the Internet is the site of struggles over political, economic and juridical powers that structure the 'flows' of globalization.

Decline of community (again?)

Another area of debate is around the effects of the Internet on communities, social capital and general social interaction that in many ways mirrors debates about globalization (Morse 1998). The idea of modernity's destructiveness has deep roots in sociology and from the late nineteenth century a sociological critique of modernity lamented the passing of communal social bonds illustrated by Tönnies' (1971) famous distinction between *Gemeinschaft* and *Gesellschaft* and Simmel's concern with the cultural effects of urban and commercial society. Here earlier progressive optimism faded behind a more nostalgic and pessimistic motif that modernity's scientific and technical achievements had destroyed something authentic and meaningful that had preceded it. Bryan Turner points out that this was not just a passing mood but that it became a dominant theme with deep resonance in European culture, illustrated by Weber's comment that acquisition of wisdom from the Tree of Knowledge involved a transgression and disqualification from the paradise of naiveté to which there was no return (Turner 1992: 133–5). Knowledge of nature that could be harnessed in an industrial–technological civilization meant that there could be no return to the enchanted cultures of the past. Current critiques of globalization and cyberspace are 'recapitulating more than a century of sociological debate about whether community has become lost, saved, or liberated since the Industrial Revolution' (Wellman and Hampton 1999).

This is illustrated by Ritzer's critique of the 'globalization of nothing' and his distinction between 'place and non-place'. Globalization tends to be associated with the proliferation of nothing

(2003: 73). He says, 'Few things seem less like a locale, and more like a flow than the Internet and its Web sites. . . . [that] offer a perfect example of the dehumanisation associated with nothing and the non-place end of the place-non-place continuum' (2003: 127–8). For Ritzer, 'nothing' is a 'social form that is centrally conceived, controlled and comparatively devoid of distinctive substantive content' such as credit cards (2003: 3). 'Something', on the other hand, is a 'social form that is generally indigenously conceived, controlled and comparatively rich in distinctive substantive content', such as credit negotiated between a banker and a customer. The broader and deeper void associated with the Internet (especially that portion associated with consumption) leads to a fear of losing oneself in an abyss of the Internet but also rending oneself into many conflicting parts as one jumps around different selves in chat rooms. Non-places are 'spaces of flows' – houses centrally planned by developers, with a limited number of designs repeated in many parts of the world (2003: 41). Thus resistance to symbols of nothing and 'grobalization' (the growth of nothing through the spread of globalization) take the form of anti-Americanism, global attacks on McDonald's, which 'reflect the . . . growing awareness that capitalism, Americanization and McDonaldization . . . are threats to indigenous cultures' (2003: 93), which is part of a struggle of the 'grobal' against the 'glocal'.

These critiques replay the old sociological trope of the critique of modernity as alienating and destructive of intimate communal social relations – impersonality versus intimacy, disembedded versus embedded relations, anonymous and fleeting versus deep and meaningful social encounters. But Ritzer attempts to establish a critique of 'nothing' that is based on what seem to be personal preferences and takes little account of social context and meanings. Disneyland may be invested with meaning to, say, a ten-year-old child, and much more 'something' than the forms of culture and life valued by adults. On the other hand, the personal loan agreed between the banker and the client will be affected by global movements in capital, interest rates and the lending targets of the bank – this may be no more than the *illusion* of a personal exchange that is as globally structured as getting a loan on the Internet. Virtual and mass-produced objects can become 'real' in the sense that they will be given multiple meanings by users and integrated into everyday lives. Community and authenticity have long since ceased to be based (if they ever were) on socially integrated contiguous locales. Ritzer's distinction between authentic and inauthentic is tied to a supposedly firm concept of natural and timeless preservation that takes no account of how the social and natural have become intertwined over hundreds of years. So he says that Rembrandt's *Night Watch* has been so altered by wear and tear and restoration that it may once *have been* authentic but it is 'clearly' no longer so (2003: 203). This is really only pointing out how through social labour objects inevitably become incorporated within social processes and frames of meaning. Ritzer acknowledges that this distinction is open to familiar objections such as those raised against other elitist judgements on popular culture, but he responds with reference to Habermas's defence of the project of modernity, in which he sees a 'standpoint' of validity for critical judgements. But this does not work. Habermas proposes a reconstruction of communication on which he founds procedural pragmatic ethics that are explicitly opposed to any foundational standpoints (Ray 2003). Instead of providing good reasons for proposing an authentic–inauthentic dichotomy Ritzer weakly concludes that if the reader had given as much thought as he has to these issues 'they too would be concerned about the long-term trend in the direction of nothing and the loss associated with it' (Ritzer 2003: 216).

More empirically based studies also identify a loss of sociality associated with the Internet. In a study based on a sample of 4,113 US adults in 2,689 households, Nie and Erbring (2000) argue that the Internet has created a 'lonely crowd in cyberspace' because the time online necessarily takes time away from friends. They found that the more time people spend using the Internet the more they lose contact with their social environment. The effect is noticeable with those spending two to five hours per week on the Internet and rises substantially for those who spend at least ten hours per week, who report a 15 per cent decrease in social activities. Unlike TV, which can be treated as background noise to ongoing conversations, the Internet requires more engagement and attention and consequently less time interacting with real human beings. Some 60 per cent of Internet users in this survey said they had reduced TV viewing and newspaper reading. Further, Nie and Erbring claim that ITCs are 'intruding into every other aspect of our lives', blurring lines between the public and private, a theme taken up in Siebel and Wehrheim (2003). The latter argue that the spheres of public and private are delocalized as boundaries between home and workplace are breached by cellphones through which informal controls of the home and workplace extend into public space. People are physically present while being emotionally occupied elsewhere. Cellphones violate the reserved indifference of Simmel's city-dweller with loud public presentation of business and family affairs no one wants to hear (Siebel and Wehrheim 2003).

Again, the claim here is that the impersonality and anonymity of the Internet erode authentic social bonds. These 'strange and strained creations lacking emotive content and means of reciprocity' allow for Net'scapism – rapid exit from online interactions that lack the stickiness of geographically centred cultures (Houston 2003). Further, computer mediated communication (CMC) limits the bandwidth of social communication especially non-verbal features of speech and facial cues. Although the Internet is primarily a visual medium, most computer mediated interaction does not involve eye contact so an important dimension of sociality is excluded. 'The eye,' Simmel comments, 'is destined for a completely unique sociological achievement: the connection and interaction of individuals that lies in the act of individuals looking at one another.' The significance of the 'shortest line' between the eyes is that 'no objective trace remains and the interaction dies in the moment in which the immediacy' of the exchange lapses (Simmel 1997: 111–12).

Poster (1995) argues that technically advanced societies are at a point in their history similar to that of the emergence of urban, merchant culture in feudal society. The Internet is a new form of identity, imitating the telephone's decentralized quality and bringing in a new electronic age with 'many to many communications'. The broadcast model breeds new consumerism, passivity, crassness and mediocrity. New subjects of the Internet are unstable, multiple and diffuse – senders are also receivers, producers and consumers upsetting the logic of the first media age. But as a consequence of this, 'real' communities are in decline. 'Real' communities had fixed, stable identities while virtual communities are fluid and 'without visual cues about gender, age, ethnicity and social status', which creates new possibilities for falsifying the self. Thus new types of subject are created through the Internet, in which time, space, body mind and subject/object are transformed (Poster 2001). Print media created the transcendental subject of reflection who read and engaged in a cognitive response, and offered a representation of an outside world, on which the reader was encouraged to reflect. Electronic media are a hyper-real techno-cultural landscape in which subjects are continually diffuse and fragmentary. The relation of representation is undermined, as digital media do not invite a cognitive response but identification with the digital text, that is, the question of how well reality is represented is eclipsed by the flow of text and graphics. Taking up Foucault's theme of the death of the author, Poster presents the digital age as 'post-author' in which 'who speaks' becomes irrelevant to the understanding of the communication. Analogue text has a resemblance to the original, representative function of communication, but digital communications dissolve the ego in many-to-many communications. The Internet dissociates communicative action from territorialized spatial relations of the body, and the subject is transformed through online communities into which one invents oneself and knows that others also invent themselves. Instantaneous global contact inserts the subject into networks, opening new social and cultural worlds already redefining what it means to be human (2001: 37). This even undermines relations between producer and consumer as the centre of the economy shifts from making objects to consumption and in cyberspace this means 'producing culture as you consume it' (2001: 48).

Poster's claim that 'electronic geographies . . .[are] redefining what it means to be human' (2001: 37) rests on the claims that online, people invent themselves through screen genders and volatile identities, which provoke a crisis of representation. The 'analogue self' (that is the offline self) has a resemblance to the original (or presumably he means that this self is grounded in ongoing practices of validation and recognition), but the 'digital self' is fully post-representational and 'exists' only in virtual space in a regime of fluidity even if it correctly depicts some online interactions. More significant perhaps is the claim that with the growth of digital surveillance and biometric archives there emerge parallel 'databased selves'. 'What makes [these] different from our actual selves,' Simon (2005) argues, 'is that databased selves are more easily accessible, observable, manageable and predictable than we are.' This raises some important issues about the relationship between online and offline identities that will now be examined, but it should be noted that the existence of 'databased selves' as the product of post-panoptic surveillance does not eradicate the socially embedded agency of 'real' people.

THE INTERNET IN EVERYDAY LIFE

Two approaches to the relationship between Internet use and social life have emerged. One emphasizes its transformative capacity for better or worse in relation to everyday life while the other emphasizes the continued importance of propinquity and face-to-face social relations as a substratum to the development of online sociality. In line with the general thesis here in relation to globalization – that complex forms of reciprocal sociation facilitate it – the Internet will be placed within this wider social context. Contrary to the claims of the critics noted above the Internet enhances social ties defined in many ways (DiMaggio *et al.* 2001) and actually facilitates the formation of social capital. Poster stresses the constitutive character of communications media in their own right, as does Houston (2003), but there is also evidence that there are complex interactions between online and offline association and that propinquity remains essential to the development of trust and enduring social connections (Boden 1994). In this way the Internet again mirrors the process of globalization that it facilitates since it is increasingly being incorporated into everyday life, where it is used in both innovative and traditional ways and which it changes but does not revolutionize.

Sociality online

Does the Internet bring social isolation, erosion of traditional community and atomization or constant communication combined with new forms of social organization? The argument here is that technology usage adapts to the patterns of its users and so has different outcomes for different people. We need to differentiate between 'communities' generated online such as Usenet[15] or the Whole Earth Electronic Link (WELL)[16] and people who meet or have met face to face and use electronic communications. Electronic gatherings meet a range of social needs – for affiliation and emotional support, to contact others with shared interests, to access information, to seek entertainment and role playing, for political and social activism, and to engage in the informal economy (Hornsby 1998). New forms of community can be created technologically as a kind of gift economy where people do things for one another out of a spirit of building something between them as Rheingold (2000) argues happens with the WELL. The Internet encourages specialized relations because it permits people to select contacts within their own homes, and feelings of closeness may be based in shared interests rather than other characteristics such as age, gender, residence and so forth.

Many studies of Internet use question the claim that the Internet is socially isolating, having markedly changed people's patterns of interaction. The Home Net project (Kraut *et al.* 1998) indicated that Internet users have larger social networks than non- or infrequent users, and rather than being isolating, Internet communities offer multiple supports. Nie and Erbring (2000) found that the Internet created a lonely crowd in cyberspace because it necessarily took time away from friends, but considerable evidence points to the opposite conclusion. Nie and Erbring identify a shift from telephone use and television watching (both viewed as social activities) to Internet use (viewed as solitary activity). But the Internet can be viewed as an interactive and social activity in its own right – in which case Nie and Erbring have only identified a change in the medium rather than a decline in social communication in itself. Katz *et al.* (2001) found that the more time people spend online the more likely they are to engage in offline activities. The Electronic Village Study (Hampton and Wellman 2002) challenges the notion that there is an absence of intimate personal acquaintanceship on the Web but that on the contrary the longer people spend online the more likely they are to build social capital. The Internet allows both asynchronous and direct one-to-one and one-to-many broadcasts and has become another communication tool among many ways in which people can interact. Asynchronous communication is a low-cost way for people to organize their lives, but it is not a distinct social system separate from existing foci of activity. They conclude that the Internet has intensified the volume and range of neighbourly relations rather than reducing social connections.

Wellman writes of a 'non-local community', castles of 'network based culture' and geography and hierarchy on the verge of losing influence. This is an exaggeration in that many social interactions still occur face to face – people still chat to neighbours, they still have line managers and many organizations are still similar to the way they looked twenty years ago. But informal networks may be growing in significance – while community solidarities depend on face-to-face interactions these may be supplemented by long-distance electronically mediated links (Davis 2004). This is made increasingly possible through social software that enables groups to communicate and collaborate online so long as these groups have some principle of selectivity that enables them to retain a collective identity. Beyond a certain size members find it hard to align individual interests with collective identities while smaller networks allow stronger ties and more trust and reputational risk. Social software is used by people in everyday lives – group-filtering mechanisms, websites designed to introduce other people such as Ryze-for-Business. One comment on the latter looks forward to the possibility of more networked links between social sites and programmes:

> None of us wants to join 10 or 20 social networks. The headache of filling out the profiles, interacting with the systems, etc. is just too time consuming for most normal people. But we'd all like to be part of LinkedIn and Ryze for business networking, Tribe for classifieds, Friendster if we are dating, etc. Will there be a way that I can have one profile like I have one email address and each social network just takes that profile applies its own business logic and rules for its particular application and delivers value to me? I don't know, but I'd like that to happen.[17]

Again, in one of the largest studies of Internet use in North America Haase et al. (2002)[18] found that most relationships formed in cyberspace continue in physical space, the Internet is used more to maintain existing ties than to create new ones and the most frequent users were the most socially integrated in the survey. Distance still constrains communications: only 30 per cent of respondents were in contact with friends and relatives living 'far away' and friendships were mostly 'local'. Further, visitors to multi-user environments (MUDs) are more likely to participate in public voluntary organizations although educational attainment was the strongest predictors of participation. People who frequently seek information from the Internet are likely to participate in organizations, although Haase *et al.* conclude that the Internet supplements political participation but does not change people's levels of involvement. There is no association between extent and length of use of the Internet and a 'sense of community' measured on a psychometric scale, but there was a greater sense of *online* community among long-term users as opposed to those who had only been online for a short time. The Internet is increasing social capital, civic engagement and a sense of belonging to an (online) community. But there is 'no single Internet effect'.

The Pew/Internet project (2004), based on telephone survey of 2,013 adult Americans' use of the Internet in 2003, found that the Internet is used in multiple ways organically as part of everyday routines. A large proportion of those surveyed (92 per cent) routinely used the Internet for getting everyday information; 85 per cent routinely used it to communicate and interact with others; 75 per cent used the Internet to conduct everyday transactions and 69 per cent as a general source of entertainment. Overall the evidence suggests that rather than being an isolating and socially maladaptive activity, communicating with others over the Internet helps maintain close ties with one's family and friends but also facilitates the formation of close and meaningful new relationships within a relatively safe environment (Bargh and McKenna 2004).

Racism on the Internet

Sociality however has many different contents and objects of communication. Just as online communication generates new forms of social capital and 'community' so it also links together disparate racists and hate communities. Racism on the Internet is expanding as racist and extreme right organizations make use of its potential as an alternative medium that is largely unregulated, is cheap and transcends national boundaries. There is growing research into the

Internet as a medium for racism and constructions of violence through chat rooms where anonymity protects participants from the usual social taboos against the expression of both racism and violence (Glasser *et al.* 2002). Balestri (2002) undertook a study of football supporter sites that were subject to content analysis and classified into 'absent' (no racist) content, 'latent' (concealed racist allusions), 'recurrent' (direct racist allusions) and 'strong' (explicitly racist and xenophobic). Reviewing a range of racist Internet sites, Back (2002a) examines the relationship between digital technologies, racism and the emergence of new patterns of racist culture in transnational and international settings. In this and other studies (Back 2002b, 2002c) he notes how cyber-technologies make new types of racist behaviour possible, for example, celebrating 'real incidents of racist violence and simulat[ing] the vicarious "pleasure" of being party to such vicious acts' (Back 2002a). Extreme violence, both real and fantasy, is a feature of racism on the Internet and there is a need for further research that examines the relationship between this cyber-violence and actual violence and its significance for the reconfiguration of racism in general.

The typical activist is much younger than in the past and less likely to be a member of a neo-Nazi organization or ideologically sophisticated and organizationally connected. However, they are part of a xenophobic culture that includes both the older organizational forms and a heterogeneous youth culture. Although the risk of hate crime varies with locality (some more dangerous than others) youth cultures such as that of the fascho-skinheads have broken out of parochial boundaries to establish international links through the Internet, which serves as a source of re-affirmation of their identity and increases their organizational capacity. 'Stormfront' is a gateway into skinhead and racist sites. Domain names will be changed periodically to evade blocking by ISPs. Watts argues that:

> There are many reports of contacts to a variegated international network, particularly in the United States, United Kingdom, Scandinavia, the Netherlands, and to a lesser degree Spain (relations with the Czechs, Poles, Hungarians, and other central Europeans are somewhat more strained, but they exist).

(Watts 2001)

In Germany, the government estimates that there are more than 200 skinhead or racist websites (in the United States, there are far more, of course); many of them are in English to broaden their impact (or because they use North American Internet providers to avoid German censorship). The growth of Internet racism and the linking of disparate individuals into global virtual hate communities follow the same social logic as other forms of Internet use.

Intimate strangers

The idea that narratives of the self can be written and re-written is part of post-Cartesian deconstructionist 'posthuman' vision of cyberspace (Hayles 1999). People may (temporarily) escape their embodied selves and the expectations and norms of behaviour with their everyday lives. So when one plays in virtual space one can be a gay man who pretends to be a heterosexual woman or whatever. As Žižek (1998) notes, this is open to the contrasting interpretations of either liberation (infinite possibilities to build new identities) or paranoiac visions of manipulation by the digital space. For Žižek neither of these views is right because the encounter with cyberspace prompts an even more profound universal doubt – that we may now become aware that there never was a 'real reality'. Reality always was virtual; we just were unaware of it. 'What if my self-awareness is merely a superficial "screen"?' Somewhat judgementally Žižek says:

> What is horrible about virtual sex is not that before we had a real partner whom we touched, embraced, squeezed and now you just masturbate in front of the screen . . . The point is we become aware of how there never was real sex. . . . What if real sex is only masturbation with a real partner?
>
> (Žižek n.d.)

For Žižek this possibility is indicative of a wider questioning of the self, prompted by the encounter with cyberspace.

An important objection to this view of the radical doubt of reality is precisely Žižek's preoccupation with the Cartesian problem of the ego, since the self is not engaged in secluded reflection but is already both intersubjective and embodied in physical and social being.

Underpinning free-floating cyber-selves there are our 'real life' bodies, situated in historically determinate lifeworlds and existing through networks of interaction with others. Intersubjectivity is not a relation between thought and object but the site of historically determinate disclosure of a horizon of possible meaning. If we worry less about the medium of digital communication and focus more on the social forms and rules constituting intersubjectivity some of the hyperbole surrounding the construction of cyber-utopias and dystopias recedes.

How people negotiate the tensions between virtual relationships within digital space and the interaction order of physical co-presence tells us about the play of personal and impersonal relations that is vital to the globalization process. It also shows how virtual and globalized spaces may be shaped by and grounded in social, bodily and cultural experiences. One example of this is Internet dating, which creates a 'seamless movement between reading descriptions, writing responses and exchanging messages' (Hardey 2002). In some ways Internet meeting is congruent with the post-traditional idea of 'pure relationships' (Giddens 1992; Hardey 2002), which value talk rather than passion, negotiation rather than commitment and advancement of the self rather than the development of the couple associated with the traditional ideology of romantic love. Email is more open and interactive than the traditional memo form of communication and has evolved into an interactional form of some intensity (Boden and Molotch 1994). Users 'chat', exchange gossip, send computer jokes, circulate tips advertise sexual preferences and argue. Compared with face-to-face interactions email allows increased disclosure and intimacy and escape from the constraints of time and biography. An example of this is the global use of sites such as the UK-based Friends Reunited – in order to revisit past loves and lost youth – and Genes Reunited – to enable contact between remote family members who would previously have known little or nothing about each other. Friends Reunited enables people's biography to escape the constraints of temporality and linearity by 'returning' to periods of one's life that in a pre-digital age would probably have remained in memories and old diaries. This kind of online community is large but bound together by a nostalgic desire to connect with lost biography. Genes Reunited claims 41 million names of ancestors and many other genealogical research sites worldwide create virtual communities of the living and the dead. In a context of greater intimacy and 'liquid love' (Bauman 2003) the Internet facilitates the search both for security but also fluidity and experimentation.

Intimacy on the Internet allows the claims both that online relationships are impersonal and shallow, and that being liberated from the constraints of physical locality they create opportunities for new kinds of relationship. It is true that in Internet interactions many relational cues are missing – non-verbal, bodily movement, facial expression – so the communications are more impersonal (Parks and Floyd 1996), but at the same time email allows for immediacy, informality and lawlessness and the disappearance of boundaries between backstage and frontstage behaviour with an absence of contextual determination of events. Email is quicker, denser and formless, and involves less commitment to what is said than in enduring face-to-face interactions (Misztal 2000: 202). This makes for easy intimacy and the construction of the other in line with one's desires to the point that some claim to know online acquaintances better than some oldest friends. McKenna *et al.* (2002) argue that people are more likely to express their 'true' selves offline – when Internet partners like each other they tend to project onto each other the qualities of friends they know in 'real' life. Many online relationships become close offline. People reveal 'true' selves online because the risks of self-disclosure are less than in face-to-face relationships. Talking with strangers is easier online – in urban environments few of us would walk up to a stranger and start chatting. Hardey reports one respondent saying:

> It is easy to get into deep issues with someone who is really a stranger. That is the best thing about the system. There are no barriers so that you get to know and trust each other well before either think to meet.
>
> (Hardey 2004)

Relationships develop as people come to depend on each other in complex ways (Parks and Floyd 1996) and relationships evolve over time with increasing experience.

Internet dating is an environment where authenticity is valued and communication is based on trust between strangers. With the increase in one-person households the Internet allows new ways of establishing intimate relationships with specific sites for the pursuit of particular interest – for all sexual identities, for long-term or fleeting relationships. There are dating sites for religious communities.[19] Stigmatized identities can find online support, such as the self-management of illness or social interaction for people who are isolated and lack mobility and so on. But while Internet presentation of the self involves strategies of marketing and a play of and with cultural stereotypes of masculinity and femininity, self-descriptions will often be shaped by the knowledge that success will involve meeting offline so there are limits to the kinds of self-presentation that can be sustained. Some argue that electronic networks alone cannot build trust relations and that online communicates are less civil, more conflictual, more risky and democratic than offline ones (Misztal 2000: 183). There may be a breach of social conventions online – as with cruelty and flaming – since with 'nothing but bits' between them people may feel they can say anything (Seabrook 1997: 119). Internet communities are self-policing and the enforcement of codes of conduct is difficult, although the notion of 'netiquette' indicates the existence of communicative rules. There are unwritten rules that may vary between sites, such as whether explicit sexual content is acceptable or not and conventions about how quickly to reply and the interaction order, and techniques to establish trustworthiness (Hardey 2004; Preece 2004). Further, one study of 'flaming' in a Usenet newsgroup identified the development of coping strategies and normative codes among participants, such as withdrawal, offering apologies, denunciation, posting poems, mediation, showing solidarity, joking and normalizing (Lee 2005). Membership of e-communities can be regulated by administrators enforcing conditions of use – such as the TinyMUD and TinySex sites where enactment of fantasy is based on mutual consent of the 'realities' being created.

Globalized space contains simultaneous multiple connections and loyalties combined with intimate space, close and sharing interaction (Kusma 2002). One example of this is the use of the Internet by migrants to overcome boundaries and inhibiting social conventions. Much work on refugees emphasizes loss, victimization and cultural adjustment but neglects the mundane experiences of developing social and intimate relationships, which relate to larger societal discourses and systems of meaning. Kusma's study of Oroma refugee women from Ethiopia argues that the space of intimacy exists where one's own and ones partner's identities interweave. Cohesion has multiple forms and levels and is enhanced by the interweaving of personal, national and global levels. In this study a sense of self-hood (of 'Oroma-ness') was interrupted when migrants moved from familiar life patterns and arrived in the globalized space of Toronto. They defended the intimate space of being Oroma against the pressures from a dominant society, from which point they attempted to venture out, but found intimacy among Oroma men difficult to find. In this context the Internet created new possibilities for actively constructing new identities and establishing new social bonds. But at the same time traditional relational patterns changed and the women's distance from Oroma society facilitated their ability to break down oppressive self/other and home/elsewhere binaries. Kusma (2002) argues that the experience of migration combined with the ability to explore intimate relationships through the relative anonymity and 'safety' of the Internet opened up creative spaces for both personal liberation and social transformation.

Sociality offline – the scaffolding for virtuality

As the example of the Oroma indicates, the Internet provides a medium in which people engage in a communicative process of building up trust, of self-disclosure and of exploring the other in relation to their reflexively constructed needs and desires. The Internet can in many different ways be the starting point for offline relationships, illustrated by dating sites like Update.com and Match.com. The establishment of contacts through textual interaction facilitates a lightening of corporal constraints, but in due course these become relevant again with the prospect of actually meeting. Thus Hardey (2002) concludes that rather than view the Internet as another life world of multiple identities it is 'just a different space where [people] . . . may meet others and make use of a vast number of services and resources'. Indeed, 'people are always somewhere', as Boden and Friedland (1994: 6) point out, and 'things have to happen in particular places and objects exist in a spatiotemporal relation to one another'. Internet technologies, like the social possibilities provided by globalization in general, are increasingly integrated into everyday life. Pew/Internet (2004) researchers also found that most Internet users still default to traditional ways of communicating, transacting affairs, getting information and entertaining themselves. Thus we find the continued geographic concentration of corporate headquarters and financial intermediaries in dominant cities of the world's most powerful nations – the scaffolding for virtual communications. In business settings a high premium is placed on co-presence because of the frequent need to develop complex understandings, arrange informal trade-offs and deal with unanticipated tensions. 'Two different measures,' they say, 'suggest that overall the virtual world of the Internet still takes second place to the real world as the place to accomplish daily tasks or enjoy recreation.' People everywhere show remarkable compulsion to talk face to face to reaffirm bonds of basic trust through co-presence, and global culture depends on local structures of action (Boden and Friedland 1994). For Boden and Molotch (1994) intimacy is the basis for advanced modernity and co-presence remains *the* fundamental mode of human intercourse. One reason for this is that co-presence is 'thick' with information since words always derive meanings from context and body talk. The latter provides cues to substantive meaning from physical movement, eye contact and facial expression, which are lost in remote communication. Power and status are communicated through posture and, as Simmel argued, musculature and eye contact signals intimacy (Simmel 1997: 109–20). Touching is a full vocabulary of deep significance that increases self-disclosure and rank – high-status people initiate touching more than lower status. Co-presence is evidence of commitment, and Boden and Molotch contrast the 'togetherness of workers, friends and lovers' with the 'civil disattention' of impersonal interactions. Conversation timings maximize the tendency for socially solidary actions to take place. Timing is important for managing solidary relations. For example, a negative response to a request can be disruptive of solidary bonds but a delay before response can allow withdrawal of the request. For actors to use time to achieve solidarity and trust there must be minimum space between them. Co-presence is thus better suited to deploying nuances in social interaction than Internet-based communication.[20]

In the end, then, online communication is not equivalent to face to face and it may be that the nature of sociality online resembles 'the characteristics of exchange at the cocktail party rather than exchange in cohesive communities' and the virtual community demands a real one prior to it in order to function successfully (Misztal 2000: 197 and 193). However, electronic networks may partially replicate face-to-face communication, as information spreads through networks very quickly, for example, evading controls and hierarchies despite a reduction in face-to-face contact (Misztal 2000: 183). People's willingness to use and especially trust Internet communications, though, is likely to be dependent on the surrounding social scaffolding underpinning the use of CMCs. Keser *et al.* (2002) found that Internet adoption across a number of countries correlated with the degree of trust locally, measured by the World Values Survey, explaining two-thirds of Internet adoption once other relevant variables such as the number of computers in the country have been statistically controlled.

CONCLUSIONS

The Internet is a source of the compression of time and space that is central to globalization and it is at the same time the most globalized public space and the most private intimate space often accessed in a solitary setting. In globalized communities people feel part of their world and a 'village' at the same time. There is a diversity of views as to whether the Internet portends a posthuman world of impersonal lost authenticity or the mirror image of this, a liberation from space and embodiment – or, again, whether it is just another medium of communication alongside many others. The view advanced here is that use of the Internet is organically embedded within existing social patterns of local lives and within culturally constraining and constituting social relationships. Actors communicating in cyberspace generate ways in which the world will be recognizable to other actors. There has been a rapid growth in the use of e-commerce, for example, but this did not come fully formed into the world – rather, it emerged from conscious decisions about the use of various logistical technologies. These technologies in turn were shaped by such decisions and the kinds of conventions that formed around them (Leyshon *et al.* 2005).

The existence of globalized spaces of communication does still presuppose that social meaning is produced in specific social, geographic and cultural contexts that are temporally bound. One effect of globalization is that previously localized capabilities become ubiquities though what is not ubiquitous is non-transferable non-codified knowledge. It is 'sticky' and arises in 'doing' social interaction. But this depends on more than spatial proximity; it includes shared norms, conventions, values, expectations and routines arising from commonly experienced frameworks or institutions. The Internet is able to connect strangers without face-to-face contact but with over 600 million users it is too vast for groups to develop close bonds unless they have offline relationships or forms of filtering that create semi-closed groups. The integration of the Internet into everyday life will proceed through software that enables people to communicate instinctively at a tacit level. Tacit knowledge is always already present in face-to-face social situations but Internet anonymity allows for its disruption through identity switching, obscene contributions and political extremism. Social software will attempt to access the tacit dimension of everyday social lives by broadening the range of symbols deployed – as, for example, MS 3 Degrees integrates music and images with text (Davis 2004: 40). Increasingly e-interactions use software such as Instant Messenger that is designed for simultaneous interaction as opposed to email that can be picked up late, although this is best suited to use in small groups and one-to-one communication. While ICT will change structures of everyday life through the invention of new traditions, software cannot recreate everyday social lives or replace them and cannot conjure a thriving community out of thin air (Davis 2004: 42). Sites such as Upmystreet can bring benefits without anyone claiming that they will do anything as dramatic as transform communities, regenerate democracy, or create rich networks of local friendships (Davis 2004: 42). They can maintain ties over distance just as well across the garden fence as across the world, creating a kind of 'local cosmopolitanism' (Davis 2004: 58) of networked organizations and individuals.

Internet communication is symptomatic of the ubiquitous 'strangeness' in a mobile world in which many are resident but potentially passing through. Many social relationships previously regarded as 'solid' have become more 'liquid' and encounters in cyberspace epitomize fluidity and rapid entry–exit and the potential for both proximity and anonymity. However, the cyber-society is one of many media of social existence and is constrained and accomplished, as are other globalization processes by situated actors within em-bodied and localized social settings.

5

GLOBAL INEQUALITIES
AND EVERYDAY LIFE

I saw innumerable hosts, foredoomed to darkness, dirt, pestilence, obscenity, misery and early death.

Charles Dickens, *A December Vision*, 1850

Two themes of this book are, first, to explore the ways in which globalization is grounded in social action and communication and, second, to argue for the continuing relevance of engagement with the central ideas in classical sociological theory. This chapter develops these with reference to global inequalities and their consequences. Between the 1960s and the 1980s debate about the relationship between rich developed and poor 'developing' nations was couched in terms of modernization versus dependency and then world systems approaches (see pp.21–4). However, events that took shape during the 1980s and 1990s radically shifted the terms of debate and significantly enhanced the process of economic globalization (Babb 2005). In the wake of the Third World debt crisis and the collapse of the post-war Bretton Woods regulatory order, World Bank and IMF policy was informed by neo-liberal ideology that insisted that it was only through liberating market forces that poor countries could 'catch up' with the developed world. The so-called 'Washington consensus' shared by the US Administration, the World Bank and the IMF held that developing countries should be given financial support only in return for conditions that generally involved reducing inflation, slashing public spending and deregulating economic activity. One major manifestation of this belief was structural adjustment lending programmes that insisted on privatization, marketization and (trade) liberalization as conditions of new or restructured loans. This global strategy (that was imposed on postcommunist countries too) opened locales to the impact of global capital to an unprecedented extent and changed the terms of debate about global poverty.

There is now extensive debate about the effects of globalization on the pattern of social inequality both within and between countries, especially between developed and developing ones. This chapter examines this debate while discussing the effects of global inequalities in everyday life. The impact of transnational corporations will be discussed. The chapter also examines the relationship between capitalist development and social solidarities on a global scale. The twentieth century has seen what might come to be regarded as one of the most significant social changes of recent times – what Araghi calls 'global depeasantization'. At the outset of the twentieth century the majority of the world's population were occupied in agriculture and lived in rural areas. By 1950 only 29 per cent of people globally and 16 per cent of people in developing countries lived in urban areas. By 2000 50 per cent of people worldwide and 41 per cent of people in developing countries lived in urban areas, and the peasantry had become a minority (Araghi 2000). This has involved, as with the growth of urban capitalism in Europe, dispossession of rural labour and the rapid extension of commercial relations into the countryside. However, whereas the framework of national capitalism provided a national context for the organization of social movements and a gradual process of mitigation of its effects, the global dislocation of the countryside is both extremely rapid and largely unregulated. Many contemporary global issues of migration and social conflict are linked to this process.

At the same time many accounts of the socio-economic impact of globalization emphasize economic processes to the exclusion of discussion of how economies are embedded within broader configurations of space, identity, family networks and social meaning and action. The case studies of global penetration of agribusiness into smallholder communities discussed in this chapter emphasize the complex integration of these dimensions of social locales. The question of livelihood, which is central to discussions of economic behaviour, involves multiple dimensions of locality, culture, structure, action and adaptation. This should reinforce the argument that we need to understand how global power and money transform but also are themselves transformed and mediated by locales in diverse ways, one consequence of which is that outcomes will often be highly uneven and disparate.

GLOBALIZATION AND INEQUALITY

There is considerable debate over the impact of globalization on global inequality and social differentiation, in which advocates of economic globalization, especially from international bodies such as the World Bank (2006), argue that globalization is good for international business but is also the best way to empower poor people and poor countries. On the other hand, critics argue that globalization enriches a global elite at the expense of labour, poor countries and the environment while eviscerating the ability of national governments to respond. This debate is driven by the old partisanship of the push and pull of distributive versus market advocating politics. There is an urgent need for sociologists and other social scientists to reflect on these debates and bring increased clarity but also complexity based on a more sophisticated understanding of the issues. For example, as sociologists know very well, measurement is crucial to how the evidence for each position here is advanced. Depending on which measures of globalization are used – global flows of finance and trade, for example, or openness of countries' regulatory regimes to investment – one will get different results as to the extent and effects of globalization. Similarly, inequality within and between nations can be measured in many ways – for example, in terms of market exchange rates, purchasing power parity and the Gini coefficient – and the combination of measures used will support different positions (Brune and Garrett 2005).

On the one hand, global enthusiasts argue that the effects are positive and that integration into the global economy increases economic activity and raises living standards. The impact of globalization has been to move countries to more outward oriented policies, which has been a main reason for growth, although this does not necessarily have much impact on inequality within countries. Even so, Shang-Jun Wei (2002) argues that there has been a decline in inequality in Chinese cities that are more open to globalization, as investment and growth have improved the prosperity of whole communities. Legrain (2002: 49–52) claims that in 2000 the global per capita income of citizens was four times greater than that in 1950. Between 1870 and 1979, production per worker became 26 times greater in Japan and 22 times greater in Sweden. In the whole world in 2000 it was double what it was in 1962. Even more significant, he argues, is the 'documented fact' that those countries that have stayed out of the global capitalist economy have done less well than those that have engaged with it. Poor countries that are open to international trade grew over six times faster in the 1970s and 1980s than those that shut themselves off from it: 4.5 per cent a year, rather than 0.7 per cent. Similarly, Dollar and Kraay (2001), who assessed data from 80 countries over four decades, argued that openness to international trade helps the poor. When GDP rises 1 per cent, the income of the poor rises by 1 per cent too, and in globalizing countries GDP increased by 5 per cent in the 1990s but in non-globalizing countries by only 1.4 per cent a year. The poor are generally getting richer in globalizing countries. Further, the World Bank claims that the percentage of people living below $1 per day (adjusted for inflation and purchasing power) halved between 1980 and 2000.[1] According to the World Bank, between 1990 and 2005 the number in extreme poverty fell from 28 to 21 per cent of the global population despite population growth during this period, which reflected a downward in trend in poverty of 15 per cent. Even so, this trend is globally highly uneven with poverty affecting 70 per cent of the population in some countries, such as those in sub-Saharan Africa. In East Asia the number of people living at the poverty level doubled between 1981 and 2005 to 313 million (UN Information Service 2005).

On the other hand, critics of these claims, such as Chossudovsky (1997), argue that more detailed variables for measuring poverty should be used. Chossudovsky argues that the one-dollar-a-day criterion is in overt contradiction with established methodologies used by Western governments and intergovernmental organizations to define and measure poverty in the developed countries. In the West, the methods for measuring poverty have been based on minimum levels of household spending required to meet essential expenditures on food, clothing, shelter, health and education. In the United States, for instance, the Social Security Administration (SSA) in the 1960s had set a 'poverty threshold', which consisted of 'the cost of a minimum adequate diet multiplied by three to allow for other expenses'. This measurement was based on a broad consensus within the US Administration,[2] but Pieterse (2004: 166n) claims that the World Bank replaced the purchasing power of $1 in 1985 with $1.08 in 1993 without adequately factoring in US inflation, and that allowing for this lowers the international poverty line by 19.6 per cent.

Indeed, it can be argued that global patterns of inequality have become increasingly polarized. Moreover, Pieterse argues that there is extensive focus on poverty, which is a relatively depoliticized concept that invites technical solutions, but little attention to inequality, which calls into question fundamental relations of power and class. A decrease in absolute poverty levels can occur alongside an increase in relative inequalities so divergent trends are quite possible. Pieterse claims that one-third of the world's population lived on less than $1 a day and 2.8 billion out of 6 billion lived in poverty (less than $2 a day) in the early 1990s. According to UN data the richest 20 per cent in the world 'own' 80 per cent of the wealth while the poorest 20 per cent own only 1 per cent (see Figure 5.1).[3] These shares represent a relative increase in global inequality since 1960 when the share of world income received by the richest 20 per cent was 70 per cent and the poorest 20 per cent 2.3 per cent. The ratio of richest to poorest in the world during this period rose from 30:1 to 61:1, and by 1991 85 per cent of the world's population received 15 per cent of the world's income (Pieterse 2004).

These inequalities predate globalization, of course, but there are global processes that are maintaining a highly unequal social system. Stiglitz (2002: 214) argues, while emphasizing the actual and potential benefits arising from globalization, that the form taken by globalization (and the role of the IMF in particular) has generated falling incomes and growing poverty in many areas of the world.

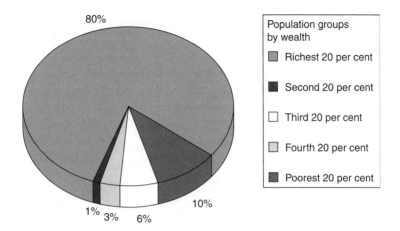

Figure 5.1   Global distribution of wealth (%)
Source: UN Development Programme 1998, p. 51

There are serious imbalances in global trading regimes that disadvantage developing countries, for example, large trading blocs such as the EU and USA have levied high tariffs against imports from developing countries which in the case of textiles can be as much as 40 per cent of their value (Oxfam 2004: 1). Again, EU farm subsidies (£3.4 billion in 2005) are greater than the EU's African aid budget (£2.3 billion) while trade barriers against both agricultural and manufactured goods from the developing world block off markets (Hale 2005).

Further, research presented to UNCTAD in 2002 suggested that in recent years developing countries have striven hard, and often at considerable cost, to:

> integrate more closely into the world economy . . .. However, in the face of deep-seated imbalances and biases in the international trading and financial systems, the gains from integration in terms of faster growth, greater employment opportunities and reduced levels of poverty have so far proved disappointing. The humbling of the Asian tigers since 1997 has revealed the heightened vulnerability of even the strongest developing countries. The extent to which liberalization policies have

themselves contributed to this disappointing. . . .The sharp deterioration in the conditions of labour, particularly among the unskilled, is a major reason why the reduction in poverty levels has so far lagged behind economic recovery in East Asia. Indeed, empirical studies show that there is a significant asymmetry in the impact of growth and crises on poverty in developing countries: the poverty-alleviating impact of a given rate of growth is significantly weaker than the poverty-augmenting impact of a comparable decline in GDP.

(Akyuz *et al.* 2002)

Liberalization and globalization of capital has driven costs down. Few workers in developed industrial economies are prepared to tolerate the conditions this new model creates. New flexible ordering systems still need not just flexible labour but excess flexible labour, because in order to adjust labour supply rapidly it is necessary to have a labour surplus. This need has been met by migrants, many of whom are drawn into Europe by collapsing agricultural prices at home, who have little market or political influence and generally take whatever they are offered, which will often be in illegal and unregulated occupations that can lead to tragedies such as the 2004 Morecambe Bay (UK) disaster when 23 Chinese migrant workers died when picking cockles against a rising tide (Song 2004). But instead of protecting migrants, the developed countries tighten border controls and attempt to remove those who are not in shortage skills areas, imagining illogically that they can enjoy the free movement of goods and capital that globalization has brought, but can shut out the free movement of labour that has inevitably accompanied it (Lawrence 2004).

Perrons (2004) argues that the poor in both rich and poor countries have experienced real reductions in living standards since 1980, as a result of changes in the organization of work, reductions in state welfare and falling public sector employment. Social reproduction is increasingly hazardous, and an increased burden falls on women because of the fragmentation of households as members migrate, both within their home country and internationally, in order to increase family earnings, which become increasingly dependent on remittances as agricultural incomes have fallen. Global migrant cites arise, such as those in the Gulf States in which nearly ten million migrants – mostly unskilled or semi-skilled – work. They are a significant part of the global economy, since their remittances reached $80 billion in 2002 (rising from $60 billion in 1998). These remittances are sent principally to India ($10 billion), to the Philippines ($6 billion) and to Bangladesh, Egypt, Jordan, Lebanon and Morocco ($2 billion) (Human Rights Watch 2003). However, migrant workers suffer discrimination, exploitation and abuse. Migrants, including large numbers of women employed as domestic servants, risk intimidation and violence at the hands of employers, supervisors, sponsors and police and security forces. Sponsors and employers often confiscate migrants' documents, including passports and residence permits, and migrants often cannot obtain an exit visa without the approval of their sponsor or employer, 'sometimes placing them in situations that amount to forced labour' (Human Rights Watch 2003).

Even so, the global trends are highly uneven. Since 1980 there has been an acceleration in economic growth in Asia, especially China, India, Bangladesh and Vietnam, but poor economic performance in Africa (Gruen and O'Brien 2001–02). Inequality in East Asia has undergone a significant increase, with widening differences between high- and low-skilled groups, rich and poor regions and urban and rural areas. At the same time there has been increased wage inequality in OECD countries during 1980–2000 as a result of many factors bound up with globalization – the decline in social welfare, technological change, deindustrialization and the decline of traditional industries, the decline of trade union collective bargaining, and the spatial clustering of businesses creating affluent corridors and depressed hinterlands. The debate over these issues is complex and several trends can be identified that point in different directions. The globalization of the commodity and market relations through the institutional frame of neo-liberalism and socio-political restructuring has had dramatic effects on global social relations and the security of life in many developing regions. This will now be examined.

CAPITALISM VERSUS SOLIDARITY

The capitalist mode of appropriation . . . produces capitalist private property. . . . The expropriation of the agricultural producer, of the

> peasant, from the soil, is the basis of the whole process. The history of
> this expropriation is different in different countries.
>
> (Marx 1976: 704)

Global capitalism links locales into global circuits of exchange so that everyday life in previously remote villages becomes intimately affected by fluctuations of world prices and supply chains, and decisions made by corporate planners hundreds or thousands of miles away. Giddens describes this process as 'time–space distanciation' (e.g. Giddens 1990: 64), which he sees as the 'necessary consequence' of modernity. The crucial dynamic here is the expansion of capital and monetary exchange, which brings a decline of traditional forms of production and ways of life, often also the mass migration of people from rural to urban areas and all the consequent effects of this on families, communities and cities, which themselves become sites of extreme dislocation of social solidarity. Hence Marx noted that capitalism 'drowns sentiment in icy waters of egotistical calculation' (1977: 225). The argument in this section is that the emergence of capitalism brings social dislocation although (contrary to Marx's expectations) post-war Western welfare capitalism mitigated these consequences and during the same period there were global efforts to do likewise. However, during the 1970s and 1980s these strategies ran counter to emerging global neo-liberalism, which had significant consequences for the pattern of globalization. The theme of these discussions is that global processes and flows are structured by multiple socio-economic relations and are embedded in social action and communication.

For Marx capitalism swept away pre-capitalist forms of production and ways of life even if – as the above quote indicates – this was to happen in different ways in different countries. Capitalism has had revolutionary and destructive effects on pre-capitalist social relations, a process that is being replicated worldwide through globalization, to some extent as Marx imagined it would. For many subsequent writers too (e.g. Moore 1969), modernization always involves extracting value from agriculture to fuel industrial capital, thus transforming rural society and either eliminating smallholder production in favour of large capitalist farms or maintaining it with more squeezed out. The commodification of labour and natural resources in the establishment of capitalism has often been the cause of bitter conflicts between (usually) the poor and relatively powerless attempting to defend customary rights and the enclosure of previously commonly accessible resources such as grazing land, forest wood and mining. These conflicts involved criminalization of people who continue to attempt to exercise traditional rights and Marx himself was politicized by the conflicts over 'thefts' of wood in the Mosel region, where exercise of the established right of peasants to collect wood conflicted with commercialization of agriculture. He noted how the numbers of convictions for 'thefts of wood' rose enormously in the early 1840s as the value of wood fuel increased, such that wood appeared to have become the 'Rhinelander's fetish' (Marx 1977: 391). Underlying this process was a more fundamental assault on pre-capitalist forms of social solidarity based in deeply unequal but complex patrimonial social relations of obligation and local traditional rights. The cash nexus, then, undermines premodern forms of social solidarity, although to imagine that this could be stopped and that life could return to some rural idyll was a romantic notion for which Marx (who referred to the 'idiocy of rural life') had only contempt. The 'necessity' of this process, however, became a matter of debate within Marx's lifetime and in the subsequent decades, as we will see below.

Although this might appear to be a teleological process occurring behind the backs of acting subjects, and Marx is certainly open to being read in this way, he also intended to demonstrate that forms of life that appear to be independent of human agency are actually the outcome of social relations and structured action. This was the main point of his critique of 'fetishism of commodities' – the commodity form appeared, especially in the works of 'bourgeois' economists, to have a life of its own within a self-equilibrating market governed by the 'laws' of supply and demand. But in reality the market and the mechanisms of price and value were embedded in social relations of power and exploitation through which value was expropriated from the direct producers. Indeed, today, markets – like the mass media – acquire the illusion of self-generating reality that masks the realities that generate it – the hands that create them are not to be seen (Araghi 2000). Further, markets and mass media along with other globalization phenomena appear in some contemporary theories as self-sustaining processes. But social life gets done through practices, norms and reciprocal relations that are embedded in everyday life and the market is one among many media for regulating social exchanges. Social life gets fixed in multiple ways through institutional structures, complex relations of dependence and exchange that can be local or stretch across continents, the 'dull compulsion of economic relations' (Marx 1974: 689) that binds people in relations of inequality, along with social relations of family, friendship and locality. We need to understand how despite inequalities and conflicts, societies can cohere and reproduce themselves through culturally embedded ties and communications.

Money exchanges and the social impact of expanding capitalism dislocate pre-modern social relations although new forms of social solidarity emerge. Polanyi (1967) argues that the principles of laissez faire do not govern all economies but are historically specific and that the self-regulating market that developed in England during the seventeenth and eighteenth centuries came, by the nineteenth century, to dominate other aspects of society to an unprecedented extent. While all societies have economies, only in capitalism does the economy apparently exist outside society, governed by its own laws, to which social relations are subordinate. In a similar way to Marx, Polanyi argued that in the capitalist market all decisions become economic decisions and all transactions are reduced to those that are consistent with the system of market relationships. This posed a grave threat to social order that was not understood by economists who assumed that self-interest was the major organizing motive in all societies. Indeed, as Holmwood (2000) argues, for Polanyi, these 'social dislocations . . . produced the crisis in European civilization, which threatened the very freedoms that liberals believed to be enshrined in market relationships'. However, the anti-social nature of the market economy provokes forms of self-protection that resist the incursion of market relations. These may be based in conservative pre-capitalist cultures of reciprocity or new principles of social solidarity. Polanyi looked forward to the re-embedding of the market in social relations that would ensure the freedom of the consumer while providing social welfare protection and planning. The post-War ethos of regulated markets was developed into Keynes' theory of demand management and indicative state interventionism.

He expressed the welfare principle as one where 'proper economic prices should not be fixed at the lowest possible level, but at a level sufficient to provide producers with proper nutritional and other standards . . . and it is in the interests of all producers alike that the price of a commodity should not be depressed below this level' (quoted in Oxfam 2002: 149).

However, relationships between economic and social processes are complex, mediated and interwoven with actions and interventions. Granovetter (1992: 9) argues that 'for all its obvious virtues Karl Polanyi's notion of embeddedness suffers from a . . . limitation'. Polanyi formulated the theory in direct opposition to the atomistic viewpoint of mainstream economics and was keen to emphasize the historical and cultural specificity of self-regulating markets. He regarded pre-industrial economies as embedded in social, religious and political institutions of reciprocity and redistribution such that tradition and political authorities rather than demand and supply set prices. But levels of embeddedness will vary considerably in different places and, as I have argued above (Chapter 4), there is no sociality without structured action and tacit knowledge. There were pre-industrial societies where markets functioned largely according to supply and demand (such as Ancient Greece and Rome, fifteenth-century north Italy and seventeenth-century Netherlands) while capitalist societies are not as disembedded as Polanyi imagined. For example, economic exchange can be organized through ethnic networks that can stretch over long distances (such as French Calvinists, Huguenots), and banks and clients often have long-term and stable relations because trust and familiarity may out weigh the costs of moving accounts. Okin (1991) argued that within capitalist societies it is possible to differentiate markets that operate in terms of auction-market prices (based on supply and demand) and customer-market prices (based on stable long-term relations and embedded loyalties) although these are not static and the nature of market behaviour will change over time.

Further, although the market cannot be transacted without institutionalized, culturally constraining and supportive normative relationships, the wider effects of commodification might still be disembedding, especially over long distances. Indeed, it might be argued that in a context of economic globalization economic relations have been uncoupled from local social spaces. At the same time, as Callon (1998) argues, the relationship between embeddedness and disembeddedness may not be an opposition but an interlinked and reversible process. Corporations are embedded in many locales and work through systems of trust, reciprocity and customer loyalty, for example, but they may have destructive effects on traditional ways of life and community – especially elsewhere in the world. In these terms, embeddedness and disembedding are not mutually incompatible. Further, since Polanyi's critique of the classical liberal belief in the unregulated market in the 1920–1930s, we have come full circle. The later twentieth century saw a revival of the idea of the global free market and embraced a new political economy of insecurity (Smart 2003: 33). The social protection advocated by Polanyi was eroded and the logic of the market constitutes the measure of all social practices – examples are evident especially in previously non-commoditized areas such as public health and education. This is, moreover, a global process in which the neo-liberal 'solutions' for the developed world are exported everywhere else.

The growth of global neo-liberalism was associated with the emergence of a de-industrialized service economy in the developed world. But this does not mean that traditional forms of labour have been eradicated, rather that they have been increasingly dispersed to less developed economies (Morris 2004). Indeed, there has been a close connection between globalization and the divergence in bargaining power of local labour, which has accompanied the increased mobility of capital. In the 1970s and 1980s there was a global realignment of production in which manufacturing output declined in industrialized countries, which in the 1980s become importers of manufactured goods from newly emerging industrialized areas of the Third World. The changing balance of trade between OECD and developing countries between 1980 and 1999 is shown in Figure 5.2, which shows exports from OECD to developing countries rising (after a dip corresponding to widespread recession in the mid-1980s), but accompanied by steadily rising imports from developing countries that exceed exports in value terms, in 1998 and 1999. However, there are deep-seated imbalances and biases in international trading and financial systems, in particular a sharp deterioration in conditions of labour among unskilled workers in industrializing regions (Akyuz *et al.* 2002). This is illustrated by the way in which the reduction in poverty levels in East Asia has lagged behind the rate of economic recovery, because the poverty-alleviating impact of a given rate of growth is weaker than the poverty-augmenting impact of a comparable decline in GDP (World Bank 2000).

The 'Agrarian Question'

I will illustrate the global effects of this process with reference to the transformation of rural society in the latter part of the twentieth century. At the turn of the nineteenth and twentieth centuries the debate over the 'Agrarian Question' arose out of Marxist predictions of the imminent disappearance of the peasantry (smallholding farmers) and the class differentiation of rural producers into capitalist farmers or landless proletarians. The model for this expectation had been the enclosures and capitalization of agriculture in eighteenth-century England and Scotland, but it became apparent by the late

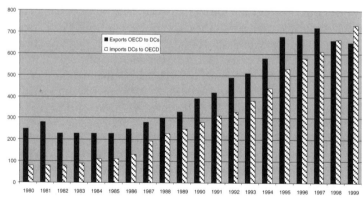

Figure 5.2   Trade in manufactures of OECD countries with developing countries 1980–99

Note: includes China
Source: Akyuz *et al.* 2002

nineteenth century that this process was not occurring uniformly in Europe and that the peasantry appeared to be adapting to capitalism and resisting the incursion of capitalism through the resources of the family labour farm, a concept developed by the Russian economist Chayanov (1986). There had actually been no unambiguous view of this by Marx himself and although he believed there was a long-term tendency for capitalism to displace peasant production he recognized that this was occurring only slowly (Marx 1963–68, II: 400ff.). He did argue, though, that where peasants remained formal owners of their land but were heavily mortgaged and forced by necessity to produce for merchants, they were effectively selling their labour (and therefore were like proletarians) and retaining 'sham property' that reduced the costs of the capitalist food companies to whom they were selling their produce (Marx 1977: 510). Much of the subsequent debate has attempted to resolve the implicit tension here between acknowledging the survival of the rural smallholding and its subordination to capitalist social relations. However, there is in addition the question of the social and cultural effects of peasant 'survivals' – small farmers who are heavily mortgaged and in debt to agribusiness corporations may be only 'nominal' owners of their land and materials in that they lack effective control over how they are put to use, but they may still regard themselves as independent producers, and the structure of land ownership will be embedded within wider cultural value systems.

A serious limitation of the debate over the Agrarian Question was that it contrasted the peasant disappearance thesis with the adaptation and survival thesis, but that both were essentialist and teleological since they attempted to define an essential nature of both capitalism and peasantry. We will actually find that the highly uneven patterns of globalization mean that the way in which these become instantiated in locales and, in turn, the reciprocal effects of these on flows of globalization will be highly varied. Further, the debate was too focused on economic processes rather than the socio-spatial dimensions of agency. This can be illustrated through the concepts of livelihood and locale – understanding the multiple ways in which global and local economic processes are intermeshed with agency and culture (De Haan and Zoomers 2003). The 'locale' (a term proposed in Giddens 1984) is space in which global processes are manifest but also transformed, and it provides a setting for human interaction and transformation. This understanding of action is neither voluntaristic nor deterministic and avoids regarding people as passive victims although their decisions will be made within the confines of structural conditions. This perspective will be developed with reference to examples of how the global can be localized in processes of commodification. We could describe this as 'glocalization' except that this ugly oxymoron does not specify the relations and processes involved and so gets us little closer to understanding them.

Global Keynesianism to commodity crisis

Development literature used to regard livelihood as occupying a highly localized, rooted, stable and socially bounded connection between people and the land, and as having a primarily economic focus. More recent approaches, though, have broadened the focus of analysis to regard livelihood as including tasks of meeting obligations, seeking security, identity and status and giving meaning to people's worlds. Assets are not only things but also the basis of agents' power to act and reproduce, change or challenge the rules that govern the transformation of resources (De Haan and Zoomers 2003). At the same time within the locale(s) in which livelihood is conducted, choices and actions are structured by wider political and policy processes while the exercise of agency by actors may also involve the deployment of power over others that is embedded in hierarchies such as age and gender. Looked at in these terms, the impact of globalization on subsistence communities will be uneven and fluid and will often involve responses to the decomposition of households and the erosion of communal solidarity; the 'persistent poverty under globalization is reflected in the large numbers of rural and urban households that exploit opportunities in different places and therefore live from both agricultural and urban incomes' (De Haan and Zoomers 2003). This will be developed with reference to changing global rural development policies.

In the interests of maintaining social solidarity post-war Western capitalist societies developed various forms of social protection and restraint on market forces, as noted in Chapter 3, typically including an extensive, non-capitalist state-owned sector and resources such as health, education, housing and income distributed according to non-market principles. But these were national solutions undertaken in the context of Fordist and protectionist systems of production, which is also discussed in Chapter 3. To mitigate the effects of capitalism on social solidarity on a global scale would have been a very different undertaking, and post-colonial states rarely had the revenue base to construct social welfare-based interventions. Nonetheless, many post-colonial states did resist global marketization, albeit through bureaucratic structures often embedded in corruption and political clientelism. A common development strategy of the neo-patrimonial state[4] involved extensive state-owned or managed economies in which producer and export prices were regulated through various bureaucratic and informal mechanisms. These were based on reciprocal and informal rather than public and accountable rules of exchange; they could also be backed up by coercion. For example, in Mexico local power brokers (the *caciques*) provided plots of land and loans, acted as intermediaries for peasants selling crops, ran local shops and in return expected political loyalty with peasants voting for the dominant party at election time (Brinkerhoff and Goldsmith 2002). Political clientelism involves an instrumental but non-market exchange of resources. While these unequal relations can survive over time they can also be destructive – neo-patrimonial economies stagnated under the weight of rent extracted by rapacious elites for conspicuous consumption to the point that the state could become a front for the extraction of resources, precipitating a general collapse of economy and society and often a descent into civil war, as happened in Sierra Leone in 1991 (Brinkerhoff and Goldsmith 2002). But clientelism can also be a viable and stable form of exchange, as with the Cane Societies in Uttar Pradesh, North India, which acted as intermediaries between cane growers and the sugar mills within a system of reciprocal exchanges that benefited client groups over others, especially untouchables (Craig 2002).

Moreover, Keynesian interventionist policies were influential for a time. During the 1950s and 1960s competition between the US and the USSR dominated politics and economics of 'development'. After the Second World War the global expansion of communist systems combined with rapidly growing anti-colonial movements and peasant movements, national development programmes were sponsored by the US as a counter to Soviet influence (especially in Japan, South Korea and Taiwan where communist-led rural unions were well organized). Araghi argues that the development formula was based on import-substitution industrialization as opposed to agricultural production for export, creating a model of 'nationalist developmentalism' that focused on the development of the national economy, state-led growth through parastatals (corporations combining state, local and international capital), instigating agricultural growth with state support and land reforms (breaking up some large estates and creating small, often family-run farms). The latter strategy had the dual objectives of expanding domestic demand in the national economy and curbing support for socialist agrarian movements (Araghi 1995). During the 1960s' development, optimism raised expectations and encouraged state-regulated and planned development. However, land reforms contributed to the proliferation of small, near subsistence farms and 'although a minority became successful capitalized family farmers, most remained petty commodity producers heavily dependent on state subsidies' (Araghi 1995). Labour patterns became varied, with households that were unable to sustain a living from their smallholding becoming dependent on seasonal migration, occasional wage labour on large estates and sub-contracting to produce for global agribusinesses (such as Del Monte, Nestlé and British American Tobacco).

This system began to unravel in the 1970s, and in response to the Third World debt crisis in 1982 the IMF and the World Bank instituted policies of structural adjustment and withdrawal of social supports.[5] These frequently entailed reducing the size of the public sector, privatization of state enterprises, the promotion of flexibility changes to remove labour protection, increasing the wage gap between public and private employees and making social welfare cuts (Giroux 2005). Rural Keynesianism was dismantled as neo-liberal strategies became dominant among Western governments, the World Bank and the IMF. The post-war social democratic policies sponsored by the Brandt Commission and North–South Commission of the 1960s gave way to risk management rather than controlling poverty. With the global hegemony of neo-liberal policies the role of the state changed to be less involved in production and ownership of the economy and more involved in attracting FDI, creating a new international framework for developing countries. As a consequence of deep penetration of commodity relations into the countryside, small owners of land become exposed to the world market. Regions that had once produced surplus grain then became deficit regions and in the developing world as a whole the ratio of food imports to food exports increased from 50 per cent in 1995–60 to 80 per cent in 1975 (Araghi 2000).

Araghi further argues that the new international division of labour in food production increasingly contradicted the established model of inward-led growth and the percentage of the labour force employed in agriculture fell by differing degrees across the world between 1960 and 1980: by 16 per cent in Latin America, 20 per cent in the Middle East, 8 per cent in Africa and 16 per cent in South-east Asia. The mid-century policies pursued by international agencies to preserve a smallholding peasantry – national protection of agriculture through state financing of inputs, price supports and subsidies – ran counter to this global reorganization of agriculture. While some smallholders accumulated capital and became capitalist farmers, most became net *sellers* of part-time wage labour. With deregulation and more unfettered market forces in the 1980s and 1990s, a shift towards outward oriented growth strategies and cuts in farm subsidies, the process of depeasantization was accelerated (Araghi 2000). There followed a massive movement of population to urban centres of accumulation and in some areas (especially Latin America, South Africa, India and Turkey) virtually all urban growth was attributable to in-migration. Further, the very division between rural and urban began to erode, with an expansion of non-agricultural activities in rural localities during the 1980s and 1990s (UN 2001: 35–6).

One consequence of these changes was the termination or liberalization of purchasing and marketing boards for primary products in developing counties. These had never functioned particularly in the interests of smallholders, having been set up by the colonial authorities and used by post-independence governments to impose heavy taxes on producers and enrich local vested interests. Smallholders were required to sell to marketing boards at regulated prices set well below export prices. Even so, marketing boards were also the main source of credit, fertilizers and other inputs, and they prevented prices falling to below subsistence levels. When the Tanzanian coffee board was dismantled these inputs were removed and many farmers were unable to continue growing coffee (Oxfam 2002: 164). The wider problems following liberalization of commodity production have been (Oxfam 2002: 164ff.):

- pressure on developing countries to reduce labour and non-wage costs, such as health, social welfare and education (to reduce public expenditure);[6]
- reduction in yields following the collapse of extension systems, lost access to credit and increased fertilizer prices;
- pressure on small farms to operate through a monopolistic private trading system;
- vulnerability to price volatility, exacerbated by the absence of functioning insurance or credit markets;
- loss of market access for the poorest and most isolated farmers following the end of pan-territorial pricing and marketing systems;
- greater exposure to global competition resulting in lower prices.

Global processes of commodification, then, undermined the attempts to generate rural property-owning communities (Araghi 1995). The UN reported that in 2003 progress on overcoming poverty in Latin America had 'stagnated' in the previous five years, with 43.4 per cent of the population (220 million) living in poverty and 55 million suffering some degree of malnutrition (UN Information Service 2003). These conditions have prompted mass migration into the cities and across national borders, and the effects of this have been to some extent to alleviate poverty through remittances.[7] However, smallholders are still recruited into global production chains as the following two cases illustrate.

Case I: the sociology of coffee

Giddens famously illustrated the sociological perspective by referring to how 'an individual who drinks a cup of coffee is caught up in a complicated set of social and economic relationships stretching across the world' (Giddens 1997: 4). Not dissimilarly, in a 1998 advertisement, Nestlé, one of the world's leading roasters and marketers of coffee, says, 'Next time you enjoy a cup of Nescafé, stop and think about how more than 100 million people involved in the coffee growing industry have worked together to help you "open your day".' Indeed, coffee is a global product that passes through a chain of intermediates and relations of power and money in which most value is added through export, processing and retaining systems. Ong'wen (2006) explains that the first intermediates are the local traders, who own a store and will be part of the local elite. More often than not they are the only people who are able to provide some means of transport – most likely some pick-up van whose roadworthiness is in doubt – and act as local financiers by offering local peasants loans, usually on condition that the farmers mortgage their coffee harvest at very low prices and/or repay the loans at high rates of interest. Next in the chain are the processors. From the processors, the coffee passes to private exporters, who are mainly transnational corporations. Exporters have the very specific role of preparing the products in accordance with the precise demands of the importer. Different roasters give different specifications for their green beans order. The exporter must ensure that the right type of coffee is sent to the right importing company at the right time. As with every intermediary, the goal of the exporter is to buy at the lowest possible price and sell at the maximum price they can get, and farmers may receive less than 1 per cent of the supermarket retail price.

Around one billion people globally depend on commodity production for their livelihood, and most of these are smallholder farmers. In Uganda, for example, about one-quarter of the population earns its living from coffee growing. However, commodity prices have fallen globally over the past two decades, in many cases by as much as 80 per cent (see Table 5.1) and coffee prices have fallen by over 50 per cent in Africa, Asia and Latin America This meant that in three years alone (1999–2002) the value of coffee exports fell from $13 billion to $7 billion, with the consequences for the growers of worsening nutrition, having to take children out of school and increased vulnerability to other adverse events such as increasing food prices and illness and the inability to buy essential materials such as cooking oil (Oxfam 2002: 150). At the same time, the terms of trade (the value of export prices against the prices of imports) have fallen in favour of industrialized countries by around 10 per cent. In Uganda small farms (*shambas*) are precariously located on hillsides where coffee is traditionally intercropped with bananas, beans and vegetables, since the deep roots of the coffee bush help bind the soil and prevent erosion. This is a sustainable system that has been passed across generations, but it is now threatened by falling prices, lack of social supports and the liberalization of production. The impact on local communities can be devastating as lower prices force (mainly) male farmers to seek work away from the farm and women farmers to spend more time earning elsewhere while retaining primary responsibility for child care. Household incomes fall despite households remaining in production attempting to increase the volume produced in order to maintain incomes. This has the counter-productive effect of increasing supply and therefore further reducing the prices paid to producers. Coffee consumption is highly price inelastic in that people are unlikely to increase consumption even if the price falls; anyway, supermarket retail prices have remained stable and have not fallen in line with producer prices. So increases in productivity (through increased exploitation of family labour) are most likely to push producer prices even further down. On the other side of the production chain, Nestlé's trading profit rose by 15 per cent between 1999 and 2000 alone (Oxfam 2002: 151).

Global markets, then, are structured by power imbalances since fragmented suppliers are competing with small groups of powerful corporate buyers. Nestlé and Philip Morris account for half the world market in roasted and instant coffee and five companies (these plus Sara Lee, Procter & Gamble and Tchibo) control over two-thirds of the market. On the other hand, producers lack power and information and are inserted into buyer-driven supply chains. There are a large number of smallholder farms driven into commodity markets by the need for cash. Here they are confronted by market driven prices without social protection or minimum pricing structures – on the contrary, the prices of raw commodities as opposed to manufactured goods have been falling for two decades. Producers confront a monopsonistic market (one with few buyers) for their

Table 5.1   Prices of selected primary commodities between 1980 and 2001

Product	Unit	1980	1990	2001
Robusta coffee	cents/kg	411.7	118.2	63.3
Cocoa	cents/kg	330.5	126.7	111.4
Groundnut oil	$/ton	1090.1	963.7	709.2
Cotton	cents/kg	261.7	181.9	110.3
Rice (Thai)	$/ton	521.4	270.9	180.2
Sugar	cents/kg	80.17	27.67	19.9
Copper	$/ton	2770	2661	1645
Palm oil	$/ton	740.9	289.9	297.8
Soya	$/ton	376	246.8	204.2
Lead	cents/kg	115	81.1	49.6

Source: Ong'wen, 2006

produce partly because there are high barriers to the entry of new buyers. These include the economies of scale in an industry with global distribution, the costs of branding (e.g. attempting to compete with highly successful brands such as Nescafé would require a great deal of risky investment), the need for market intelligence and the limited possibilities for entry into retail markets that are already controlled by a few supermarkets. These power imbalances are exacerbated by the nature of certain cash crops such as coffee, tobacco, tea and cocoa that have no or negligible food value. The family cannot consume the crop if things go wrong, such as the price structure collapses or the purchaser does not judge the quality adequate.

However, coffee can bring benefits too. In Machahos (Kenya) seriously eroded landscapes of the 1930s were turned into prosperous countryside with terraces, trees, coffee and farmsteads in the 1990s, while the population has increased six-fold and the acreages per capita more than halved. This recovery followed the migration of men to Nairobi when women formed working parties to look after the land and used knowledge, training support in soil and water conservation, and new varieties of coffee provided by development agencies and the Kenya government. This illustrates the potential of collective agency and learning in a supportive context (Tiffin *et al.* 1994). It is also true that particularly in coffee production (but in other agricultural products, too) the Fair Trade movement has been one of the most powerful responses to problems facing commodity producers. The movement is premised on the willingness of developed world consumers to pay higher prices for 'ethical commodities' that address the three problems of low prices, price instability and low value-added activity. Some Fair Trade cooperatives such as the Kuapa Kokoo in Ghana have more than 30,000 members and operate as a trust fund for members, a marketing organization and a political lobby attempting to raise awareness of the problems outlined here. Kuapa Kokoo sells cocoa to the Fair Trade market at a guaranteed minimum price, and surpluses are invested in community-level development programmes such as school construction, health care provision and water supply and sanitation. Fair trade organizations work through international NGOs, such as Oxfam, Café Direct, Tradecraft and Twin Trading, and some mainstream companies such as the Body Shop and Green and Black's chocolate company. This is, in turn, an indication of the increasing purchasing power and influence of 'ethical consumers' in developed countries.[8] However, for all its achievements there are limits to what the fair trade movement can do – fair trade markets remain small niches and have not fundamentally changed world markets. Less than 1 per cent of total tea, coffee and cocoa sales are carried out on a fair trade basis (Oxfam 2002: 167).

Case II: going up in smoke

The classical debate about the Agrarian Question posed the issue in terms of either the class polarization of the peasantry (into landless workers or capitalist farmers) or the adaptation and survival of the family labour farm. It should be apparent by now that diverse patterns and combinations of forms appear in different places and people adapt to the global context in multiple ways – farm proprietors may work for a period of time for wages on another farm or outside the agricultural sector; they may also employ labour on a casual or seasonal basis. Contract farming is an example of how global processes can both sustain small-scale economic activity while also undermining the independence this once might have promised, prompting in turn complex forms of agency and power. In particular, farmers may remain nominal owners of the means of production (land and other assets) but lose control of the means of subsistence (what and how to grow) since indebtedness and prior investment decisions mean that what is produced is dictated or strongly influenced by global agribusiness.

One controversial example of contract farming is the global tobacco growing scheme of British American Tobacco (BAT), which extends to some 250,000 farmers worldwide in 23 countries (BAT 2005). Tobacco is a powerful and high-revenue earning global industry. In 2002 the world's three largest multinational cigarette companies (Philip Morris, Japan Tobacco and British American Tobacco) had combined tobacco revenues of more than \$121 billion, a sum greater than the total *combined* GDP of Albania, Bahrain, Belize, Bolivia, Botswana, Cambodia, Cameroon, Estonia, Georgia, Ghana, Honduras, Jamaica, Jordan, Macedonia, Malawi, Malta, Moldova, Mongolia, Namibia, Nepal, Paraguay, Senegal, Tajikistan, Togo, Uganda, Zambia and Zimbabwe (WHO (World Health Organization) 2004). In Kenya tobacco is a significant foreign exchange earner, leaf exports generating \$10.5 in 2004 and cigarettes \$126m.[9] The operation is expanding, with British American Tobacco (Kenya) (BAT(K)) contracting tobacco growing to 17,500 smallholders cultivating 15,000 hectares, compared with 7,000 growers in 1972 and 11,000 in 1991 (Kariuki 2000). BAT insists that their leaf-growing programmes include integrated crop management, soil and water conservation, appropriate use of agrochemicals, environmental, occupational health and safety standards in green leaf-threshing operations, eliminating exploitative child labour and promoting afforestation programmes for the farmers who require wood for tobacco curing to obtain it from renewable sources (BAT 2005).

In the early 1980s I conducted research into the promotion of tobacco growing in Kenya by BAT(K), which was then the only tobacco transnational company operating in the country (Currie and Ray 1984, 1985, 1986).[10] Unlike Tanzania, Kenya had not previously been thought suitable for tobacco cultivation but in conjunction with the Kenyan government, BAT(K) was encouraging small farmers (with around two hectares) to join a tobacco extension scheme that involved diversifying from subsistence crops, such as maize, to tobacco. The contracting arrangements through which farmers are recruited to the growing scheme are typical of many global purchasing chains. The transnational company avoids the risks and costs involved in establishing estates and processing plants and buys cured tobacco from the farmers who remain responsible for the growing and curing process. This way the company is protected from the risks of production – such as the vagaries of the weather, crop failure, pests, and errors in the curing process – but is guaranteed a supply of tobacco leaf since farmers have no other outlets for their product. Competition appeared in the early 1990s from a small Kenyan company, Mastermind Tobacco Kenya (MTK), which was offering higher prices to growers for cured leaf. BAT(K) claims that conflict between extension staff and MTK employees along with over-production of leaf had caused and 'a total breakdown in law and order in some areas' (Patel *et al.* 2007). According to Patel *et al.* BAT(K) used political influence to re-establish its dominance in leaf purchasing and commit farmers to offer produce to only one purchaser.[11]

The underlying structural exchange between producers and the company are relatively unchanged from the 1980s. Tobacco cultivation is a labour-intensive process, requiring constant watering, weeding and ridging, followed by harvesting in summer and curing, during which family members often sleep round the kiln to maintain the right temperature. It also requires capital inputs – seeds, fertilizer, curing kiln, drying shed, pesticides (the crop is particularly vulnerable to pests) and wood for fuel – which most farmers are unable to provide without loans from the company. They also have to acquire the skills to cultivate and cure a crop of tobacco leaf that would be of sufficiently high quality to be purchased by BAT(K), which are again provided by the extension scheme. Being tied into one purchaser means that the income farmers receive is dependent on how the crop is graded by the purchasers. Advertising for the scheme emphasized the high earnings that farmers could expect from tobacco cultivation although in practice the financial benefits have been highly uneven. While some farmers have used tobacco income to invest in a tractor and expansion, several reports claim that after repayment of credit, incomes are low and some lose money on cultivation (Christian Aid 2004; Kariuki 2000). Ogara and Ojode (2003) found that most farmers receive 50,000 Kenyan shillings per hectare but are left with 20,000 after deductions and that if labour was costed at day rates for agricultural workers, then farmers could be said to be losing 40,000 Kenyan shillings on the exchange.

Further, there is evidence that tobacco farming exacerbates deficiencies in food production. After tobacco is harvested in July farmers have one season, until November, to cultivate food before the rains begin. But one season of maize will not be enough to feed most communities and some tobacco growing regions (such as Migori) have reported problems of under-nutrition (Kariuki 2000). In Kuria, an arid region where there is already poor food supply, Rimmer and Willmore (2004) argue that tobacco cultivation is exacerbating a situation where 52 per cent of children suffer from chronic or acute under-nutrition and the region is in constant need of famine relief. In Meru most of the fertile land was given over to tobacco and because the topsoil was eroded by deforestation heavy rains wash away the maize (Chacha 2001). In various ways, then, remaining farmers are incorporated into global circuits of capital and decision making in which life chances are highly dependent on world markets and commodity prices, the vagaries of the weather, financial movements and corporate strategies.

In this global and institutional context households make decisions about the pursuit of livelihoods although, as De Haan and Zoomers (2003) argue, these will not always be strategic decisions but based on paths already entered into. That is, once locked into a particular activity that has been invested with meaning and that has become a source of identity, and having acquired relevant knowledge and skills, there will be a bias towards continuing with it. Moreover, the family labour farm is able to sustain itself against global forces partly by instantiating and reproducing gender and age hierarchies. Research on decisions within households found that while the decision to grow tobacco is largely a man's, actual work largely lies on the shoulders of the woman (wives where there is polygamy). Children also bear the burden of working on tobacco farms, but men usually control marketing and the utilization of money. These structures are crucial to the global commodity chain since the low incomes from tobacco leaf (for many farmers) are subsidized by uncosted family labour and the household bearing the risks (and hazards) of production (Asila 2004). These risks include the health risks not only of consuming but also of growing tobacco, arising from the use of pesticides, the inhalation of smoke during curing and the absorption of nicotine (Christian Aid 2004).

Further, global commodification has environmental effects. Curing places heavy demands on wood fuel, and in semi-arid areas where forests are already declining (such as the Kunati valley on the slopes of Mount Kenya) deforestation is exacerbated by tobacco cultivation (Chacha 2001). In Meru (a major growing area) the top-soil is highly eroded and washes away in heavy rain. BAT(K) encourages reforestation and requires farmers to replant felled forest, but this is generally done with fast growing eucalyptus trees. They need to be fast growing to match the loss of wood each year, but eucalyptus makes heavy demands on water and lowers the water table so exacerbating water shortages. Anyway, Rimmer and Willmore (2004) claim that farmers prefer to use traditional species of tree for curing since this affects the tobacco aroma and therefore the selling price. They conclude that the rate of deforestation is too fast to be replaced by replanting and quote a local member of parliament (Samson Mwita Marwa), who said in 2001:

> The lands are increasingly becoming bare and barren, unproductive, caked, ugly and blistering. BAT claims to be engaged in reforestation programmes [but] . . . the rate of deforestation is far too fast to be equal to the rate of reforestation. Surely that much cannot be in doubt.
>
> (Rimmer and Willmore 2004)

The extension of commodity relations and their insertion into local production chains have multiple effects that are subject to contestation and negotiation. Despite the problems engendered by the contracting scheme, there is no evidence that smallholders are actually being forced from the land, although indebted farmers may not receive further inputs (Kweyuh 1998); rather, they are increasing the exploitation of family labour in order to sustain a livelihood. To understand this we need to appreciate the traditionally patriarchal relations of rural Kenya but also the political and cultural centrality of land ownership. It would not be politically acceptable for large numbers of farmers to be dispossessed (although increasing numbers are away from their farms as temporary migrants) while ownership is a key factor in status and identity. Control of land is linked to the complex interplay of social and political power and gives meaning to people's lives. Even so, the nature of rural society is changing:

> for most small scale land holders, the greater proportion of incomes are from off-farm activities . . . [and] . . . up to 36 percent have at least a single salaried member living away from the farm. . . [and] 33 percent receive remittances from members working away.
>
> (Kodhek and Maina 2000)

End of patriarchy?

These changes have had profound effects on rural patrimonialism, and statistics do not convey how rapid changes impact on structures in complex ways. For Castells (1997) the dislocation of traditional societies had brought an 'end of patriarchy' although the discussion of contract farming indicates that a contrary trend can be identified, too. The impact of globalization on gender relations has been highly varied. The transformation of rural social relations and the new international division of labour has involved the increased participation of women in global labour markets.[12] On one hand, one effect of male migration from the countryside might be to increase the social and juridical status of women, who might then have responsibility for running a farm, dealing with loans and so forth (Babb 2005; De Haan and Zoomers 2003). With enhanced power in households women may exercise greater control over the use of household income, other resources and their fertility (Perrons 2004: 84). Rather than simply be family helpers on a subsistence smallholding, some women's power and status may increase as they enter the paid sector. Indeed, Perrons argues that paid work:

> provides a sense of freedom, a space and time where [women] can be themselves, and some enjoyment from socializing with other women. Paid employment is also found to raise self-confidence, self-esteem and

respect from other people in their household, so overall women are to some degree empowered by independent incomes.

(Perrons 2004: 117)

With these changes comes new spatial mobility, income, consumption and greater autonomy, for example to negotiate with parents over potential partners, evade arranged marriages and experiment with new forms of romance and transgressive relationships (Mills 2003).

On the other hand, it would be premature to view this as signalling the 'end of patriarchy'. Increases in women's autonomy also engender ambivalence, conflict and violent reactions from men for whom the decline of traditional work opportunities and the rising status of women might be perceived as a 'crisis of masculinity' (Mills 2003; Perrons 2004: 119). Further, the increased participation of women in the new international economy has also created new global chains of dependence and subordination. Structural adjustment strategies have required cuts in social expenditures, which in turn presuppose that households have the flexible capacities to absorb the costs of social support for the workforce. This assumes an increased domestic role for women who are also forced into the labour market or self-employment by the squeeze on households. Feminization of employment has been concentrated in electronics and garments, agribusiness and services (especially call centres). International capital often relies on gendered ideologies and social relations to recruit and discipline women employees who are regarded as more compliant and dextrous than men and who can also be paid less (Mills 2003). In developed countries, too, women are over-represented in care, nurturing, clerical work and sales, and women in professional occupations are often managing mainly other women (Perrons 2004: 86). Further, the ILO (International Labour Organization) (2003) reports that:

- Women are more likely than men to find employment in the informal economy, outside legal and regulatory frameworks, with little if any social security benefits and a high degree of vulnerability.
- Family responsibilities are still very much assigned to women. When they have to combine child-raising activities with work

activities, women are required to find a solution for balancing these two roles.

- Women everywhere typically receive less pay than men. This is in part because women often hold low-level, low-paying positions in female-dominated occupations.
- Increases in labour force participation rates have so far not been matched by improvements in job quality, and the working conditions of women have not led to their true socio-economic empowerment.
- As a result, the share of women that are employed but still are unable to lift themselves and their family above the US $1 a day poverty line – the so-called working-poor share – is higher than it is for men. Out of the total number of 550 million estimated to be the working-poor, around 60 per cent or 330 million are women.

These patterns of global gender and employment both reflect pre-existing social structures but also articulate and reinforce them in various ways. Thus, as well as generating new forms of sociality, globalization flows in ways structured by and reinforcing deeply embedded hierarchies of power and domination. These uneven effects are for the most part unintended consequences of particular combinations of global commodity chains, the intermeshing of local and transnational culture and power relations along with the multiple ways in which people inscribe these processes with meaning and deploy resources in the course of maintaining livelihoods.

CONCLUSIONS

Globalization has, for the first time in world history, created a global market and dense network of production and commodity chains, which has had profound effects on social relationships in the past few decades. But these effects are subject to controversy, such as the debate over the relationship between globalization and inequalities. While many international agencies focus on poverty (and the debates over the direction of the trends) there is evidence that global inequalities between and within countries have risen along with increasing global socio-economic integration. Overall reductions in global poverty are, of course, consistent with widening relative global and regional inequalities and contrary trends in certain places, since there are always globalization 'winners' and 'losers'. One global consequence of these processes has been large-scale depeasantization – the disappearance of rural peasant life that had – at the outset of the twentieth century – been the way of life for the majority of people worldwide but that had – by its close – given way to massive (generally unplanned) urbanization. This is a complex and uneven process that manifests in different ways in particular locales. As the examples of coffee and tobacco production illustrated, there are situations in which small-scale rural production may be sustained by global commodity chains that reach from the rural village to the metropolitan supermarkets. However, although extension schemes and production for agribusiness can increase incomes and re-generate local communities, the unequal terms of exchange mean that more widespread effects are to deplete local environments and exacerbate the drift from the countryside to new, expanding urban areas. Even where farms remain under 'family' ownership (which in turn entails structured but changing hierarchies of gender and generation), they rarely remain the sole source of income, and labour becomes an increasingly flexible mix of cash cropping, subsistence, casual labour and short- or long-term migration. The very distinction between the rural and the urban and between permanent and temporary residence becomes blurred in the process as a decreasing proportion of 'rural' residents are engaged in agrarian activities.

The Marxist debate over the Agrarian Question attempted to understand how these processes were creating new patterns of class formation. Marx's argument was that capitalism necessarily subordinated the countryside to the logic of the market, thereby undermining traditional forms of social solidarity and in the process creating polarization between a minority of capitalist farmers and a mass of landless proletarians. This was important to Marxists because the process of social differentiation (in industrial and rural settings) was itself the prelude to the socialist revolution, although by the early twentieth century it was apparent that the countryside was not following this pattern quite as expected. Indeed, not only did the 'family farm' seem to have a capacity for survival but also in the postwar period there were both national and global strategies aimed at increasing social protection and mitigating the destructive social impact of market forces. Alongside the national welfare systems in developed capitalist countries there were attempts to develop a 'rural Keynesianism' that would foster some rural stability in developing countries. Many agribusiness transnationals also sustained small-scale enterprises that would then bear a considerable share of the risks and costs of production. These strategies came increasingly under strain with the global economic crisis and the growth of structural adjustment programmes from the 1980s onwards, and the process of rural decomposition has again intensified.

However, the terms of the Agrarian Question were overly essentialist. I have argued for an understanding of the intersection of global and local processes in which collective outcomes are the result of decisions made in locales, albeit within the constraints of power relations, established practices, states of knowledge and the institutional governmental context. However, Marxist expectations have not been matched by these new realities in a further respect, namely that the anticipated process of class formation was to be linked to the development of new productive forces – the growth of the industrial system of production. While this is, of course, happening in parts of the developing world, much unregulated urban growth is detached from the expansion of new industries or forms of employment and many of the new urban populations live on the edge of subsistence. One result of this is that the informal economy, long considered incompatible with economic growth and industrialization, has been rapidly expanding in both developed and developing countries. There is, moreover, a strong relationship between informal, unregulated and sometimes illicit work and poverty (Carr and Chen 2001). The upshot of these processes, then, is that global depeasantization is a stimulus to large-scale population movement and has produced impoverished cities in which many are removed from sources of solidarity and connectedness. This in turn has an impact on global ideological divisions. Davis (2004) comments: 'If God died in the cities of the industrial revolution, he has risen again in the postindustrial cities of the developing world', where radical Islam and Christian Pentecostalism are gaining ground, especially in the ideological vacuum created by the global collapse of socialist movements.

6

GLOBAL TERRORS AND RISKS

Night is here but the barbarians have not come.
And some people arrived from the borders,
and said that there are no longer any barbarians.
And now what shall become of us without any barbarians?
Those people were some kind of solution.

Constantine P. Cavafy Expecting the Barbarians (1904)

This book has addressed in different ways the question of the appropriateness of sociological theory for understanding globalization and everyday life. Beck has argued that sociology clings to 'zombie categories' such as nation, class and gender that are dead (that is, removed of content and relevance) but are still living. They embody nineteenth-century horizons of experience, horizons of the first modernity that still mould our perceptions and are blinding us to the real experience and ambiguities of the second modernity (Beck 2000b). Further, his claim that there has been a 'democratization of risk' and consequent obsolescence of traditional sociological concerns with structure is one of fundamental claims of risk society thesis. This underpins the claim shared by many writers discussed here that globalization poses a challenge to conventional sociology because it entails the fragmentation of society and state systems, an implosion of boundaries and a new permeability of borders, such that the previously established divisions of nature/society, bodies/

culture no longer apply. Indeed the distinctiveness of the social itself is called into question, and Law (1994) and Urry (2003: 106) argue that social ordering is 'not simply social' but is 'materially heterogeneous' combining 'talk, bodies, texts, machines, architectures'. This book takes issue with these views. In relation to Urry and Law, one may ask which among talk, bodies, texts, machines and architectures are not 'social'? All these activities (talk, bodies, texts, machines and architecture) are ordered, organized, placed within sometimes stable and sometimes contested frames of meaning, become objects of discourse and the resources around which sociality can occur. Sociology concerns itself with the forms of sociality that constitute the global as an object of reflection and intervention and maintain the substratum of global relations. Goffman (1983) argued that the 'human condition is that for most of us, our daily life is spent in the immediate presence of others' so all our 'doings' will be socially situated. To this we might add that this is true too in global interactions through the medium of digital communications technologies as I argued in Chapter 4. Further, the concepts of structure, class, bureaucracy, gender, ethnicity, power and commodity are crucial for understanding the ways globalization is embodied in locales, as the analysis of global inequalities in Chapter 5 attempted to demonstrate. Nonetheless, the collapse of traditional social forms and divisions engendered by globalization (combined with the appearance of new ones) means that the experience of fluidity, fragmentation and, above all perhaps, permeability has multiple effects on patterns of everyday lives. Among these the dislocations of living every day with new real and imaginary terrors has changed perceptions of living in the global. It is to these issues that this chapter turns.

'HAPPY' TO 'SAD' GLOBALIZATION

The global order is in part the combined effect of complex sets of networks grounded in social, political, economic and virtual communications and organization. But participating in the global order also, as Robertson (1992: 8) argues, entails a form of consciousness – or, rather, multiple and fluid forms of global imagining, we might say. This final chapter explores some aspects of both processes – the power dynamics of structures and patterns of global integration but also the changes and dimensions of global consciousness and imagining in the face of risks and terrors.

With the end of Cold War there was a widespread sense of global optimism epitomized by people such as Friedman and Fukuyama who expressed the idea of what Holmes (2001) calls the 'long postcommunist "decade" (1989–2001)' as 'the heyday of happy globalization' during which time there was widespread optimism that as capitalism gained access to the whole planet it opened a decade of 'frictionless competition', bringing prosperity to the poor, peaceful dialogue and progress towards democracy and rule of law. Fukuyama (1992) argued that liberal democracy and free market capitalism, being the most satisfying and efficient form of government and method of organizing the economy, represent the final stage of human government. In due course all competing ideologies will fade away and states that are not presently liberal democracies must justify their rule to indicate that they are moving towards liberal democracy. They must promise freedom and democratic voting, because the legitimacy of the state is in question if they do not. He claimed that capitalism is ultimately the only viable economic system in the modern world and that all states will eventually adopt free market capitalism. Further, all human societies, regardless of their particular cultural inflection, will inevitably be drawn into a global consumer culture. He did not mean that 'history' in the sense of the happening of events would end but that the eventual triumph of liberal democracy and consumer societies would signal the end of History (capitalized) as a set of beliefs geared to a final (generally utopian) state of affairs, a belief that was epitomized by Marxism.[1] Similarly, Friedman said, 'The world is 10 years old. It was born when the Wall fell in 1989. . . . And technology, properly harnessed and liberally distributed, has the power to erase not just geographical borders but also human ones' (Friedman 2000: 1). Again, Habermas wrote of the end of communism offering Europe a 'second chance' to realize the idea of a communicative civil society in both East and West – but this time free from 'Eurocentric narcissistic self-absorption' (Habermas 1994: 72). This optimism (that was never shared by everyone of course) gave way to greater pessimism after September 11th 2001 (hereafter September 11th) and the increased focus on new terrors that appeared to arise precisely from the globalization process itself. The appearance of powerfully ideological global movements, especially Islamist, seemed further to question the notion of an end of History.

Further, the very permeability of borders and collapsed space and time that epitomized globalization now gave rise to new fears of violent incursion and dislocation of the naively assumed trust, or what Goffman (1983) calls 'civic disattention' of public spaces in contemporary societies. Moreover, since global mobility occurs across borders and border controls are forms of the regulation of bodies, the border can serve both as a territorial threshold and a metaphor for the boundaries of the body threatened by violent incursion. Fears after September 11th accentuated existing anxieties about the violent pollution of the nation, body and culture. The very permeability and openness of borders became a threat, and mobility and fluidity also came to be perceived in terms of threats of violence. The 'non' vote in the French referendum on the EU constitution was fuelled in part by the 'fear from the East' of unregulated and alien migratory bodies that tapped into already potent 'resistance' to global forces, such as José Bové's *Confédération Paysanne*, one of the leaders of the 'no' vote in France (Ireland 2005).

Images of a peaceful global order have been replaced by ones of violence and threat. In contrast to Fukuyama's optimism about the end of History and the eventual triumph of liberal democracy, there have recently, and especially since September 11th and the 'war on terror', been suggestions that the world is entering a new phase of bi- or multi-polar divisions, in which in particular 'the West' confronts 'Islam'. One of the best-known advocates of this view is Samuel Huntington (1999) whose 'clash of civilizations' thesis reflects thinking among the neo-conservative group of Republicans close to President Bush.[2] Huntington's thesis is that the fundamental source of global conflict after the end of the Cold War will be cultural and between 'civilizations'. This is because the end of the Cold War released cultural and civilizational forces that had been developing in non-Western societies for centuries (1999: 39). The basis of these conflicts appears to be primal:

> Civilizations are the ultimate human tribes, and the clash of civilizations is tribal conflict on a global scale. In the emerging world, states and groups from two different civilizations may form limited, ad hoc, tactical . . . coalitions to advance their interests against entities from a third civilization . . . Relations between groups from different civilizations however will almost never be close, usually cool and often hostile.
>
> (Huntingdon 1999: 207)

There will be various phases in these relations – Cold War, trade war, quasi-war, uneasy peace, troubled relations, intense rivalry, co-existence and arms races – but 'trust and friendship will be rare' (1999: 207). He initially sets out a multi-polar model of potential conflict between several civilizations – 'Western', Latin American, African, Islamic, Sinic, Hindu, Orthodox, Buddhist and Japanese – but it is the potential conflict between Islam and the West that has occupied most attention. Indeed, Huntington says himself that 'some Westerners . . . have argued that the West does not have problems with Islam but only with violent extremists'; however, 'fourteen hundred years of history demonstrate otherwise' and this conflict will make that between democracy and Marxism–Leninism appear 'superficial and fleeting' (1999: 209). Thus his thesis focuses on a new, apparently bipolar conflict in which the language and materiel of the Cold War can be redeployed.

It does appear that the post-Cold War world has become a dangerous and less predictable place than it was when the balance of terror between the US and the USSR exercised some checks on the potential for regional conflicts to go global. But the post-Cold War world is one in which collective identities can be radically altered and in which 'memories' are elastic and changing, so the 'clash' thesis is flawed in assuming that there are timeless and intractable historical conflicts. Indeed the personification of enormous entities of 'West' and 'Islam' overlooks the internal dynamics and plurality of both (Said 2001). Islamist movements struggle for hegemony *within* Islamic societies as much as with the 'West' and are the focus of bitter conflicts with local states. A less bipolar focus would make connections between the violent activities of Islamist groups and various kinds of religious and political violence elsewhere, such as the Branch Davidians, Japanese Aum Shinrikyo, the Oklahoma bombers, neo-nazis and the KKK and fundamentalist Christians who bomb abortion clinics (Hewitt 2002: 14ff). The appearance of such hate groups with access to resources and the capacity to commit mass murder is a global phenomenon but does not support a bipolar view of the world. Further the polarity of the West and Islam activates what Said and others have described as deep antipathies towards Islam in the Western imagination, which ignore the extent to which Islam was *within* the West from the start – there is a long history of cultural exchange and the Renaissance drew on Arab humanism, science, philosophy and historiography (Said 2001). In addition, there patently is no bipolarity comparable to the Cold War and there will not be, unless al-Qaeda comes to power in (say) Saudi Arabia and half a dozen other major states (Outhwaite and Ray 2005: 141).

There is, further, the bifurcated view of socio-cultural struggle in Barber's (2003) thesis of 'McWorld' versus 'Jihad' – a clash between the homogenizing and conflictual elements of globalization, in particular consumerist capitalism versus religious and tribal fundamentalism. On the one hand, consumer capitalism on the global level is rapidly dissolving the social and economic barriers between nations. On the other hand, ethnic, religious and racial hatreds are fragmenting the political landscape into smaller and smaller tribal units. But as Kellner (2002) says (of an earlier version of the thesis), 'Barber's model oversimplifies present world divisions and conflicts and does not adequately present the contradictions within the West or the "Jihad" world', although unlike Friedman (2000) Barber does point to some of the limitations of globalization. More generally, binary mind-sets still inform much thinking about global issues whereas the multidimensional process of globalization cannot be reduced to simple stereotypes, especially in view of the meaning that people locally attach to globally distributed goods and images. The crucial point about globalization is that cultures do not passively absorb foreign and global influences, but rather they may resist (e.g. as with the Iranian prohibition of satellite dishes) but more often actually incorporate foreign influences into their lives, as we saw in relation to digital communications in Chapter 4. For example, ethnographic studies of McDonald's (e.g. Caldwell 2004) show that the meaning of McDonald's has been changed enormously by local culture and customers and by local competition. In Moscow, for example, the *Russkoe Bistros* sell traditional pirozhki as a fast food snack and, despite some business problems, have become a well-established local competitor (Konnander 2006). In this respect Hannerz (1990) writes of a process of *creolization* – the creativity of local expressions that are adaptations of global interconnections. Again, writers such as Hanif Kureishi mix languages and express in their writing the diversity and richness of diverse cultural influences. In a 'culture of cultures' (Sahlins 2001), an important frame of reference for people is to claim a specific 'culture' – indigenous peoples, ethnic minorities, transnational alliances of 'black people' with a particular 'memory' and history. So people reclaim 'lost' identities – from 1970 to 1980 the number of North American Indians increased from 70,000 to 1.4 million – not the result of a population explosion but of the rapidly growing number who acknowledge indigenous ancestry, a phenomenon itself part of the global pursuit of genealogy-identity (Breidenbach and Zukrigl 1999). Living in globalized world does not therefore generate either homogeneity or polarization but rather a creative and eclectic mix of identities.

Another version of binary thinking is that of Hardt and Negri (2000), who argue that nation states are being replaced by 'empire' or by 'imperial sovereignty' – the emergence of dynamic and flexible systemic structures articulated horizontally across the globe. This new form of sovereignty is de-territorialized and decentred. 'Empire', however, generates its opposite – rebellious multitudes that are the 'other' of empire – 'the resistances, struggles and desires of the multitude' (Hardt and Negri 2000: xvi, 398). But their use of the term 'empire' here is ambiguous and misleading in that they are essentially describing the process of globalization and the supra-territorial hegemonic project of the US rather than traditional notions of empire as a centralized and territorially based organization. This gives their work the appearance of a novelty that it might not otherwise have. Further, they do not explain the appearance of 'resistances' or the particular forms these might take – for example, Islamist as opposed to secular socialist and anarchist movements. Similarly, Johnson (2000) argues that violence that appears to arise from outside the West – from 'terrorists' or 'rogue states' 'often turn[s] out to be a blowback from earlier American operations', such as support for the Afghan mujahedin against the Soviets in the 1980s (2000: 8). This is not a very nuanced explanation of why and how opposition arises within the global system, but it does point to the way in which violent conflicts in the global arena may be the unintended consequences of actions on a global scale. An anti-systemic challenge to the global American 'empire' comes from Islamist movements that in some ways occupy the previously communist space of an 'anti-imperialist bloc' and mobilize energies of fanatical devotion and unquestioning loyalty and a Jacobin ethic of violence and the purging of the old society to usher in a new purified utopia (Ray 1999a).[3] In some ways the old territorially based ideological divide between capitalism and communism has been replaced by fluid transnational identity politics and anti-globalization protest movements.

However, although globalization generates hybridity and sociocultural heterogeneity, it may well be the case that there is a new global bipolarity that is significant for the social imaginary of international relations.[4] Likewise, the spatially distanced Other represent 'harbingers of disorder and ambiguity against which security is written into the symbolic order [in ways that] variously include communism drugs, alien migration and sexual deviance' (Spence 2005). Indeed, although Huntington's thesis is implausible in many respects there is a risk that it is becoming a self-fulfilling prophesy since it (or a version of it) is fed by the dual fantasy ideologies of al-Qaeda and Washington, for both of whom the world is viewed in terms of Manicheistic divisions between irreconcilable Good and Evil. Kellner says:

> While Huntington's model seems to have some purchase in the currently emerging global encounter with terrorism, and is becoming a new dominant conservative ideology, it tends to overly homogenize both Islam and the West . . . [and] . . . lends itself to pernicious misuse.
>
> (Kellner 2002)

One example of this is its combination with the belief in the particularities of 'Arab mind' – asserted, for example, in Patai's (1976) influential book – that entered US strategic thinking, and De Atkine's (1999) linking of Huntington's thesis with US global strategic considerations. The use of sexual humiliation in the torture of Iraqi prisoners in 2003–04 were apparently rooted in the belief derived from Patai (1976: 216), that 'Arabs only understand force and . . . the biggest weakness of Arabs is shame and humiliation', especially around sexuality. The use of pseudo-social science combined with ideological fantasies of a global war on terrorism threatens to bring into fruition a 'clash of civilizations'.

In these ways globalization creates its Other – its new barbarians in the zones of turmoil – just as it incorporates the world into the neoliberal market. Just after the September 11th attacks, Hendrik Hertzberg wrote in *The New Yorker* that globalization:

> relies increasingly on the kind of trust – the unsentimental expectation that people, individually and collectively, will behave more or less in their rational self-interest . . . The terrorists made use of that trust. They rode the flow of the world's aerial circulatory system like lethal viruses.
>
> (Herzberg 2001)

The virus metaphor was significant because just as the body has been a metaphor for the state so disease and political violence have often been associated and linked by their common properties of threat, foreignness and capacity to permeate national borders. The political philosopher Thomas Hobbes, for example, claimed that with the social contract comes a separation between political and civil society, which he describes as two systems, that is 'numbers of men joyned in one Interest as parts of the body' (Hobbes 1994: 131). The metaphors of bodies/borders and virus/invasion will be examined further below.

TERROR AND THE GLOBAL RISK SOCIETY

Beck argues that three global risks – ecological crises, financial crises and terrorism – promote the global risk society and fundamentally change the relationships between individual and social life. The war on terror is in part a war of ideas and the imagination – for example the 'Great Satan' against the 'Axis of Evil' and an ideological struggle over the meaning and values of Islam in relation to the West. Unlike the Cold War this is a more diffuse and less territorially grounded conflict of identities, loyalties and belonging – which is illustrated by the renewed disputes over the integration of ethnic and religious minorities into Western societies. Shannon (2002) suggests that a world dominated by non-state entities may be a more historically relevant condition of global power relations as we enter a 'post-Westphalian' age in which familiar distinctions between soldier, civilian and state break down. The old model of territorially based conflict has been eclipsed to some extent by insurgency and intra-national warfare. Global, post-Westphalian conflicts are more likely to involve intra-state violence, for example conflict over the attempted session of a unit claiming independence on grounds of its ethnic, linguistic, religions or other claim to cultural particularity. In this case an official state armed force is in conflict with irregular non-state based insurgents. Indeed, as Urry says:

> Before September 11th there was a peace that was not a peace, there has now been a war that is not a 'war' between sovereign nation-states, and there has now been a world on the edge of chaos not at all at peace with itself.

> (Urry 2002)

Global terrorism is different from earlier forms of terrorism and more consistent with the notion of post-territorial global processes (Hudson 1999).[5] Following the analysis by Bergesen (2003) this could be said to be so in at least six senses. First, there has been an organizational shift to international networks that form loosely coupled organizations rather than professionally trained and hierarchical organizations. Second, contemporary groups less often explicitly claim responsibility for violent acts where in the past these would have been occasions for issuing a political statement. Third, demands are often vague and hazy – al-Qaeda did not explicitly claim responsibility for September 11th for some time, nor was this atrocity accompanied by any set of demands. Groups engaging in political violence in the past pursued specific objectives such as the removal of British rule in Northern Ireland for the IRA (Irish Republican Army), or ethnic-national separatism for the Basque. Fourth, there has been a shift from largely political motives to religious motives – for example, among Islamist groups, Christian fundamentalists and Aum Shinrikyo. Fifth, there has been a global dispersion of targets and victims beyond the immediate site of grievance. Targets may have global symbolic significance as with the World Trade Center, or local significance as with the Jewish social centre in Casablanca, bombed in May 2003. Finally, contemporary violence is more indiscriminate and makes no distinction between combatants and civilians, and often specifically targets the latter. It does not suggest a replaying of conflict between territorially based blocs. We might add to these the increasing importance of symbolic targets. The Japanese attack on Pearl Harbor, with which September 11th was initially compared, had a strategic, pre-emptive purpose of devastating the American navy. But September 11th had little strategic purpose in this sense; it was an attack on *symbols* of American (and Western) global power (the Pentagon) and finance (the Twin Towers). There has been a profound shift in violent conflict away from war between territorially based sovereign states that eventually ends in the formal cession of hostilities either through the surrender of one party or through a negotiated peace. The global pattern of violent conflict is one of insurgency in which states combat the 'asymmetric' force of irregular non-state armed forces whose capillary networks are often internationally organized. Although non-state armed forces such as the IRA may declare an end of hostilities, these conflicts are much more diffuse and indeterminate, often lacking the end point presupposed by traditional inter-state conflicts. Overall, then, globalization facilitates global–local networks that are bound together by identity and digital communications rather than closely linked and spatially fixed solidarities. The era of territorial bipolarity has given way to one of multiple, often non-state forms of violent conflict in which the politics of the spectacle may be more significant than clearly defined strategic objectives.

It is ironic that the ability of global terrorism to strike at large numbers of countries simultaneously was facilitated by globalization and has now become its biggest challenge. September 11th itself was a mega-event in a global media world of spectacle combined with the lethal power of modern technology. Kellner (2002) argues that September 11th 'dramatized that globalization is a defining reality of our time, and that the much-celebrated flow of people, ideas, technology, media and goods could have a downside as well as an upside'. The relationship between representation and reality was inverted, Davis (2001) suggests, since:

> The attacks on New York and Washington DC were organized as epic horror cinema with meticulous attention to *mise en scène*. Indeed the hijacked planes were aimed to impact precisely at the vulnerable border between fantasy and reality. In contrast to the 1938 radio invasion,[6] thousands of people who turned on their televisions on 9.11 were convinced that the cataclysm was just a broadcast, a hoax. They thought they were watching rushes from the latest Bruce Willis film.
>
> (Davis 2001)

He notes that this illusion has continued with 'a succession of celluloid hallucinations' of filmic representations of September 11th and, further, that September 11th 'is obviously a *global event* that could only happen in a networked society that is interconnected, where technology is available for anyone'.

Beck (2003) argues that terrorism is the harbinger of further globalization and has introduced a new era of globalization in which the focus is on the transnational reinvention of the political through networking and cooperation between states:

> Terrorist resistance to globalization has caused the precise opposite of what it aimed at, it has introduced a new era of globalization of politics and the state – the transnational intervention of the political through networking and cooperation. In an age in which belief in God, class, nation and government disappears, the known and recognized globality of danger is transformed into a source of associations, opening up new global political prospects for action.
>
> (Beck 2003)[7]

September 11th was, he says, the 'Chernobyl of globalization' in that where the 1986 explosion of the nuclear reactor dramatized the risks of nuclear power, September 11th 'laid to rest' neo-liberalism's promise of salvation. The disengagement of the economic from the political cannot solve the problems of humanity and the withdrawal of the state and privatization (in this case of air safety) increases vulnerability. However, the solution is not the return to a self-closed nation state (impossible, in his view, anyway) but rather to increased international cooperation and legality and cosmopolitanism. David Held (2002) makes a similar argument about the need for global political legitimacy and ethics in response to terrorism.

However, it is difficult to see these as much more than aspirations. Beck is viewing globalization here as a top-down process that is governed by states' actions rather than as (also) a bottom-up process that is the unplanned and unintended consequence of actors' choices and decisions. At least two processes need to be differentiated here. There is the question of whether September 11th and subsequent terrorist attacks have encouraged increased political networking and cooperation and there is the question of terrorism's impact on the economic processes that sustain globalization. One possibility is that since business generally dislikes instability and increased risk, FDI in areas at risk of terrorist attack has declined and will continue to do so. A review of the literature on the effect of terrorism on FDI argues that the evidence is mixed. FDI flows to the developing world increased 200 per cent between 2000 and 2004, up from 18 per cent to 36 per cent of global FDI, while FDI flows to developed countries fell by 27 per cent, from 81 per cent to 59 per cent of global FDI. In every category of developing country the inward FDI trend is rising, despite the vast majority of recent terrorist attacks having taken place in developing countries. On the other hand, there is some evidence of that September 11th cost the US some $660 billion by 2005 and has significantly reduced global investment levels. The IMF has estimated that the loss of US output from terrorism-related costs could be as high as 0.75 per cent of GDP, or $75 billion per year in the future (Wagner 2006). The likelihood is that the effects of global terrorist risks are uneven across the world and therefore have no uniform implications for economic globalization.

Nonetheless, there is little evidence for a rolling back of neo-liberalism and corporate freedom. According to Giroux (2005), 'markets are still presented to an increasing extent as the driving forces of everyday life while government is disparaged.' Citizenship is increasingly a function of consumerism as politics is reconstructed as freeing corporations from controls through deregulation and privatization. Indeed, for Giroux anti-terrorism exhausts itself in a discourse of moral absolutes that removes politics from state power and suppresses dissent. Thus 'the destruction of the welfare state has gone hand in hand with the emergence of a prison-industrial complex and a new state that is largely used to regulate, control, contain and punish those who are not privileged by the benefits of class' (Giroux 2005). Rather than provoke a rethinking of the political in terms of transnational legality and cooperation the (unwinnable yet indefinite) war on terror has increased state powers while increasing the freedom of corporations from political limitations.

Indeed, there is a strong link between neo-liberal restructuring and globalization – the latter being both a result and a medium of the former (Köhler and Wissen 2003) since it results from capital being freed from national boundaries by neo-liberal politics and shapes the conditions which are favourable to further neo-liberal restructuring. Further, as Held points out, the 'focus of the liberal international order is on the curtailment of the abuse of political power, not economic power. It has few, if any systematic means to address sources of power other than the political' (Held 2002). Thus there is a conflict between a global deregulating neo-liberal model and the kind of entrenchment of cosmopolitan values of equal dignity and worth of all human beings that Beck hopes will emerge in a global risk society. As we saw in the last chapter, global economic liberalization and the unregulated growth of capitalist markets across the world have resulted in heightened levels of social inequality that states have a reduced will or capacity to address. Hertz (2001: 11) has described this as a 'silent takeover' in which, following the end of the Cold War, 'the balance of power between politics and commerce has shifted radically', so that 'corporations are taking on the responsibilities of government'.

At the same time neo-liberalism has been the focus of global social movements attempting to fight its influences in everyday life and create lived spaces of alternative social and economic infrastructures. Such movements, often locally situated but transnationally networked, are 'interlocking various spatial scales from sub-local to the global' contributing to the 'emergence of global but diverse movement' (Köhler and Wisssen 2003). For example there was the civil society network that originated with French groups aimed at establishing and international tax on currency speculation (the Tobin tax) and spread across global social movements. There were the *piqueteros*, organizations of unemployed workers in Argentina that began to occupy factories abandoned in the 2001 economic crisis while local exchange systems and networks aimed to develop cooperative exchanges outside the market. It might be these areas of local politics and social activism that are more likely to decide the fate of neoliberal strategies rather than the war on terror. In this context, Rheingold (2000) writes of 'smart mobs' that emerge when communication and computing technologies amplify human talents for cooperation. The technologies that are beginning to make smart mobs possible are mobile communication devices and pervasive computing – inexpensive microprocessors embedded in everyday objects and environments. The impacts of smart mob technology are both beneficial and destructive – used by some to support democracy and by others to coordinate terrorist attacks. Already, governments have fallen, youth sub-cultures have blossomed from Asia to Scandinavia, and new industries have been born and older industries have launched furious counterattacks. Street demonstrators in the 1999 anti-WTO protests used dynamically updated websites, cellphones and 'swarming' tactics in the 'battle of Seattle'. Glasius and Kaldor (2002) point to the accelerating numbers of and connections between INGOs since 1990, and the growth of 'parallel summits' since 1990, such as the 2001 Porto Alegre meeting in Brazil attended by 11,000 people to protest against the Davos (Switzerland) World Economic Forum. These parallel summits along with the extensive and interconnected anti-capitalist, ecology and peace movements provide an alternative vision of a world order based on global norms of human rights, environmental protection and social justice.

One difficulty here, though, is that, contrary to Beck, the global risk society is one in which strengthening state and intergovernmental surveillance inhibits local forms of resistance and organization. Indeed, Rheingold (2000) continues to point out that media cartels and government agencies are seeking to reimpose on 'smart mobs' the regime of the broadcast era that would deprive users of the technology of the power to create, leaving only the ability power to consume – through battles over file sharing, copy protection and regulation of the radio spectrum. Not only this but the increased surveillance and polarization associated with the war on terror also has the effect of encouraging conspiracy theories among anti-globalization activists. For example, the website of the Canadian-based Center for Research on Globalization sells books and videos that 'expose' how the September 11th attacks were 'most likely a special covert action' to 'further the goals of corporate globalization'. This kind of conspiracy thinking is not exceptional. Moreover, as Strauss (2003) argues, antisemitism has been a specific and growing feature of anti-globalization analysis – 'conspiracy theories must always have a conspirator, and all too often, the conspirators are perceived to be Jews.' In the face of a worldwide stock market, new forms of money, open borders and concepts such as country and nationality being called into question, anti-globalists look for the ones who are guilty for this new situation and they find the Jews. In the wake of the war against Iraq, it was argued that a cabal of Jewish neocon advisors had forced the US into conquering Iraq to safeguard Israel. The backlash against globalization unites elements across the political spectrum – the far right's conception of the Jew (a fifth column, loyal only to itself, undermining economic sovereignty and national culture), the far left's conception of the Jew (capitalists and usurers, controlling the international economic system) and the 'blood libel' Jew (murderers and modern-day colonial oppressors). In the process, the Tsarist forgery, the 'Protocols of the Elders of Zion', that depicts a world Jewish conspiracy is increasingly cited and given credibility (Ben-Itto 2005).

Finally, we should also note that 'September 11 was a moment when international law might have been taken seriously . . . [since] terrorists, human rights violators, and criminals are best defeated by scrupulously upholding the rule of law' (Glasius and Kaldor 2002: 27), but this is not what happened. Despite the activities of multiple INGOs and civil society networks, there is (again *pace* Beck) no developed effective global (or cosmopolitan) civil society in which both corporate and state powers are embedded within normative frameworks. Rather than enhancing these optimistic expectations the aftermath of September 11th and the war on terror casts doubt on the possibility of developing a global civil society. While there are beginnings of cross-national trades union organization (e.g. a fifteen-month dispute by Group 4 workers in India, Uganda, South Africa and Kenya in 2005–06) it is still generally the case that capital gains maximum mobility across national boundaries, taking command of *space* in a way that voluntary organizations rooted more in locality and *place* cannot do (Harvey 1994: 238). Similarly, Susan Buck-Morss (2003: 65) argues that national security and threat dominates political discourse while neo-liberalism eliminates the possibility of critical thinking.

TERROR, BODIES AND SOCIAL INTERACTION

The context of global threats and perceived danger enters everyday life in complex and contradictory ways. In public places state sovereignty is written onto the body by practices designed to subject it to authority. Both licit and illicit movement invokes the control of bodies, a process that will be enhanced with the growth of stored biometric data and technologies enabling the virtual encoding of bodies in movement. One example of this is the suggestion that air travellers be electronically tagged.[8] Borders are sites of transparency and potential violation of the privacy of the body, such as strip searches, and airports are liminal spaces where the usual Western conventions of bodily contact cease to apply (Donnan and Wilson 1999: 130). State power is imposed on the most intimate element of our being – our body, 'where the raw power of the state can be found' (Donnan and Wilson 1999: 132).

The experience of the everyday in public places is closely bound up with naively assumed trust that others are what they appear to be. Goffman (1983) argued that 'once in one another's immediate presence, individuals will necessarily be faced with personal-territory contingencies'. To follow Goffman further, 'there are enablements and risks inherent in co-bodily presence' since to participate in (offline) social situations we bring our bodies with us, which gives rise to vulnerabilities. These include risks of physical assault, sexual molestation, robbery and obstruction of movement, and breaches of psychic reserves, and at the same time we command the resources to make others similarly vulnerable to us, although these risks and vulnerabilities will be structured on lines (especially) of gender and race. At the same time everyday interaction in public spaces requires 'civic disattention' – disengagement from anonymous people in one's shared space, which presupposes the benign intent of the other's appearance and manner.

In contrast, terrorism violates trust and weakens public order by threatening the security of identities in public space. But for Goffman (1983) the assassin 'must rely on and profit from conventional traffic flow' and the appearances of someone who does not 'abuse free passage'. Thus 'normalcy is a fragile façade as self and other interpret situations not for what is manifest but for what the manifest may hide'. Indeed 'at the heart of public order is a profound paradox: The rules and expectations that generate order are the very rules and expectations that allow for hiding threats to that order' (Weigert 2003). A pragmatic acceptance of the public performance of others at face value allows the real possibility of not being who one appears to be – the apparent identity of airline passenger or subway traveller may override the apparent identities of terrorist and suicide (from the victims' frame) or hero and martyr (from the perpetrators' frame).

For Goffman and Weigert terrorism (or more significantly its threat) creates a self-fulfilling dynamic in which people will tend to see situations as dangerous and this leads to a decline of public trust and increased barriers and surveillance. On the other hand, it could be argued that there is a normalization of surveillance and risk calculus that enters the routine rituals of everyday life, especially those involving transport and global travel. The security questions at airports and on visa applications become routinized along with the increasingly elaborate compartmentalization of space into zones of surveillance and regulation, generating what Foucault (1977: 135ff.) called 'docile bodies' subject to exploration and re-arrangement. Indeed Spence (2005) argues that: 'Terror is . . . insinuated within the structures of the social world, part of the background of prejudgements, assumptions and understandings that shape the reception, experience and reproduction of everyday life.' The state of emergency, he says, 'becomes normal', but it is also, surely, normal*ized*. So at the same time the exigencies of the everyday exercise a dull compulsion that often overrides the apocalyptic moment – as the *Baltimore Sun* journalist Susan Reimer put it:

> I wrote five years ago that my life would not permit any fundamental changes in the aftermath of Sept. 11 . . . .. The mundane intrudes relentlessly, even on our worst days. And it turns out, I was correct. I am too busy to assess my personal terror level – orange, yellow or red – so I

> can't really say if I feel less safe or not. . . . I haven't got the time to worry
> about whether my mall is safe from a suicide bomber or whether my
> water supply is vulnerable to bioterrorism.
>
> (Reimer 2006)

The idea that on the level of everyday life the triple threats of ecological crisis, financial collapse and terrorism prompt an on going reflexivity and individualization needs to be balanced against the everyday routines through which counter-terrorism passes unreflectively. On the other hand the insinuation of threat into everyday rituals of increased surveillance, queuing, data collection and checking and the need to prove in certain public spaces that one is not a terrorist is also highly structured and subject to 'ethnic profiling', an activity that brings into play deep structures of inclusion and exclusion. Everyday civic disattention remains a precondition for the existence of public space, perhaps even more in liminal interstices of departure lounges, but one that is inflected with increased distrust. For example, the increasingly global debate about the appropriateness of the Muslim veil is situated in a visual culture where, as Simmel noted (1997: 109–19), mutual eye contact indicates reciprocity. But a visual culture is also one of surveillance and transparency in which the veil is a symbol of both exclusion and visibility – in particular the visibility of an Other whom many at a subliminal level view as symbolic of threat.

MOBILITY, BORDERS AND FEAR

Global change in the past two decades has had an enormous impact of human mobility, following such factors as collapsing empires, civil and interstatal wars, ecological disasters and processes of depeasantization discussed in Chapter 5, de-industrialization and outsourcing to the periphery, the role of global media and cheap air travel. These have propelled some people in uncertain directions while creating heightened awareness of global interconnections and possibilities. Many contemporary fears are bound up with mobile bodies. The relationship between globalization and migration, for example, is complex since deregulation in one area does not automatically imply loosening restrictions in another. Contrary to claims that the significance of borders is eroding, some states are working to endow them with meaning in innovative ways, and immigration policy is crucial to the maintenance of the national community (Goff 2000). Flows of global movement are proliferating while the fortification of national boundaries is becoming more vigilant – a trend intensified since September 11th and by the rise of anti-migrant politics in Europe. Borderlands are taking on increased significance as resources and means of exploitation since human beings have considerably less freedom to move across international borders than capital has (Donnan and Wilson 1999). States are seeking to maximize investment opportunities for transnational corporations while closing their doors to the forms of migration that these economic shifts stimulate (Papastergiadis 2000: 2–3). The 1998 Schengen Agreement institutes extensive systems of control on and surveillance of migration into the EU from further east, especially the former Soviet Union and Middle East. These controls include expansion of the Eurodac computerized fingerprint database to refugees and asylum seekers, harmonization of sanctions on carriers of illegal migrants, and a raft of policing measures and requirements for controls on external borders.

Various kinds of forced migration have produced at least 140 million migrants and refugees worldwide and this differential arose along with the process of globalization in the twentieth century. Some borders are permeable, at least for people with the right documents, while others are heavily barred. For those who have the passports or the appropriate visas and have the means to buy the technologies of actual and virtual mobility, the world is a space of mobilities. But the world presents a very different lived experience for those who are poor or homeless and have nowhere to go in a hurry. In this context Bauman distinguishes between 'tourists' and 'vagabonds'. The former move through choice, move easily, and despise and fear the vagabond, who in turn moves through necessity, does not choose where to go, moves with difficulty and admires and envies the tourists – 'The tourists travel *because they want to*; the vagabonds because *they have no other bearable choice*' (Bauman 1998: 94). The vagabond is a pilgrim without a destination, a nomad without an itinerary, while the tourist pays 'for their freedom; the right to disregard native concerns and feelings, the right to spin their own web of meanings . . . The world is the tourist's oyster . . . to be lived pleasurably – and thus given meaning' (Bauman 1993: 241). Both vagabonds and tourists travel through other people's spaces – for both this involves the separation of physical closeness from moral proximity, and for both it sets standards for happiness and the good life. For Bauman the good life has come to be thought of as somewhat akin to a 'continuous holiday' (1993: 243) while the vagabond is a 'flawed consumer' (1999: 77).

There are very different social and economic processes that generate a global culture of consumer tourism on the one hand and some 10 million migrants and 25 million displaced persons on the other. Both processes are of global significance but arise in very different ways. Tourism is one of the largest global industries[9] but is premised not on mobility as such but rather on temporary sojourn in which many 'home comforts' and familiar forms of consumption will be available. Migration, however, is itself a highly differentiated process that includes temporary migrant workers, highly skilled voluntary migrants, forced and trafficked migrants and refugees, each variety generated by different sets of social relationship. Underlying economic migration is the way in which capital increasingly defines labour costs in terms of lowest global costs and, through sub-contracting in home and overseas markets, is able to achieve lowest costs in some sectors, such as textiles. Low cost and often forced labour migration is a crucial facet of global mobilities (Papastergiadis 2000: 40). The presence of undocumented workers in advanced capitalist economies has the important effect of reducing costs in sectors that are structurally dependent upon them, such as textiles, minicab services, cleaning services, food service and agriculture (Rivera-Batiz 1999). Migration and ethnic divisions epitomize the differential way in which global elements are localized, labour markets are constituted, and culture de- and re-territorialized (Sassen 1998). There are indeed decentred, flexible and knowledge-rich networks continually restructuring themselves according to the signals of a fast fluid nexus of global scapes and flows. So Bauman's metaphors of 'vagabond' and 'tourist' may conceal more than they reveal, while the patterns of global population movement can be accounted for in terms of existing theories and concepts of global capital, and class, gender and racialized structures. There is a global industry in trade of people (Salt 2000: 106) that follows the appearance of global networks of migration agents, smugglers and traffickers and is therefore in part also a product of late twentieth-century globalization of international crime. Border controls have an ambiguous role here in that they increase the risk and therefore the premium for trafficking – for sex, body parts and labour – and may therefore make such trafficking even more lucrative. Further, migration is located at the crossroads between two very different political semantics: those based on economic and functional issues, on the one hand (e.g. the need to meet labour shortages) and those based on culture, identity and tradition, on the other (Zolberg 1999). A less noted consequence of this cross-cutting location is that discursive political loyalties over migration issues cannot be efficiently policed by the use of a binary code of political activity, the distinction between conservative and progressive (Luhmann 1982: 166–89). This explains why some immigration policy may be changed only through temporary hybrid 'discursive coalitions' (Jacobs 1998). At the same time, however, the impossibility of consistently linking immigration and general issues, under conditions of high politicization, makes further room for free-floating adaptations and swift changes (Sciortino 2000).

For this reason, perhaps, there are multiple fears associated with movement of people across borders. A review of print media between October and December 2002 (Article 19 2003) found that media reporting of migration was overwhelmingly negative and hostile – constructing a crisis and panic about 'invasion' – especially following September 11th. Issues of crime, negative effects on local communities, fraud, illegal employment and accommodation dominated stories, and this was true of both the broadsheet and tabloid papers. This illustrates how migration operates as a floating issue, evading dominant political codes of 'left' and 'right'.

Fears associated with migration often invoke metaphors of war to justify the need to repel whatever is hostile or threatening. Immigration controls become matters of national security; a national emergency requires full deployment of the armed forces on a prime defence mission to detect incursions. Representing asylum seekers who arrive in the UK without prior refugee determination as bogus and phoney implicitly legitimizes policies that move beyond policing and into detention and deterrence for the sake of the nation. The recurring panics about asylum that get increasingly over-determined by the fears of terrorism encourage the exclusion of domestic minority communities while justifying expansionist penal policies. For example some headlines in UK newspapers in recent years have claimed:

> 3000 gypsies coming to Britain to sponge off the cushy benefit system.
> (*The Sun* 20 October 1997)

> Gypsies invade Dover hoping for a handout.
> (*The Independent* 21 October 1997)

> We want to wash this dross down the drain.
> (*Dover Express* October 1998)[10]

When writing about asylum seekers and refugees, the press often elide the vocabulary of war with that of crime. Following the *closure* of the Sangatte refugee camp on the French side of the Channel amid fears of illegal migration to the UK, the UK newspaper, *The Daily Mail* announced on 6 September 2003, 'They're back – the new asylum army massing in numbers, the migrants are readying themselves for a renewed invasion of Britain.' Again, on 19 February 2004, an unspecified 'Official report' – hence with implicitly authoritative sources – was cited in the *Daily Mail* and the *Express,* claiming that '1:20 people in London is migrant' and '£600m or 1% of NHS budget is going on "immigrants".' Fears of asylum were attached to wider fears of crime, with young male asylum seekers being portrayed as already criminalized – with photographs of groups of young men taken close up to camera suggesting a menacing but obscured presence. Subsequently and especially after the 7 July 2005 London suicide bombings, panics shifted from preoccupation with asylum to threats posed by Muslim separation and difference from mainstream society.

Borders and disease

'The dominant political concerns and anxieties of society tend to be translated into disrupted and disturbed images of the body' (Turner

2006). The *danse macabre* gave gruesome expression to the devastation of medieval society by the Black Death and in modern society AIDS 'has often been imagined in military metaphors of invading armies' (Turner 2006). Bodies that flow from the inside to outside are dangerous and contaminating because they challenge our sense of orderliness. 'Part of the centuries-old conception of Europe as a privileged cultural entity is that it is a place which is colonized by lethal diseases coming from elsewhere' (Sontag 1988). Further, epidemics throw into relief deeply held social tensions and anxieties especially where these are infused with tensions over sexuality. Buchholtz and Reich (1987) use Habermas's theory of the intrusion of lifeworld by system to identify a violent process of rationalization in which people displace threats and fears onto clichés provided by the mass media. Disease, like the above example of fears of asylum and migration, offer potent images for this.

However, this also indicates the continuing importance of understanding the inequalities of vulnerability to risk. According to Beck (1992: 36) 'poverty is hierarchical; smog is democratic' and equality of vulnerability is fundamental to the concept of Beck's global risk society. But this assertion does not take sufficient account of the social structuring of disease on a global scale, the very process of the inscription of inequalities onto bodies. Social divisions and inequalities have a direct effect in patterns of illness and health. Global patterns of illness are structured according to social location and hierarchical position. This is especially the case in developing countries, where many millions of people experience the cycles of malnutrition, underweight babies, high infant mortality, slow child development and repeated illnesses in childhood leaving weaker immune systems and longer periods of infectivity. These, combined with the lack of clean water and (often) adequate shelter, generate high levels of morbidity and mortality, especially among children under five years old. The most common forms of death among the under-fives in developing countries are pneumonia, diarrhoea, malaria, measles and respiratory infections. Infant mortality is higher in rural areas and urban shantytowns than in urban areas were there is some semblance of organized facilities and adequate housing. Lack of clean water means that diseases transmitted by faeces are common (WHO 2004b).

Further, although the link between social inequality and disease is well known, few have examined the contribution of social inequalities to disease emergence (Farmer 1996). But Farmer argues that inequalities have affected not only the distribution of infectious diseases but also the course of the disease in those affected. Outbreaks of Ebola, AIDS and TB suggest that disease models need to be dynamic and critical and incorporate analysis of global complexity. This suggests the need for a strongly societal view of the pathogenicity of viral processes in which microbial mutations are responsive to human actions. For example, malaria is often thought of as a 'tropical disease', but during the nineteenth century it affected around a million a year in the US southern states and it declined largely because of agricultural development, improved housing and land drainage – many 'tropical diseases' are predominantly distributed by inequality rather than latitude. For example, the Harlem age-specific death rate (from infectious disease and violence) is higher in several groups than that in Bangladesh (Farmer 1996).

Epidemic disease is usually constructed as coming 'from outside'. Many borders represent transmission of 'an infection', leaking not just people but also contaminated substances (Seremetakis 1996: 490). The beginnings of cross-border regional collaboration between Bulgaria, Albania, Romania, Turkey and Greece in the early 1990s was accompanied by 'media panic stories about waves of infectious diseases crossing the Greek frontier: AIDS, hepatitis B, cholera, Ebola and the list goes on. Borders were not only leaking people but . . . contaminating substances' (Seremetakis 1996). During the 1980s AIDS was the epitome of global risk and threat. The association of global air travel and sexual promiscuity was a powerful metaphor for the anxieties around the permeability of borders and bodies. This was illustrated by the myth that AIDS was brought to the US by 'Patient O', a flight attendant believed to have infected 40 of the 248 people known to be infected by AIDS in 1983. The media profile of AIDS was very high, with hardly a day passing without news and commentary on AIDS along with extensive literature and fiction, such as Randy Shilts' *And the Band Played On* (1987) and the film *Philadelphia* (1993). This faded during the 1990s and has in some ways been replaced by terrorism as a global fear. This was partly because in developed countries the rate of incidence slowed, and HIV became for many people a chronic and manageable, rather than terminal, condition. But this was also because the developing world and Africa, in particular, became the main site of the epidemic.[11]

For a time AIDS came to be symbolic of the permeability of borders/bodies and the feedback effects of fears and panics. For example, in 1982 the US National Cancer Institute announced that the epidemic was an endemic Haitian virus that had been brought into the US by homosexual tourists. This proved incorrect, but the damage had then been done to Haitian tourism with the results of increased poverty and a steeper slope of inequality and vulnerability to disease (Farmer 1996). This false claim was also a coded statement that exoticized Haiti, deployed folk beliefs about Haitians and Africans and conflated poverty and cultural difference. Yet at the same time the virus was crossing borders *into* Haiti and across in the world following contours of the transnational socio-economic order. Thus 'much of the spread of HIV in the 1970s and 1980s moved along international "fault lines" tracking along steep gradients of inequality, which are also paths of migrant labour and sexual commerce' (Farmer 1996). Like earlier infections such as TB, HIV became a disease of poverty, and disparities in the course of the disease among those affected are similarly socio-economically structured – a phenomenon that has been heightened by global inequalities of access to antiviral agents. The IMF's structural adjustment programmes (discussed in Chapter 5) are 'pushing poor people even deeper into poverty [thereby] . . . increasing vulnerability to HIV infection, and reinforcing conditions where [it] . . . can flourish' (World Development Movement 1999).

There are high levels of turbulence at borders not just between nations but also between differential health status and social entitlements. These are contours of global socio-economic inequality around which there is the continual movement and regulation of bodies and deployment of law and power. For example, the Mexican–US border, described as 'the most extreme economic precipice on the planet' (Davis 2004), divides countries in which the average national income is four times higher and the rate of infant mortality three times lower on one side than the other. On any one day, while young Americans will cross the border so they can illegally drink alcohol, some Mexicans will die of thirst trying to cross it legally so they can work. But whereas policing the border used to be an immigration issue it has, since September 11th, become a security issue symbolizing the permeability of the US political body/border.[12] Rather than usher in an open world of frictionless movement, globalized mobility displays the disciplinary practices of quarantine and the manufacture of docile bodies – at borders, zones of transit and in many forms of internal and transnational transport. Although these become routinized, the principle of naively assumed trust and disattention in everyday public encounters may also be eroded in a state of permanent watchfulness. In the process existing and new forms of structural exclusion are likely to be maintained, along with a blurring of the idea of bodies/borders and disease and threat. Globalization does not necessarily therefore bring a 'democratization of risk', nor did September 11th spell the end of neo-liberalism and its replacement by an era of transnational cooperation. However, the post-September 11th phase of globalization does indicate the contradictory and complex indeterminacy of the process.

CONCLUSION

In Chapter 5 I argued that global economic strategies, especially structural adjustment programmes, were generating dislocation of everyday life in many parts of the world and prompting local solutions including large-scale migration and extended transnational forms of sociality. Economic globalization generated increased inequalities (as well as increased growth) and in its wake has exacerbated global divisions of vulnerability and access to resources. These vulnerabilities crucially include risks of poverty and illness, which in turn shape most other life chances. In these senses notions of social division and structural patterning of social effects – the issues at the core of much sociology – remain essential points of reference for explaining the form taken by global connections. Smog may be 'democratic', but the hierarchical ordering of risks is still fundamental to lived experience in the global community. At the same time, the shrinking of space that globalization entails has increased global population mobility and consciousness of the disparities in life chances. This in turn, and especially since September 11th, has generated new globalization terrors since the threats are perceived to arise from the social infrastructures that generated globalization itself.

At the centre of the global imagination is the idea of permeability of borders, which have frequently been metaphorically understood not just territorially but also as membranes of a body politic. For many, especially in the years following the end of the Cold War, globalization was positively viewed as creating opportunities for cosmopolitan and fluid identities, increased security and economic growth. But it has also been perceived in terms of threats to the security, integrity and identity of cultures, nations and traditional ways of life. There is often a highly emotively charged metaphorical elision between violent threats to security and viral contagion, such that the boundaries of the nation and body become fused. Such perceptions are not confined to particular political positions and can appear both on the traditional right and in anti-globalism movements. Since September 11th the awareness of global terrors has increased and I have argued that the optimistic gloss on this as stimulating a more cosmopolitan transnationalism is overstated for the present at any rate. In some respects the exigencies of increased surveillance and background fears are routinized in everyday life. But they are mobilized as fears of new 'barbarians' and transform the nature and perception of interaction in public space.

CONCLUSIONS

Globalization is an accomplishment of everyday life involving human agents engaged in the active construction of global forms of sociality. Debates about globalization raise some central sociological questions about the extent to which social processes are indirect and self-steering as opposed to constituted and sustained through the ways in which actors make choices and meaningfully construct social life. Within this context, sociological problems of power and social divisions such as social class, gender, nationality, ethnicity, institutional organization and capitalism remain as central as they have ever been. I have attempted to illustrate this in a number of places through engagement with classical sociologists such as Marx and Durkheim and Simmel. In contrast, I have argued that some dominant approaches to globalization in contemporary sociology emphasize the systemic properties of globalization as an emergent phenomenon and often highlight how it undermines pre-existing social bonds, but they have relatively little to say about how social life nevertheless 'gets done'. In particular, theories of reflexive individualization risk (so to speak) becoming pre-social because of the absence of any account of how everyday life is sustained nor any critique of how the ideology of individualism might belie a reality of more complex social bonds and interdependencies. It may be true that there is a tendency for globalization to lift forms of life out of specific contexts – for example, through long-distance monetary or institutional networks – and in the process previously localized, tacitly organized capabilities become ubiquitous and therefore codified knowledge. The logic of the market, for example, is to generate homogeneity, impersonality and routinized exchanges over long distances. Nonetheless markets, even globally organized ones, require complex social, cultural and institutional underpinning, and I have argued that even long-distance social relations have a 'stickiness' since participants often consolidate communications through face-to-face interactions. Moreover, spatially stretched communications and networks still presuppose shared norms, conventions, values, expectations and routines arising from commonly experienced frameworks or institutions – just as much as those within spatial proximity.

I began by asking whether globalization renders 'society' an inappropriate unit of analysis. Those who talk about the end of the 'container theory of society' base their argument largely on the putative end of the national state. Beck refers to the nation and other core sociological structural concepts as 'zombies' derived from nineteenth-century sociology. But the idea of the nation state as an ethnically homogenous realm is relatively new and has co-existed with other forms of state organization throughout the modern period. The key issue here is not where the boundaries of 'society' might be drawn – for example, around the 'nation' – but of understanding the dynamics of social solidarity in cosmopolitan, globalized societies. Sociology never actually was wedded to a national concept of society, and this debate has been addressing a straw argument. Rather, classical sociology was centrally organized around concepts such as capitalism, civil society, industrialism, bureaucracy, world religions, and so forth that are not particularly 'territorial' and anticipate post-national forms of society. In any event, because populations are culturally diverse, and economic, cultural and political life is complex, it does not follow that the state and territoriality are no longer significant units of analysis. On the contrary, the state has arguably become more significant as an actor in the global area than it was previously, and not only in relation to surveillance, regulation of borders and anti-terrorism but also in its attempts to counter the socially destructive consequences of global neo-liberalism.

In this context states attempt to mediate and regulate the tension between the relative mobility of capital, which must nonetheless be spatially embedded, and relatively (though perhaps decreasingly) immobile labour, and this exercises an important constraint on unfettered global integration. Among the consequences of global economic restructuring has been a weakening of social solidarity and institutional supports (notably welfare), increased uncertainty and fluidity of work experience, and, partly as a consequence of this, the undermining of some traditional forms of masculinity and an increased perception of global risks. The global 'social cohesion' agenda attempts, on the one hand, reflexively to reconstruct sociality (by building local social capital, for example) while, on the other hand, it attempts to police communal, often inter-ethnic, divisions that have themselves been exacerbated by the vicissitudes of global capital. In the process state actors have given rise to a complex mixture of intended and unintended consequences, some of which have had the effect of creating novel forms of social networks and action (such as the contradictory effects of migration controls on migration).

Globalization debates clearly pose important questions about what it is that sociologists study. The abiding object of sociology is sociality, by which I mean both the tacit and explicit knowledge and meanings that underpin social life and provide a scaffold for apparently self-determining processes of money, the market and other systemic media. I have attempted to emphasize throughout this book how global flows must be realized and manifest in spaces that variously become terrains of integration and conflict. The existence of globalized spaces of communication still presupposes that social meaning is produced in specific social, geographic and cultural contexts that are temporally bound. In the process of the localization of the global and globalization of the local there are social structures, cultures and forms of power that are enacted, summoned up, reproduced and, of course, transformed through everyday interactions. The results of recent research into digital communications are, in my view, good examples of this. The Internet is a source of the compression of time and space that is central to globalization, and it is at the same time the most globalized public space and the most private intimate space often accessed in a solitary setting. In globalized communities people feel part of their world and a 'village' at the same time. There is a diversity of views as to whether the Internet portends a posthuman world of impersonal lost authenticity or liberation from space and embodiment. Or again it may be just another medium of communication alongside many others. The view advanced here is that use of the Internet is organically embedded within existing social patterns of local lives and within culturally constraining and constituting social relationships. Actors communicating in cyberspace generate ways in which the world will be recognizable to other actors. Indeed, while virtual worlds epitomize the fluidity and 'placelessness' of globalized interaction we find that virtual communications are governed by social norms (which inevitably get breached, of course), institutional contexts (regulators, list managers, etc.) and tacit understandings, and that people who communicate online often also have or develop offline relationships and so on. Because offline sociality is important to developing trust and enduring social bonds, many transnational corporations will fly executives around the world to face-to-face meetings when it would be a lot cheaper and more efficient to arrange videoconferences. 'The global', then, 'is not a pre-given entity external to other spatial scales. Instead it is produced, reproduced, modified and challenged in a multiplicity of actions on various spatial scales' (Köhler and Wissen 2003).

Globalization has for the first time in world history created a global market and dense network of production and commodity chains, which has had profound effects on social relationships in the past few decades. While many international agencies focus on poverty (and the debates over the direction of the trends) there is evidence that global inequalities between and within countries have risen along with increasing global socio-economic integration. One global consequence of these processes has been large-scale depeasantization – the disappearance of rural peasant life that had at the outset of the twentieth century been the way of life for the majority of people worldwide and that by its close had given way to massive (generally unplanned) urbanization. This is a complex and uneven process that manifests itself in different ways in particular locales, one of which is large-scale urbanization that is often detached from new sources of employment and generates high levels of unemployment or semi-employment in informal economies. This in turn is pushing both legal and illicit migration into higher-wage economies, which in turn further extend global interconnections between people, and remittances sent 'back home' become a major flow of cash in the global economy.

This unprecedented population mobility in the twentieth century has generated new forms of cultural hybridity, and transnational identities have emerged, in which many people have overlapping memberships of national, religious and ethnic communities. In the process cosmopolitanism becomes rooted in the fabric of modern societies, too, which calls for new strategies (among state and non-state actors) of regulation and integration. As people are less bound together by common values or ways of life, formal procedures (such as liberal democracy and guarantees of rights) have become crucial to the articulation of substantive differences. Thus rooted cosmopolitanism and 'constitutional patriotism' are proposed as post-national forms of political and civic identity. This is a matter of cultural hybridity and negotiation, which – like all complex social relations – may give rise to tensions. People manage multiple identities and points of reference, including hybrid identities with overlapping historical, national and global references – such as African-American, Asian-American, British-Asian, Chinese-British, British Muslim, British-Jewish, Christian-Arab etc., although at times these may give rise to conflicts of loyalty both within the self and with others. People's lives are enacted within particular spaces that are both invested with memory and meaning and are also spaces of governance. The urban landscape itself is subject to competing meanings, histories and claims to authenticity, which is illustrated by the important public meanings given to monuments, streets and commemorations – I discussed the example of disputes over the meanings of Auschwitz in Polish and European history but many examples can be found where landscape and buildings are invested with conflicting meaning, such as disputes over indigenous people's land rights, or Native Americans' challenges to battlefield commemoration in the US. Global space is organized within territorially bounded civic communities, definitions of citizenship, institutions, official language(s), political, educational, cultural systems etc. Governments themselves are not neutral in these disputes but attempt to secure loyalty from diverse constituencies in the public stances taken. However, to complicate things further this is not only a cultural process since global migration and patterns of ethnic differentiation are also driven by and recreate social divisions and exclusions. The fear of 'migration from the East' in western Europe is in part a displacement of complex anxieties about global cultural incursion but also the concern to protect the labour market position among groups who perceive themselves in competition with new migrants. Cosmopolitanism will remain merely an aspiration unless the multiple sources of these tensions are addressed.

In the Introduction I asked whether globalization was an outcome of complex socio-economic developments or an emergent process in its own right. Is it the effect of a complex combination of social, economic, cultural and political changes? The analysis here has suggested that the multiform processes that are described as 'globalization' are the outcomes of a whole complex of socio-economic and cultural changes, the collective consequences of which are unintended and to a degree unpredictable. Two of the defining global events of recent times – the fall of the Berlin Wall and the fall of the Twin Towers – were the outcome of globalizing forces but were largely unanticipated. So globalization is primarily an outcome of a set of processes that are themselves only loosely connected, although the relationship is dialectical in that once global consequences and forms of sociation take shape, they in turn act back on the actions and structures from which they emerged. Further, the idea of globalization has preoccupied contemporary discourses and become an object around which multiple governmental, corporate, social movement and policy actions have been orientated, illustrating again that if people believe circumstances are real, they are real in their consequences.

I also asked whether globalization creates a homogeneous, especially visual global culture, or whether, on the contrary, it brings increased differentiation between globalization winners and losers along with eclectic hybrids of local and global cultures. The answer to this question is implicit in the foregoing. In some ways globalization enables economic and cultural communicative action to span geographical space and establish globally recognized commodities, buildings, languages, lifestyles, foods and so on. Transnational corporations promote a global consumerist culture, in which standard commodities, promoted by global marketing campaigns exploiting basic material desires, create similar lifestyles such as 'CocaCola-nization'. Western ideals are established as universal, threatening to override local traditions. Modern institutions are inherently rational-izing, driving towards making all human practices more efficient, controllable and predictable, as exemplified by the spread of fast food 'McDonaldization'. But at the same time it would be rather superficial to imagine that because one can get Sky Sports or a Big Mac in almost any city in the world that this creates any common-ality of meanings or cultural perceptions. Not only will global commodities acquire different meanings in particular locales but the transmission of cultural commodities is multi-directional – for example, the appropriation of Jamaican hip hop in Western music or of Japanese animation in Western cinema. Cultural flows occur differently in different spheres and may originate in many places, while integration and the spread of ideas and images provoke reac-tions and contestation. Further, diversity has itself become a global value, promoted through international organizations and move-ments – and, indeed, states – leading to an institutionalization of difference.

Globalization is inescapable but it is a complex multifaceted process with highly uneven effects and consequences for human welfare. As I argue in the Introduction, it is not one thing and cannot be judged 'good' or 'bad' in itself. In some ways it has become a metaphor for multiple and often unsettling changes that impact on everyday lives. But at the same time multiple resistances to globalization themselves produce 'the global' both as an object of loathing and a space within which cooperation and action take place. This is because of the ineluctable nature of the social – rebellious and revolutionary practices achieve mutual intelligibility and pro-duce practices that have shared meaning for participants. So 'Creativ-ity, nonconformity and rebellion only meaningfully occur against a background of mutually constituted intelligibility' (Rawls 2002: 25). This remains the thread that links global sociality.

NOTES

INTRODUCTION

1 UN bodies have their origins in the attempt by the Second World War allies to recreate the globalism of the late nineteenth and early twentieth centuries but within a framework of international regulation that would offset the kinds of major crises that predicated fascism and world war.

2 Quah describes the weightless economy as one where 'the economic significance of knowledge achieves greatest contemporary resonance' and has four main features: (1) information and communications technology (ICT) and the Internet; (2) intellectual assets – not only patents and copyrights but also, more broadly, name brands, trademarks, advertising, financial and consulting services, and education; (3) electronic libraries and databases, including new media, video entertainment and broadcasting; (4) biotechnology – carbon-based libraries and databases, pharmaceuticals (Quah 2002).

3 China's merchandise exports rose 28.3 per cent in 2005 following 30 per cent growth in the previous two years, reflecting an annual 10 per cent GDP growth 2000–05 (Cohen, *Business Week* 2006).

4 See WHO warning www.who.int/mediacentre/factsheets/avian_influenza/en/.

5 See www.confederationpaysanne.fr/index.php3 (in French).

1 WHAT'S NEW ABOUT GLOBALIZATION?

1 Durkheim's work also reflects this approach, which sees national life as the highest form of social phenomenon. See Durkheim and Mauss (1971) and Nelson's (1973) and Mandalios's (1996) discussions of this.

2 This theory was named after the Soviet economist Nickolai Kondratieff, who proposed it in 1926. Each cycle lasts 50–60 years and goes through development and boom to recession. The first cycle was based on steam

power, the second on railways, the third on electricity and the motorcar, and the fourth on electronics and synthetic materials. Kondratieff argued that one of the forces that initiate long waves is a large number of discoveries and inventions that occur during a depression and are usually applied on a large scale at the beginning of the next upswing. The downswing of the cycle is likely to be accompanied by wars and violent reorganization of production (Chase-Dunn 1983: 132–3).

3 'Latifundia' refers to landed property covering tremendous areas, today found only in South America. The most widely spread form is the hacienda (facenda), which is an economic and social entity, similar to a small state, that strives to be self-sufficient and autarkic, and is centred upon the 'patron'.

4 Radice (2000) points out that it is hard to find academic writers who have seriously argued the 'hyper-globalist' position. There is also Held's' 'transformationalist' view that local institutions such as states have been transformed by globalization but remain significant. This is discussed in Chapter 3.

5 That is, value added by organizing the production process transnationally – for example, exporting commodities in unprocessed form for manufacture or refining elsewhere. But this may not actually be a measure of globalization so much as the existence of trade barriers in the EU and the US against the import of manufactured sugar, cocoa and other commodities from developing countries (Oxfam 2002).

6 In other words, with modernity the 'space' within which social interactions take place gets lifted out of immediate concrete places and spread across time – an example is the way in which money stores value over time and facilitates complex social exchanges that are removed from one another in time and space.

7 On 16 July 1945, the 'Big Three' leaders met at Potsdam, Germany, near Berlin. The Second World War heads of state – President Truman, General Secretary Stalin and British Prime Ministers Churchill and Atlee – discussed post-war arrangements and national boundaries in Europe.

8 In 1945 Poland's borders were redrawn, the eastern territories that the Soviet Union had occupied in 1939 were permanently annexed, and most of their Polish inhabitants were expelled. Today these territories are part of Belarus, Ukraine and Lithuania. In return, Poland was given former German territory, the southern two-thirds of East Prussia, Pomerania, Brandemburg and Silesia up to the Oder-Neisse Line. These territories were repopulated by Poles expelled from the eastern regions.

9 One example is the New Zealand prime minister (in 1873 and 1876) and entrepreneur Julius Vogel, the son of Russian Jewish migrants to London, who raised loans to facilitate mass migration to New Zealand in the 1870s.

His commitment was more to the international idea of 'Crown and Empire' than to a British national project.

10 Marxist and Keynesian economic theories are not usually hyphenated – they are conventionally seen as opposing theories of, on the one hand, the inevitable crisis and breakdown of capitalism as opposed to its potential for stabilization and social justice through government interventions, on the other. The usage here reflects neo-liberal belief that both theories share a (false) view that the 'free market' is dangerous, chaotic, unworkable and crisis-prone.

11 See www.globalpolicy.org/socecon/ffd/2003/0722fight.htm.

12 'Glocalization' refers to the 'interlacing of social events at a distance from locales', an intersection of presence and absence (Giddens 1990: 21). This rather awkward term captures the important point that the local and global are tightly linked but does not offer much in the way of theorization of its articulations. The term is not greatly used in this book.

13 Actually to suggest that the fall of the Wall had the effect of prompting the collapse of the Soviet Union is not a 'complexity' analysis but a simplification of a much more complex set of structural and systemic processes.

2 GLOBALIZATION AND THE SOCIAL

1 Solidarité was to be diffused through the educational system, promoting social justice as repayment of a 'social debt' by the privileged to the underprivileged. This assumed mutual interdependence and quasi-contractual obligations between all citizens and implied a programme of public education, social insurance and labour and welfare legislation. Solidarism advocated state intervention, social legislation and voluntary associations to create a middle way between laissez-faire liberalism and revolutionary socialism. (Lukes 1973: 350–4)

2 For Durkheim this cult of individuality is 'neither anti-social nor egoistic' but involves 'sympathy for all that is human, pity for all sufferings, miseries and greater thirst for justice' (Durkheim 1969).

3 'There is no such thing as society. There are individual men and women and there are families' (Thatcher talking to *Women's Own*, 3 October 1987).

4 Although it was noted in the last chapter that the *national* state was never a universal model and the presence of national, linguistic, ethnic and religious minorities within the borders of state jurisdictions have been widespread since classical antiquity.

5 Singh (2004) argues that two kinds of trust are involved – 'hard' trust (authentication, encryption and security) and 'soft' trust (loyalty, user information, and social and cultural confidence).

6 Parliamentary debates indicated that the currency limit was frequently evaded, especially through Swiss banks, which suggested that already money was not necessarily restricted by borders (*The Times* 1969 p. 4).

7 The Stock Exchange Automated Quotation system replaced the trading floor of the stock exchange with a screen-based quotation system used by brokers, while restrictions on ownership of UK stockbrokers were abolished.

8 This typically involved re-launches of the currency, dramatic devaluation (which had disastrous impact on many people's savings) and the introduction of tight monetary policies to differing degrees in different places.

3 BEYOND THE NATION STATE?

1 The constitution had been ratified by Austria, Germany, Greece, Hungary, Italy, Lithuania, Slovakia, Slovenia and Spain, but following rejection of the constitution in referenda in France (29 May 2005) and the Netherlands (1 June 2005), the European Council, meeting on 16 and 17 June 2005, considered that it did 'not feel that the date initially planned for a report on ratification of the Treaty, 1 November 2006, . . . [was] still tenable' (http://europa.eu/constitution/index_en.htm).

2 In the UK, for example, between 1945 and the mass privatization programme of the Conservative government (1979–97) extensive areas of the British economy were nationalized – including British Coal, British Gas, British Petroleum, British Rail, British Steel, British Leyland (motor corporation), British Airways, the Bank of England, the Post Office (including the telephone division), and the Central Electricity Generating Board – creating one of the largest state-owned economies outside the Soviet bloc.

3 It is not just a matter of proliferation of INGOs but of how effectively networked and mobilized members have re-shaped world politics. At the 1992 Earth Summit in Rio for example, 17,000 NGO representatives staged an alternative forum while 1,400 were engaged in official proceedings. At the Beijing Fourth World Conference on Women 35,000 NGOs staged an alternative forum while 2,600 participated in the official multilateral negotiations (McGann and Johnstone 2005).

4 Path dependence refers to an evolutionary process in which successive developments do not tend towards an optimum equilibrium state of maximum efficiency but maximize the advantages of practices that have already been locked into the development processes. A frequently cited example is the QWERTY keyboard, which was initially designed to slow

typists down and reduce the risk of typewriters jamming but was then inscribed into training manuals and production processes and would have been expensive to undo even when more efficient typewriters were available.

5 The Uruguay Round was an international trade negotiation between September 1986 and April 1994 that transformed the General Agreement on Tariffs and Trade (GATT) into the World Trade Organization (WTO). It was launched in Punta del Este, in Uruguay (hence the name).

6 Amis comments that 'Right up to 1989 the Auschwitz Museum itself was a monument to Holocaust denial' (Amis 2002: 222).

7 Similarly, the Romany Holocaust, previously 'forgotten' in European history, is subject to remembrance and the search to document witness from survivors. See Kapralski (2001).

4 VIRTUAL SOCIALITY

1 'K-waves' (Kondratieff waves) are described on pp. 207–8 n. 2.

2 A network is simply a set of interconnected nodes with no centre. The crucial logic in networks is not stability but inclusion or exclusion. Networks are highly fluid but also generate structures (relatively stable and permanent) of insiders and outsiders.

3 Although many call centre staff are required to create an illusion of familiarity and personal service by introducing themselves by their first names and adopting a friendly manner.

4 Although bureaucracy often has a negative connotation there are many areas of life in which impersonality is highly valued. For example, employers are required by law to provide equal employment opportunities to all qualified persons without regard to race, age, colour, sex, religion, national origin, pregnancy, physical handicap, marital status or medical condition. Processes of evaluation such as essay marking are required to be impersonal both in that the same criteria must be applied to all students and substantively in that they are often anonymously marked.

5 One should beware hyperbole and rogue statistics, however. In an otherwise well-argued discussion Castells (1999) claims that the 'Internet today is used by about 100 million people and doubling this number every year'. No source for this figure is cited. If we assume 100 million in 1998, then at this rate of increase there would have been 6,400 million online by 2004 – roughly the whole world's population that year! It would be better to apply the model of the S-diffusion graph, in which take-up of new technologies rises steeply initially then levels out as it becomes saturated within a population.

6 The correlation coefficient for Internet users' share of population and GDP per capita is 0.77, computed from International Telecommunications Union Yearbook of Statistics (2000). The distribution of hosts also correlates positively with the proportionate population; online at http://news.netcraft.com/.

7 But there are deviations from this where affluent countries have lower than average Internet use (such as Saudi Arabia and India), which could be explicable in terms of high levels of internal income inequality and/or cultural restrictions on Internet use (Norris 2001: 60).

8 See for example Urry's discussion of 'automobility' as a 'machinic complex' – a system of fluid interconnections forming a self-organizing system of technologies and signs such that social life is locked into a mode of individualized mobility (2003: 68–9).

9 http://en.wikipedia.org/wiki/Main_Page.

10 See Union for the Public Domain: http://english.ohmynews.com/.

11 See, for example, http://en.wikipedia.org/wiki/Internet_censorship_in_China.

12 See International Herald Tribune: www.iht.com/.

13 The Internet is not always profitable, though, which was shown by he collapse of dot-com companies in 2003 that has had lasting regional effects on regions where dot-com companies were a significant part of the local economy such as California's Bay Area (*San Francisco Chronicle* 8 May 2005).

14 See www.public-domain.org/?q=node/47.

15 See for example www.groups.google.com.

16 See www.well.com/. Actually people who 'meet' on the WELL meet offline too.

17 http://avc.blogs.com/a_vc/2004/02/social_networki.html.

18 This was a survey of 20,075 North American visitors to the National Geographic Society website in 1998 of whom 88 per cent were Americans and 12 per cent Canadians.

19 Such as 'Jewish Dating' (www.jewishdating247.com/); Hindu Dating (http://hindu.indiandating.de/); Parsee dating (www.kamaconnection.com/parsi-singles-dating.php); and Christian singles (www.linkchristians.com/?gclid=CLPeoorFkogCFRMQZwodelSUAw).

20 This might reveal that it is the timing of responses to communications rather than co-presence itself that is crucial for determining the level of trust and solidarity in an interaction – thus real time 'chat' may prove to be more solidary than asynchronous email (Bargh and McKenna 2004).

5 GLOBAL INEQUALITIES AND EVERYDAY LIFE

1 See http://iresearch.worldbank.org.PovcalNet/jsp/index.jsp.

2 See www.transnational.org/features/chossu_worldbank.html.

3 Care in the use of these figures is needed because they are composites based on highly diverse national data collected in very different ways. Patterns of ownership will be culturally varied and single investors in equities such as insurance and pension funds can represent millions of individual people. The role of personal and corporate taxation in different countries, too, will have a significant impact on relative equality and inequality.

4 So-called because of its similarity to Weber's concept of bureaucratic patrimonialism where centralized bureaucrats were connected trough payments for service, or benefices (Turner 1981: 245).

5 The origins of the debt crisis are complex and beyond the scope of this book to discuss in detail. But in brief – during the 1960s (partly because of the cost of the Vietnam War) the US budget rose from 0.8 to 2.1 per cent of GDP, which put downward pressure on the value of the US dollar and on interest rates. The oil price rises in 1973 generated large volumes of petro-dollars and high levels of borrowing among Third World governments. But in the global recession that followed, commodity prices fell and many governments were unable to generate sufficient foreign exchange to cover interest payments. In 1982 Mexico defaulted on its debt payment, threatening the international credit system. The IMF and the World Bank restructured Mexico's debt and that of other nations facing similar problems, prescribing their loans and structural adjustment policies to ensure debt repayment.

6 One consequence of this is that while by the end of the 1990s in developed countries all children spent 15–17 years in full-time education, in sub-Sahara Africa the average for boys was 3.7 years and for girls 2.2 years, in South Asia 5 years for boys and 2.6 years for girls, and in Latin America 5 years for both girls and boys (Oxfam 2002: 82). This further disadvantages developing countries' participation in the global knowledge economy.

7 The UN reported in 2005 that indices of poverty had fallen to 40.6 per cent of the population and that 2.5 million escape poverty because of remittances from abroad of $45 billion, which is higher than combined FDI and development aid (UN Information 2005).

8 According to one report roughly one in six shoppers in the UK says they frequently buy or boycott products because of the manufacturers' reputations. They buy overtly ethical consumer products currently worth

well over £1.3 billion. A further £3.3 billion is invested in ethical funds, while significant sales of products from companies such as the Body Shop are also driven by concerns about the impact companies have on communities and the environment (Cowe and Williams 2000).

9 Although tea is the largest earner of foreign exchange, at $463.7m. See FAO (Food and Agricultural Organization) 2004, www.fao.org/es/ESS/toptrade/trade.asp?dir=exp&country=114&ryear=2004.

10 BAT(K) no longer has a monopoly of supply or monopsony of purchase of tobacco but remains dominant in both markets – it currently has 55 per cent of the Kenyan market, SanCom Co. has 25 per cent and Mastermind Tobacco Kenya has 20 per cent. BAT(K) was heavily involved in drafting legislation in 1994 to require farmers to grow tobacco under contract to only one company and to prevent farmers growing tobacco 'out of season', thus limiting competition among leaf purchasers (Christian Aid 2002).

11 The 1994 Crop Production and Livestock (Tobacco Growing and marketing Rules), details of which are in Patel *et al.* (2007).

12 Between 1975 and 1995 74 per cent of developing and 70 per cent of developed countries had increases in women's labour market participation while rates for men declined by a few percentage points (Perrons 2004: 82).

6 GLOBAL TERRORS AND RISKS

1 Although Fukuyama envisaged this global convergence occurring through a necessary process of social development the belief that liberal capitalist democracy is both the most efficient social system and what, given a choice, most people would want has underpinned recent US and NATO military interventions aimed as installing democratic political systems in various parts of the world, notably, of course, in Iraq. The failure of this intervention to achieve this objective (at the time of writing) has raised widespread doubts about the viability and rightness of military intervention – and has prompted Fukuyama to distance himself from some of his former views. See www.spiegel.de/international/0,1518,407315,00.html where he argues that the impact of the rapid collapse of communism in 1989 'skewed the thinking about the nature of dictatorships . . . [and] made a wrong analogy between Eastern Europe and what would happen in the Middle East'.

2 Also known as 'neocons', the people in this group, including Donald Rumsfeld, William Kristol, Elliott Abrams, Paul Wolfowitz, John Bolton and Richard Perle, organized themselves in the 1990s as the 'Project for the American Century' that lobbied for regime change in Iraq.

3 These other non-Islamic opponents of US hegemony such as Venezuelan President Hugo Chavez regard the Islamic Republic of Iran as an ally in the global struggle against 'imperialism'.

4 I use the term 'imaginary' in the sense of powerful and pervasive constructions of the world that do not correspond to 'rational' or 'real' elements but become the symbolic ground on which actions take place and therefore have real effects.

5 The term 'terrorist' is ambiguous and there are well-known difficulties of distinguishing terrorism, insurgence, guerrilla war and indeed any other act of war. I take terrorism to mean the deployment of violence as a spectacle aimed primarily at civilian populations in pursuit of political, religious or other ends. The literature on terrorism is vast and this brief section does not attempt to address it, which would require another book.

6 Orson Wells' reading of H. G. Wells' *War of the Worlds* on 30 October 1938 was believed by many listeners to be a real news broadcast.

7 This is, on the face of it, a curious claim in view of the central significance of religious belief in present global conflicts. What Beck seems to mean is that there has been a loss of faith in religious belief in developed Western countries (though this may not be the case at all in the US) and this in turn leads to the need for new transnational responses.

8 See, for example, www.tiscali.co.uk/travel/guardian/news/2006/10/13/how-tagging-passengers-could-improve-airport-se.html.

9 Figures produced by the World Travel and Tourism Council (WTTC) indicate that tourism generates 11 per cent of global GDP, employs 200 million people, and transports nearly 700 million international travellers per year – a figure that is expected to double by 2020. International tourism accounts for 36 per cent of trade in commercial services in advanced economies and 66 per cent in developing economies; it constitutes 3–10 per cent of GDP in advanced economies and up to 40 per cent in developing economies; it generated US$464 billion in tourism receipts in 2001; and it is one of the top five exports for 83 per cent of countries and the main source of foreign currency for at least 38 per cent of countries. See www.uneptie.org/pc/tourism/library/mapping_tourism.htm.

10 The *Dover Express* continued 'illegal immigrants, asylum seekers, bootleggers . . . and scum of the earth, drug smugglers have targeted our beloved coastline . . . We are left with the backdraft of a nation's human sewage and no cash to wash it down the drain' (*Dover Express* 1999)

11 Over 40 million people are estimated to be infected with HIV, of whom 25.8 million live in sub-Saharan Africa, where in 2006 there were 2.4 million of the 3.1 million AIDS-related deaths worldwide. Thus it is among the heavily indebted and impoverished African population that AIDS is most prevalent

and will have the most devastating effects on society and economy. See 'AIDS in Africa' Global Issues, www.globalissues.org/Geopolitics/Africa/AIDS.asp.

12 See, for example, 'Arrest Adds to Fears of Terrorist Presence on Mexican Border' (*Business Journal of Phoenix* 2005). http://phoenix.bizjournals.com/phoenix/stories/2005/11/21/daily23.html.

BIBLIOGRAPHY

Abu-Lughod, J. L. (1989) *Before European Hegemony: The World System A.D. 1250–1350*, New York: Oxford University Press.

Akyuz, Y., Flassbeck, H. and Kozul-Wright, R. (2002) *Globalization, Inequality and the Labour Market*, Geneva: UNCTAD, www.britishcouncil.org/netherlands-networks-apeldoorn-young-globalization-inequality-and-the-labour-market.pdf, accessed 30 October 2006.

Albrow, M. (1997) *The Global Age*, Stanford, CA: Stanford University Press.

Amin, S. (1990) *Delinking – Towards a Polycentric World*, London: Zed Books.

Amis, M. (2002) *Koba The Dread – Laughter and the Twenty Million*, London: Jonathan Cape.

Ananiadis, B. P. (2003) 'Globalization, Welfare and "Social Partnership"', *Global Social Policy* 3, 2: 213–33.

Araghi, F. A. (1995) 'Global Depeasantization, 1945–1990', *The Sociological Quarterly* 36, 2: 337–68.

Araghi, F. A. (2000) 'The Great Global Enclosure of our Times', in Magdoff, F., Foster, B. and Buttel F. (eds) *Hungry for Profit: The Agribusiness Threat to Farmers, Food, and the Environment*, New York: Monthly Review Press, pp. 145–59.

Article 19 (2003) *What's the Story? Results from Research into Media Coverage of Refugees and Asylum in the UK*, www.article19.org/pdfs/publications/refugees-what-s-the-story-.pdf, accessed 30 October 2006.

Asila, J. (2004) 'No Cash in This Crop', *New Internationalist*, July, 369.

Aye A (2001) 'Astronaut Families: A Review of Their Characteristics', *New Zealand Journal of Psychology* 30, 1: 9–15.

Babb, S. (2005) 'The Social Consequences of Structural Adjustment: Recent Evidence and Current Debates', *Annual Review of Sociology* 31: 199–222.

Back, L. (2002a) 'Aryans Reading Adorno: Cyber-culture and Twenty-first Century Racism', *Ethnic and Racial Studies* 25, 4: 628–51.

Back, L. (2002b) 'New Technologies of Racism', in Goldberg, D. T. and Solomos, J. (eds) *A Companion to Racial and Ethnic Studies*, Oxford: Blackwell, pp. 365–77.

Back, L. (2002c) 'When Hate Speaks the Language of Love', *Opendemocracy* 20, 25 April.

Baldwin, P. (1990) *The Politics of Social Solidarity*, Cambridge: Cambridge University Press.

Balestri, C, (2002) *Racism, Football and the Internet*, Vienna: Study carried out on behalf of the European Monitoring Centre on Xenophobia and Racism (EUMC) by Unione Italiana Sport per Tutti, http://eumc.europa.eu/eumc/material/pub/football/Football.pdf, accessed 30 October 2006.

Barber, B. R. (2003) *Jihad Vs. McWorld: Terrorism's Challenge to Democracy*, New York: Ballantine Books.

Barbesino, P. (1997) 'Towards a Post-foundational Understanding of Community', *Kybernetes* 26, 6/7: 689–702.

Bargh, J. A. and McKenna, K. Y. A. (2004) 'The Internet and Social Life', *Annual Review of Psychology* 55: 573–90.

BAT (British American Tobacco) (2005) *Social Report 2005*, www.bat.com/OneWeb/sites/uk__3mnfen.nsf/vwPagesWebLive/C1256E3C003D3339C125715A004FA7D8?opendocument&SID=&DTC=, accessed 30 October 2006.

Bauman, Z. (1992) 'Blood Soil Identity', *Sociological Review* 40: 675–701.

Bauman, Z. (1993) *Postmodern Ethics*, Oxford: Blackwell

Bauman, Z. (1998a) 'Europe of Strangers', Transnational Communities Programme WPTC 98–03, www.transcomm.ox.ac.uk/working%20papers/bauman.pdf, accessed 30 October 2006.

Bauman, Z. (1998b) 'What Prospects of Morality in Times of Uncertainty', *Theory, Culture and Society* 15,1: 11-22.

Bauman, Z. (1999) *Globalization*, Cambridge: Polity.

Bauman, Z. (2001) *Liquid Modernity*, Oxford: Polity.

Bauman, Z. (2003) *Liquid Love*, Oxford: Polity.

Beck, U. (1992) *Risk Society – Towards a New Modernity*, London: Sage.

Beck, U. (1994) 'The Reinvention of Politics', in Beck, U., Giddens, A. and Lash, S. *Reflexive Modernization – Politics, Tradition and Aesthetics in the Modern Social Order*, Oxford: Polity, pp. 1–55.

Beck, U. (1998) *World Risk Society*, Cambridge: Polity.

Beck, U. (2000a) *What is Globalization?* Cambridge: Polity.

Beck, U. (2000b) 'The Cosmopolitan Perspective: The Sociology of the Second Modernity', *Sociology* 51,1: 79–106.

Beck, U. (2001) 'An Interview', *Journal of Consumer Culture* 1, 2: 261–77.

Beck, U. (2003) 'The Silence of Words: On Terror and War', *Security and Dialogue* 34, 3: 255–67.

Beck, U. and Beck-Gernsheim, E. (2001) *Individualization: Institutionalized Individualism and its Social and Political Consequences*, London : Sage.

Beck, U. and Giddens, A. (2005) 'Nationalism Has Now Become the Enemy of Europe's Nations', *The Guardian*, 4 October.

Beck, U. and Lau C. (2005) 'Second Modernity as a Research Agenda: Theoretical and Explorations in the 'Meta-Change' of Modern Society', *British Journal of Sociology* 56, 4: 526–57.

Beck, U., Bonss, W. and Lau, C. (2003) 'The Theory of Reflexive Modernization: Problematic, Hypotheses and Research Programme', *Theory, Culture and Society* 20, 2: 1–33.

Bell, D. (1987) 'The World and the US in 2013', *Daedalus* 116, 3: 1–32.

Ben-Itto, H. (2005) *The Lie That Wouldn't Die – The Protocols of the Elders of Zion*, London: Vallentine Mitchell.

Berger, S. and Dore, R. (eds) (1996) *National Diversity and Global Capitalism*, London: Cornell University Press.

Bergesen, A. J. (2003) 'Is Terrorism Globalizing?', *Protosociology* 18–19: 32–55.

Bernal, M. (1989 [1991]) *Black Athena*, London: Vintage.

Billig, M. (1997) *Banal Nationalism*, London: Sage.

Boden, D. (1994) *The Business of Talk: Organizations in Action*, London: Polity.

Boden, D. and Friedland, R. (eds) (1994) *NowHere: Space, Time and Modernity*, London: University of California Press.

Boden, D. and Molotch, H. (1994) 'The Compulsion of Proximity' in Boden, D. and Friedland, R. eds., *Now/Here: Space, Time and Modernity*, pp. 257-86.

Bourdieu, P. and Wacquant, L. (1999) 'On the Cunning of Imperialist Reason', *Theory Culture and Society* 16, 1: 41–58.

Boyer, R. (1996) 'The Convergence Hypothesis Revisited: Globalization But Still the Century of Nations?', in Berger, S. and Dore, R. (eds) *National Diversity and Global Capitalism*, London: Cornell University Press, pp. 29–59.

Breidenbach, J. and Zukrigl, I. (1999) 'The Dynamics of Cultural Globalization: The Myths of Cultural Globalization', *International Cultural Studies*, www.inst.at/studies/collab/breidenb.htm, accessed 30 October 2006.

Brinkerhoff, D. W. and Goldsmith, A. A. (2002) 'Clientalism, Patrimonialism and Democratic Governance', Abt Associates, USAID.

Brune, N. and Garrett, G. (2005) 'The Globalization Rorschach Test: International Economic Integration, Inequality and the Role of Government', *Annual Review of Political Science* 8: 399–423.

Buchholtz, M. B. and Reich, G. (1987) 'Panik, Panikbedarf, Panikverarbeitung. Sozio-psychoanalytische Anmerkungen zu zeitgenossischen Desintergrations-prozessen aus Anlass von Tschernobyl und AIDS', *Psyche* XLI: 610–40.

Buck-Morss, S. (2003) *Thinking Past Terror: Islamism and Critical Theory on the Left*, London: Verso.

Business Journal of Phoenix (2005) 'Arrest adds to Fears of Terrorist Presence on Mexican Border', 22 November, http:\\phoenix.bizjournals.com/phoenix/stories/2005/11/21/daily23.html.

Caldwell, M. L. (2004) 'Domesticating the French Fry – McDonald's and Consumerism in Moscow', *Journal of Consumer Culture* 4, 1: 5–26.

Calhoun, C (1991) 'Indirect Relationships and Imagined Communities: Large-Scale Social Integration and the Transformation of Everyday Life', in Bourdieu, P. and Coleman, J. S (eds) *Social Theory for a Changing Society*, Boulder, CO: Westview Press and New York: Russell Sage Foundation, pp. 95–120.

Callon, M. (ed.) (1998) *The Laws of the Markets*, Oxford: Blackwell.

Carnoy, M. (2000) *Sustaining the New Economy: Work, Family and Community in the Information Age*, New York: Harvard University Press.

Carr, M. and Chen M. A. (2001) 'Globalization and the Informal Economy: How Global Trade and Investment Impact on the Working Poor', www.wiego.org/papers/carrchenglobalization.pdf, accessed 30 October 2006.

Castells, M. (1997) *The Power of Identity* Oxford: Blackwell.

Castells, M. (1999) *Information Technology, Globalization and Social Development* UNRISD Discussion Paper 114, Geneva; www.unrisd.org/unrisd/website/document.nsf/d2a23ad2d50cb2a280256eb300385855/f270e0c066f3de77802 56b67005b728c/$FILE/dp114.pdf, accessed 30 October 2006.

Chacha, B. K. (2001) 'From Pastoralists to Tobacco Peasants: The British American Tobacco and Socio-ecological Change in Kuria District Kenya, 1969–1999', http://archive.idrc.ca/ritc/winner2.pdf, accessed 30 October 2006.

Chase-Dunn, C. (1983) 'The Kernel of the Capitalist World Economy – Three Approaches', in Thompson, W. *Contending Approaches to World Systems Analysis*, London: Sage, pp. 55–78.

Chayanov, A. V. (1986) *On the Theory of the Peasant Economy*, translated by T. Shanin, Manchester: Manchester University Press (first published 1918).

Chossudovsky, M. (1997) *The Globalisation of Poverty*, London: Zed Press.

Christian Aid (2004) *Behind the Mask: The Real Face of Corporate Social Responsibility*, www.christian-aid.org.uk/indepth/0401csr/csr_behindthemask.pdf, accessed 30 October 2006.

Cohen, D. (2006) 'The Global Reverb of China and India,' Business Week Online 9/2/06, www.businessweek.com/investor/content/feb2006/pi20060209 469282.htm.

Cowe, R. and Williams, S. (2000) *Who are the Ethical Consumers?* Cooperative Bank, www.co-operativebank.co.uk/servlet/Satellite?blobcol=urlpdffile&blobheader =application%2Fpdf&blobkey=id&blobtable=PDFFile&blobwhere=10825322 76181&ssbinary=true, accessed 30 October 2006.

Craig, J (2002) 'Caste, Class, and Clientalism: A Political Economy of Everyday Corruption in Rural North India', *Economic Geography* 78, 1: 21–42.

CRNM (Caribbean Regional Negotiating Machinery) (2005) 'Private Sector Trade Brief' Vol. 2 March, www.crnm.org/documents/private_sector/Brief2.htm, accessed 30 October 2006.

Crow, G. (2002) *Social Solidarities: Theories, Identities and Social Change*, Buckingham: Open University Press.

Currie, C. C. and Ray, L. J. (1984) 'Going Up in Smoke: The Case of British American Tobacco in Kenya', *Social Science and Medicine* 19, 11: 131–9.

Currie, C. C. and Ray, L. J. (1985) 'Trend Report: Class Formation and the Peasantry', *Sociology* 19, 4: 573–85.

Currie, C. C. and Ray, L. J. (1986) 'On the Class Location of Contract Farmers in Kenya', *Economy and Society* 15, 4: 445–75.

Davis, M. (2001) 'The Flames of New York', *New Left Review* 12, Nov–Dec, pp. 34–50.

Davis, M. (2004) 'Planet Of Slums', *New Left Review* 26, March-April, pp. 5–34.

Davis, W. (2004) *You Don't Know Me, But . . . . Social Capital & Social Software*, The Work Foundation, www.theworkfoundation.com/Assets/PDFs/you_ dontknowme.pdf, accessed 30 October 2006.

De Atkine, N (1999) 'Why Arabs Lose Wars', *Middle East Quarterly*, VI, 4: 17–27.

De Haan, L. and Zoomers, A. (2003) 'Development Geography at the Crossroads of Livelihood and Globalization', *Journal of Economic and Social Geography* 94, 3: 350–62.

DiMaggio, P., Hargittai, E., Neuman, W. R. and Robinson, J. P. (2001) 'Social Implications of the Internet', *Annual Review of Sociology* 27: 307–36.

Dollar, D. and Kraay, A. (2001) *Trade, Growth and Poverty*, World Bank Policy Research Working Paper No. 2615.

Donnan, H. and Wilson, T. M. (1999) *Borders: Frontiers of Identity, Nation and State*, Oxford: Berg.

Doogan, K. (2005) 'Long-term Employment and the Restructuring of the Labour Market in Europe', *Time and Society* 14, 1: 65–87.

Dore, R. (1996) 'Convergence in Whose Interest?', in Berger, S. and Dore, R. (eds) *National Diversity and Global Capitalism*, London: Cornell University Press, pp. 366–74.

Durkheim, E. (1969) 'Individualism and the Intellectuals', *Political Studies* 17: 14–30.

Durkheim, E. (1984) *The Division of Labour in Society*, translated by Wilfred Douglas Halls, London: Macmillan.

Durkheim, E. and Mauss, M. (1971) 'Note on the Notion of Civilization', *Social Research* 38, 4: 808–13.

Eade, J. and O'Byrne, D. (eds) (2005) *Global Ethics and Civil Society*, Aldershot: Ashgate.

Eisenstadt, S. N. (1973) *Tradition, Change and Modernity*, London: John Wiley.

Eisenstadt, S. N. (ed.) (1987) *Patterns of Modernity*, London: Pinter.

Elliott, A. (2003) *Critical Visions – New Directions in Social Theory*, Oxford: Rowman and Littlefield.

Farmer, P. (1996) 'Social Inequalities and Emerging Infectious Diseases', *Emerging Infectious Diseases* 2, 4: 259–69.

Featherstone M. and Lash S. (1995) 'Introduction', in Featherstone, M., Lash, S. and Robertson, R. (eds) *Global Modernities*, London: Sage.

Figstein, N. (2001) *Architecture of Markets*, Princeton, NJ: Princeton University Press.

Financial Services Authority (2000) *In or Out? Financial Exclusion: A Literature and Research Review*, London: FSA.

Food and Agriculture Organization of the UN (2004) 'Key Statistics on Kenya', www.fao.org/es/ESS/toptrade/trade.asp?dir=exp&country=114&ryear=2004

Foresight (2002) *Britain Towards 2010*, www.foresight.gov.uk/Previous_Rounds/ foresight_1999_2002/Financial_Services/Reports/Britain_Towards_2010

Foucault, M. (1977) *Discipline and Punish: the Birth of the Prison*, London: Allen Lane.

Friedman, T. (2000) *The Lexus and the Olive Tree*, New York: Anchor Books.

Fukuyama, F. (1992) *The End of History and the Last Man*, London: Hamish Hamilton.

Fulcher, J. (2000) 'Globalisation, the Nation-state and Global Society', *The Sociological Review* 48, 4: 522–43.

Gadamer, H. (1975) *Truth and Method*, New York: Seabury Press.

Gallagher, S. (2004) 'The Personal *Is* Political. Now What? Privacy, Publicity, and Gender in American Politics', http://faculty.uml.edu/sgallagher/personalis political.htm, accessed 30 October 2006.

Garmadi, F. (2001) 'Économie solidaire une troisième voie', www.local.attac.org/ attac86/Telechargements/Economie_solidaire.PDF, accessed 30 Octo-ber 2006.

Garrett, G. (1992) 'International Cooperation and Institutional Choice: The European Community's Internal Market', *International Organization* 46: 533–58.

Garrett, G. (2001) 'Globalization and Government Spending Around the World', *Studies in Comparative International Development* 35,4: 3–29.

Gergen, K. (1991) *Saturated Self*, New York: Basic Books.

Gertler, M. S. (2003) 'Tacit Knowledge and the Economic Geography of Context, or The Indefinable Tacitness of Being (There)', *Journal of Economic Geography* 3: 75–99.

Gibney, M. J. (2001) *Outside the Protection of the Law: The Situation of Irregular Migrants in Europe*, Refugee Studies Centre Working Paper No. 6, www.rsc. ox.ac.uk/PDFs/workingpaper6.pdf, accessed 30 October 2006.

Giddens, A. (1984) *The Constitution of Society*, Berkeley, CA: University of California Press.

Giddens, A. (1990) *Consequences of Modernity*, Cambridge: Polity.

Giddens, A. (1992) *The Transformation of Intimacy*, Cambridge: Polity.

Giddens, A. (1994a) 'Living in a Post-Traditional Society', in Beck, U., Giddens, A. and Lash, S. *Reflexive Modernization: Politics, Tradition and Aesthetics in the Modern Social Order*, Oxford: Polity, pp. 56–109.

Giddens, A. (1994b) 'Foreword', in Boden and Friedland (1994) *NowHere: Space, Time and Modernity*.

Giddens, A. (1997) *Sociology*, Cambridge: Polity.

Giddens, A. (1999) *Runaway World*, Cambridge: Polity.

Giddens, A. (ed.) (2001) *The Global Third Way Debate*, Cambridge: Polity.

Gilpin, R. (1987) *The Political Economy of International Relations*, Princeton, NJ: Princeton University Press.

Gilpin, R. (2000) T*he Challenge of Global Capitalism: The World Economy in the 21st Century*, Princeton: Princeton University Press.

Giroux, H. A. (2005) 'The Terror of Neoliberalism: Rethinking the Significance of Cultural Politics', *College Literature* 32, 1, Winter.

Glasius, M. and Kaldor M. (2002) 'The State of Global Civil Society', in Anheier, H., Glasius, M. and Kaldor, M. (eds) *Global Civil Society 2001*, Oxford: Oxford University Press.

Glasser, J., Dixit, J. and Green, D. P. (2002) 'Studying Hate Crime with the Internet: What Makes Racists Advocate Racial Violence?', *Journal of Social Issues* 58, 1: 177–93.

Glover S., Gott, C., Loizillon, A., Portes, J., Price, R., Spencer, S., Srinivasan, V. and Willis, C. (2001) *Migration: An Economic and Social Analysis*, RDS Occasional Paper No. 67, London: Home Office.

Goff. P. M. (2000) 'Invisible Borders: Economic Liberalism and National Identity', *International Studies Quarterly* 44, 4: 533–62.

Goffman, E. (1983) 'The Interaction Order', *American Sociological Review* 48: 1–17.

Gordon, P. H. (2004) 'Globalization: Europe's Wary Balance', *Yale Global Online*, http://yaleglobal.yale.edu/article.print?id=4790, accessed 30 October 2006.

Granovetter, M. (1992) 'Economic Action and Social Structure: The Problem of Embeddedness', in Granovetter, M. and Swedberg R. (eds) *The Sociology of Economic Life*, Boulder, CO: Westview Press, pp. 53–84.

Gruen, D. and O'Brien, T. (2001–02) 'Introduction', in Gruen, D. and O'Brien, T. (eds) *Globalization, Living Standards and Inequality: Recent Progress and Continuing Challenges*, Royal Bank of Australia Annual Conference Volume, Canberra: Royal Bank of Australia, pp. 1–8, www.rba.gov.au.publications andresearch/conferences/2002/introduction.pdfd.

Guéhenno, J.-M. (1996) *The End of the Nation-State*, translated by Victoria Elliott, Minneapolis, MN: University of Minnesota Press.

Guillén, M. F. (2001) 'Is Globalization Civilizing, Destructive or Feeble? A Critique of Five Key Debates in the Social-Science Literature', *Annual Review of Sociology* 27: 235–60.

Haase, A. Q., Wellman, B., Witte, J. and Hampton, K. (2002) 'Capitalizing on the Internet – Social Contact, Civic Engagement, and Sense of Community', in Wellman, B. and Haythornwaite, C. (eds) *The Internet and Everyday Life*, Oxford: Blackwell.

Habermas, J. (1989) *The Theory of Communicative Action, Lifeworld and System: A Critique of Functionalist Reason*, Vol. 2, Cambridge: Polity.

Habermas, J. (1994) *The Past as Future*, Cambridge: Polity.

Habermas, J. (1996) *Between Facts and Norms Contributions to a Discourse Theory of Law and Democracy*, Cambridge: Polity.

Habermas, J. (2001) *The Postnational Condition*, Cambridge: Polity.

Hale, D. (2005) 'How Marginal is Africa?', *Resource Investor*, 25 February, www.resourceinvestor.com/pebble.asp?relid=8425, accessed 30 October 2006.

Hampton, K. N. and Wellman, B. (2002) 'Neighboring in Netville: How the Internet Supports Community and Social Capital in a Wired Suburb', *City and Community* 1, 4:277–311.

Hannerz, U. (1990) 'Cosmopolitans and Locals in World Culture', in Featherstone, M. (ed.) *Global Culture*, issued as *Theory, Culture & Society* 7, 2–3.

Hannerz, U. (1996) *Transnational Connections*, London: Routledge Comedia.

Hardey, M. (2002) 'Life Beyond the Screen: Embodiment and Identity Through the Internet', *Sociological Review* 50, 4: 570–85.

Hardey, M. (2004) 'Mediated Relationships: Authenticity and the possibility of romance', *Information, Communication and Society* 7, 2: 207–22.

Hardt, M. and Negri, A. (2000) *Empire*, London: Harvard University Press.

Harvey, D. (1994) *The Condition of Postmodernity*, Cambridge, MA: Blackwell.

Hayles, N. K. (1999) *How We Became Posthuman: Virtual Bodies in Cybernetics, Literature and Informatics*, London: University of Chicago Press.

Hayward, C. (2004) 'Constitutional Patriotism and Its Others', Paper to 2004 Annual Meeting of the American Political Science Association, Chicago, IL, 2–5 September, http://psweb.sbs.ohio-state.edu/intranet/poltheory/Constitutional_Patriotism.pdf, accessed 30 October 2006.

Held, D. (2002) 'Violence, Law and Justice in a Global Age', OpenDemocracy.net www.ssrc.org/sept11/essays/held_text_only.htm.

Held, D. and McGrew A. (eds) (2000) *The Global Transformation Reader: an Introduction to the Globalization Debate*, Cambridge: Polity.

Held, D., McGrew, A., Goldblatt, D. and Perraton, J. (2000) *Global Transformation*, Cambridge: Polity.

Hertz, N. (2001) *Silent Takeover*, London: Heinemann.

Hertzberg, H. (2001), 'Tuesday, And After', *The New Yorker*, 24 September.

Herrera-Lima, F. (2001) 'Transnational Families: Institutions of Transnational Social Spaces', in Pries, L. (ed.) *New Transnational Social Spaces: International Migration and Transnational Companies in the Early 21st Century*, New York: Routledge, pp. 77–92.

Hess, M. (2004) 'Spatial Relationships? Towards a Reconceptualization of Embeddedness', *Progress in Human Geography* 28, 2: 165–86.

Hewitt, C. (2002) *Understanding Terrorism in America*, London: Routledge.

Hirst, P. and Thompson, G. (1996) *Globalization in Question*, Oxford: Blackwell.

Ho, E. S. and Farmer, R. (2004) 'The Hong Kong Chinese in Auckland', in Skeldon, R. (ed.) *Reluctant Exiles: Migration from Hong Kong and the New Overseas Chinese*, London: Sharpe.

Hobbes, T. (1994) *Leviathan*, London: Everyman (first published 1660).

Holmes, S. (2001) 'Introduction to "From Postcommunism to Post-September 11"', *East European Constitutional Review*, Winter, pp. 78–81.

Holmwood, J. (2000) 'Three Pillars of Welfare State Theory: T. H. Marshall, Karl Polanyi and Alva Myrdal in Defence of the National Welfare State', *European Journal of Social Theory* 3, 1: 23–50.

Hooghe, L. (2003) 'Globalization and the European Union: Shared Governance on a Regional Scale', in Lazar, H. and Telford, H. (eds) *The Impact of Globalization on Federal Systems*, Montreal: McGill University Press.

Hornsby, A. (1998) 'Surfing the Net for Community: A Durkheimian Analysis of Electronic Gatherings', in Kivisto, P. (ed.) *Illuminating Social Life*, London: Pine Forge Press, pp. 63–106.

Houlton, R. (2005) *Making Globalization*, Basingstoke: Palgrave.

Houston, D. A. (2003) 'Can the Internet Promote Open Global Societies?', *Independent Review* 7, 3: 353–69.

Huber, E. and Stephens, J. D. (2001) *Political Choice in Global Markets: Development and Crisis of Advanced Welfare States*, Chicago, IL: Chicago University Press.

Hudson, R. (1999) *Who Becomes a Terrorist and Why: the 1999 Government Report on Profiling Terrorists*, Guilford: Lyons Press.

Human Rights Watch (2003) 'Dubai: Migrant Workers at Risk', http://hrw.org/english/docs/2003/09/19/uae6388.htm, accessed 30 October 2006.

Huntington, S. (1999) *Clash of Civilizations and the Remaking of World Order*, London: Touchstone.

ILO (International Labour Organization) (2003) *Global Employment Trends Model*, Geneva: ILO.

International Telecommunications Union (2000) *Yearbook of Statistics*, Geneva: ITU.

Ireland, D. (2005) 'A Political Revolt in France: What Rejection of the European Constitution Means', *Spectrezine*, www.spectrezine.org/europe/FrenchNo. htm, accessed 30 October 2006.

Jacobs, D. (1998) 'Discourse, Politics and Policy: The Dutch Parliamentary Debate About Voting Rights for Foreign Residents', *International Migration Review* 32: 350–73.

Jacoby, T. (1999) 'The African American Absence in High Tech', *New Republic*, 29 March.

James, H. (2002) *The End of Globalization: Lessons from the Great Depression*, Cambridge, MA: Harvard University Press.

Jenson, J. (1998) *Mapping Social Cohesion: The State of Canadian Research*, Canadian Policy Research Networks Study No. F/03, Ottawa: Canadian Policy Network.

Jessop, B. (2000) 'The Crisis of the National Spatio-Temporal Fix and the Ecological Dominance of Globalizing Capitalism', *International Journal of Urban and Regional Studies* 24: 273–310.

Johnson, C. (2000) *Blowback: the Costs and Consequences of American Empire*, New York: Henry Holt and Company.

Kapralski, S. (2001) 'Battlefields of Memory: Landscape and Identity in Polish-Jewish Relations', *History and Memory* 13: 35–58.

Kariuki, J. (2000) 'Tobacco Cultivation Threatens Food Security in Kenya', *Panos Features*, http://lists.essential.org/intl-tobacco/msg00111.html, accessed 30 October 2006.

Katz, J. E., Rice, R. E. and Aspden, P. (2001) 'The Internet, 1995–2000: Access, Civic Involvement, and Social Interaction', *American Behavioral Scientist* 45, 3: 405–19.

Kellner, D. (2002) 'September 11, Social Theory and Democratic Politics', *Theory, Culture and Society* 19, 4: 147–59.

Kellner, D. (2003) 'Theorizing September 11: Social Theory, History, and Globalization', www.gseis.ucla.edu/faculty/kellner/essays/theorizingsept11essay. pdf.

Kennedy, P. (2002) 'Transnationalism in a Global Age', in Kennedy, P. and Roudometof, V. (eds) *Communities Across Borders: New Immigrants and Transnational Cultures*, London: Routledge, pp. 1–26.

Kennedy, P. and Roudometof, V. (2001) 'Communities Across Borders under Globalising Conditions: New Immigrants and Transnational Cultures', Transnational Communities Programme WPTC-01–17, www.transcomm. ox.ac.uk/working%20papers/WPTC-01–17%20Kennedy.pdf.

Keohane, R. O. and Nye, J. S (2000) 'Globalization: What's New? What's Not? (And So What?)', *Foreign Policy* 118 (Spring issue): 104–19.

Keser, C., Leyland J., Shachat, J. and Huang, H. (2002) *Trust, the Internet, and the Digital Divide*, IBM Res. Rep. RC22511, New York: Yorktown Heights.

Klein, E. (2001) *The Battle for Auschwitz: Catholic-Jewish Relations under Strain*, London: Vallentine Mitchell.

Kobrin, S. (1998) 'Back to the Future: Neomedievalism and the Postmodern Digital World Economy', *Journal of International Affairs* 51, 2: 362–86.

Kobrin, S. (2003) 'Sovereignty@Bay: Globalization, Multinational Enterprise, and the International Political System', in Rugman, A. and Brewer, T. L. *The Oxford Handbook of International Business*, Oxford: Oxford University Press, Chapter 7.

Kobrin, S. (2005) 'The End of Globalization?' *American Institue for Contemporary German Studies*, www.aicgs.org/analysis/911/kobrin/aspx.

Kodhek, G. A and Maina, W. (2000) 'Reassessing Kenya's Land Reform', *The Point*, Bulletin of the Institute of Economic Affairs, Nairobi 40: 1–8.

Köhler, B. and Wissen, M. (2003) 'Glocalizing Protest: Urban Conflicts and Global Social Movements', *International Journal of Urban and Regional Research* 27, 4: 942–51.

Konnander, V. (2006) 'Russkoe Bistro vs. McDonald's', http://vilhelmkonnander. blogspot.com/2006/07/russkoe-bistro-vs-mcdonalds.html.

Krasner, S. D. (2001) 'Globalization, Power and Authority', paper to the American Political Science Association meeting, San Francisco 29 August to 2 September.

Kraut, R., Patterson, M., Lundmark, V., Kiesler, S., Mukophadhyay, T. and Scherlis, W. (1998) 'Internet Paradox: A Social Technology that Reduces Social Involvement and Psychological Well-being', *American Psychologist* 53, 9: 1017–31.

Kumm, M. (2005) 'Thick Constitutional Patriotism and Political Liberalism: On the Role and Structure of European Legal History', *German Law Journal* 6, 2: 319–54.

Kusma, M. K. (2002) 'Negotiating Intimacies in a Globalized Space: Identity and Cohesion in Young Oromo Refugee Women', *Affilia* 17, 4: 471–96.

Kweyuh, P. (1998) 'Does Tobacco Growing Pay? The Case of Kenya', in Abedian, I., van der Merwe, R., Wilkins N. and Jha, P. (eds) *The Economics of Tobacco Control: Towards an Optimal Policy Mix*, Rondebosch: University of Cape Town Press, pp. 245–50.

Kymlicka, W. and Norman, W. (1995) 'Return of the Citizen: A Survey of Recent Work on Citizenship Theory', in Beiner, R. (ed.) *Theorizing Citizenship*, New York: SUNY Press, pp. 283–322.

Landolt, P. and Da, W. W. (2005) 'The Spatially Ruptured Practices of Migrant Families: A Comparison of Immigrants from El Salvador and the People's Republic of China', *Current Sociology* 53, 4: 625–53.

Law, J. (1994) *Organizing Modernity*, Oxford: Blackwell.

Lawrence, F. (2004) 'The 19 Dead Cockle-Pickers were Victims of Modern Business Practices', *The Guardian*, 9 February.

Lechner, F. (2000–2) 'The Globalization Website', www.sociology.emory.edu. globalization/theorieso3.html.

Lee, H. (2005) 'Behavioral Strategies for Dealing with Flaming in an Online Forum', *The Sociological Quarterly* 46, 2:385–403.

Legrain, P. (2002) *Open World: The Truth About Globalization*, London: Abacus.

Levy, D. and Sznaider, N. (2002) 'Memory Unbound – The Holocaust and the Formation of Cosmopolitan Memory', *European Journal of Social Theory* 5, 1: 87–106.

Ley, D. (2004) 'Transnational Spaces and Everyday Lives', *Transactions of the Institute of British Geographers* 29, 2: 151–64.

Leys, C. (2001) *Market-Driven Politics: Neoliberal Democracy and the Public Interest*, London: Verso.

Leyshon, A., French, S., Thrift, N., Crew, L. and Webb, P. (2005) 'Accounting for E-commerce: Abstractions, Virtualism and the Cultural Circuit of Capital', *Economy and Society* 34, 3: 428–50.

Lipietz, A. (2000) 'L'économie solidaire: "reminiscence" de l'économie sociale?', Presentation to an International Colloquium on Michel-Marie Derrion, 8 June 2000, http://lipietz.net/spip.php?article191.

Luckmann, T. (1996) 'Some Problems of Pluralism in Modern Societies', http://stud.unisg.ch/~cems/review/luckmann.html.

Luhmann, N. (1982) *The Differentiation of Society*, New York: Colombia University Press.

Luhmann, N. (1992) *Risk: A Sociological Theory*, Berlin: de Gruyter.

Luke, R. W. (2002) 'Bring Back Big Government', *International Journal of Urban and Regional Research* 26, 4: 815–22.

Lukes, S. (1973) *Emile Durkheim: His Life and Work*, Harmondsworth: Penguin.

Luo, Y. (1997) 'Guanxi: Principles, Philosophies and Implications', *Human Systems Management* 16, 1: 43–52.

McGann, J. and Johnstone, M. (2005) 'The Power Shift and the NGO Credibility Crisis', *Brown Journal of World Affairs*, Winter/Spring, www.globalpolicy.org/ngos/credib/2006/01shift.htm.

McGrew, A. (2004) 'Power Shift: From National Government to Global Governance?', in Held, D. (ed.) *A Globalizing World? Culture, Economics, Politics*, London: Routledge and Open University.

McKenna, K. Y. A., Green, A. S. and Gleason, M. E. J. (2002) 'TI Relationship formation on the Internet: What's the Big Attraction?', *Journal of Social Issues* 58, 1: 9–31.

McLuhan, M. (1992) *The Global Village: Transformations in World Life and Media in the 21st Century*, Oxford: Oxford University Press.

Mandalios, J. (1996) 'Historical Sociology', in Turner, B. S. (ed.) *The Blackwell Companion to Social Theory*, Oxford: Blackwell, pp. 278–306.

Marx, K. (1963–8) *Theories of Surplus Value II*, Moscow: Lawrence & Wishart.

Marx, K. (1976) *Capital: A Critique of Political Economy*, vol. 1, Moscow: Progress Publishers.

Marx, K. (1977) *Karl Marx: Selected Writings*, edited by David McLellan, Oxford: Oxford University Press.

Marx, K. and Engels, F. (1967) *Manifesto of the Communist Party*, Moscow: Progress Publishers.

Mattsson, H. (2003) 'Demystifying Tacit Knowledge: Fine-Tuning the Instruments of Economic Geography', paper to the DRUID Summer Conference on Creating, Sharing and Transferring Knowledge, 12–14 June 2003. Copenhagen, www.druid.dk/uploads/tx_pictured/ds2003-834.pdf.

Melucci, A. (1984) *Nomads of the Present*, Philadelphia, PA: Temple University Press.

Mennell, S. (1995) 'Civilisation and Decivilisation, Civil Society and Violence', *Irish Journal of Sociology* 5: 1–21.

Merton, R. K. (1957) *Social Theory and Social Structure*, Glencoe, IL: Free Press.

Meyrowitz, J. (1985) *No Sense of Place: The Impact of Electronic Media on Social Behavior*, Oxford: Oxford University Press.

Michael, B. (2003) 'Theorising the Politics of Globalization: A Critique of Held *et al.*'s "Transformationalism"', *Journal of Economic and Social Research* 5, 1: 3–17.

Mills, M. B. (2003) 'Gender Inequality in the Global Labor Force', *Annual Review of Sociology* 32: 41–62.

Misztal, B. (2000) *Informality*, London: Routledge.

Misztal, B. (2003) *Theories of Social Remembering*, Maidenhead: Open University Press.

Mitchell, D. (2000) 'Globalization and Social Cohesion: Risks and Responsibilities', The Year 2000 International Research Conference on Social Security, Helsinki 25–27 September, www.issa.int/pdf/helsinki2000/topic/zmitchell.pdf.

Moore, B. (1969) *Social Origins of Dictatorship and Democracy*, London: Penguin.

Moore, G. E. (1965) 'Cramming more components onto integrated circuits', *Electronics* 38, 8.

Morin, E. (2002) 'European Civilization: Properties and Challenges', in Mozaffari, M. (ed.) *Globalization and Civilizations*, London: Routledge, pp. 125–50.

Morris, J. (2004) 'The Future of Work: Organizational and International Perspectives', *International Journal of Human Resource Management* 15, 2: 263–75.

Morse, M. (1998) *Virtualities, TV Media Art*, Bloomington, IN: Indiana University Press.

Nelson, B. (1973) 'Civilizational Complexes and Intercivilizational Encounters', *Sociological Analysis* 34, 2: 79–105.

Nie, N. H. and Erbring, L. (2000) 'Internet and Society: A Preliminary Report', *IT & Society* 1, 1: 275–83.

Norris, P. (2001) *Digital Divide: Civic Engagement, Information Poverty, and the Internet Worldwide*, Cambridge: Cambridge University Press.

Obokata, T. (2001) '"Trafficking" and "Smuggling" of Human Beings in Europe: Protection of Individual Rights or States' Interests?', *Web Journal of Current Legal Issues* 5, http://webjcli.ncl.ac.uk/2001/issue5/obok5.html.

OECD (Organisation for Economic Co-operation and Development) (1997) Societal Cohesion and the Globalizing Economy Paris: OECD.

Ogara, E. A. A. and Ojode, L. A. (2003) *Framework on Tobacco Control Readiness: Kenyan Tobacco Farmers and Leaf Suppliers*, Bloomington, IN: University of Indiana.

Ohmae, K. (1994) *The Borderless World: Power and Strategy in the Interlinked Economy*, London: HarperCollins.

Ohmae, K. (2000) *The Invisible Continent: Four Strategic Imperatives of the New Economy*, London: Nicholas Brealey.

Okin, A. (1991) *Prices and Qualities*, Washington, DC: Brookings Institution Press.

Ong'wen, O. (2006) 'Externalization of Third World Resources' *The African Executive* http://www.africanexecutive.com/modules/magazines/articles.php?articles8 64.

O'Rourke, K. and Williamson, J. (2001) *Globalization and History: The Evolution of a Nineteenth-Century Atlantic Economy*, Cambridge, MA: MIT Press.

Outhwaite, W. and Ray, L. J. (2005) *Social Theory and Postcommunism*, Oxford: Blackwell.

Oxfam (2002) *Rigged Rules and Double Standards: Trade, Globalisation and the Fight Against Poverty*, www.maketradefair.com/assets/english/report_english.pdf, accessed 30 October 2006.

Oxfam (2004) *Stitched Up – How Rich Country Protectionism in Textiles and Clothing Preventss Poverty Alleviation* www.oxfam.org.uk/what we do/issues/trades/ downloads/bp60textiles.pdf.

Pahl, J. (1999) *Invisible Money*, Bristol: The Policy Press JRF.

Papastergiadis, N. (2000) *The Turbulence of Migration*, Oxford: Polity.

Parks, S. and Floyd, K. (1996) 'Making Friends in Cyberspace', *Journal of Communication* 46, 1: 80–97.

Parsons, T. (1979) 'The American Societal Community', *Parsons Papers* Harvard University Archives HUG (FP) 42.45.2.

Patai, R. (1976) *The Arab Mind*, New York: Charles Scribner's Sons.

Patel P., Collin J. and Gilmore A. (2007) '"The Law was Actually Drafted by us but the Government is to be Congratulated on its Wise Actions": British American Tobacco and Public Policy in Kenya', *The Journal Tobacco Control*, in press.

People's Daily Online (2005) 'China Shuts 50,000 Illegal Internet Cafes' 27 February, http://english.peopledaily.com.cn/200502/25/eng20050225_174750.html.

Perrons, D. (2004) *Globalization and Social Change*, London: Routledge.

Petras J. and Veltmeyer H. (2001) *Globalization Unmasked: Imperialism in the 21st Century*, London: Zed Books.

Pew/Internet (2004) *The Internet and Daily Life* by Fallows, D., Pew Internet and American Life Project, www.pewinternet.org/pdfs/PIP_Internet_and_Daily_ Life.pdf, accessed 30 October 2006.

Pierson, C. (1998) *Beyond the Welfare State?* Cambridge: Polity.

Pieterse, N. (2004) *Globalization or Empire?* London: Routledge.

Pinto, D. (1996) 'A New Jewish Identity for Post-1989 Europe', Jewish Policy Research paper, No. 1, www.jpr.org.uk/Reports/CS_Reports/PP_no_1_1996/index. htm, accessed 30 October 2006.

Plan – Commissariat Général du Plan (1997) *Cohésion sociale et territories*, Paris: La Documentation Française.

Polanyi, M. (1967) *The Tacit Dimension*, London: Routledge Kegan Paul.

Portes, A. (1997) 'Globalization from Below: The Rise of Transnational Communities', Transnational Communities Programme Working Paper 98–01, www.trans comm.ox.ac.uk/working%20papers/portes.pdf, accessed 30 October 2006.

Poster, M. (1995) *The Second Media Age*, Oxford: Blackwell.

Poster, M. (2001) *What's the Matter with the Internet?* Minneapolis, MN: Minnesota Press.

Preece, J. (2004) 'Etiquette and Trust Drive Online Communities of Practice', *Journal of Universal Computer Science* 10, 3: 294–302.

Quah, D. T. (1996) *The Invisible Hand and the Weightless Economy*, London: London School of Economics and Political Science, Centre for Economic Performance, Occasional papers No. 12.

Quah, D. (2002) 'The Weightless Economy', http://econ.lse.ac.uk/staff/dquah/ tweir10.html.

Radice, H. (2000) 'Responses to Globalisation: A Critique of Progressive Nationalism', *New Political Economy* 5, 1.

Rawls, A. W. (2002) 'Editor's Introduction', in Garfinkel, H. *Ethnomethodology's Program*, Oxford: Rowman & Littlefield, pp. 1–64.

Ray, L. J. (1993) *Rethinking Critical Theory – Emancipation in an Age of Global Social Movements*, London: Sage.

Ray, L. J. (1996) *Social Theory and the Crisis of State Socialism*, Cheltenham: Edward Elgar.

Ray, L. J. (1999a) '"Fundamentalism", Modernity and the New Jacobins', *Economy and Society* 28, 2: 198–221.

Ray, L. J. (1999b) *Theorizing Classical Sociology*, Buckingham: Open University Press.

Ray, L. J. (2002) 'Crossing Borders? Sociology, Globalization and Immobility', *Sociological Research Online* 7, 3, www.socresonline.org.uk/7/3/ray.html, accessed 30 October 2006.

Ray, L. J. (2003) 'Pragmatism and Critical Theory', *European Journal of Social Theory* 7, 3; 307–21.

Ray, L. and Smith, D. (2004) 'Racist Offending, Policing and Community Conflict', *Sociology* 38, 4: 681–700.

Reimer, S. (2006) 'Everyday Life Protects and Heals after Tragedies such as Sept. 11', *Baltimore Sun*, 12 September.

Remmler, K. (1997) 'Memorial Spaces and Jewish Identities in Post-Wall Berlin', in Peck, J. (ed.) *German Cultures Foreign Cultures: The Politics of Belonging*, American Institute for Contemporary German Studies Research Report no. 8, Johns Hopkins University, pp. 41–54.

Rheingold, H. (2000) *The Virtual Community*, Cambridge, MA: MIT Press.

Rimmer, L. and Willmore, I. (2004) *BAT's Big Wheeze The Alternative British American Tobacco Social and Environmental Report*, www.foe.co.uk/resource/reports/ bats_big_wheeze.pdf, accessed 30 October 2006.

Ritzer, G. (2003) *Globalization of Nothing*, London: Pine Forge Press.

Rivera-Batiz, F. (1999) 'Undocumented Workers in the Labor Market', *Journal of Population Economics* 1: 91–116.

Robertson, R. (1992) *Globalization*, London: Sage.

Rosenberg, J. (2000) *The Follies of Globalisation Theory: Polemical Essays*, London: Verso.

Rosenberg, J. (2005) 'Globalization Theory: A Post Mortem', *International Politics* 42: 2–74.

Rycroft, T. (2002) 'Technology-Based Globalization Indicators: the Centrality of Innovation Network Data', Occasional Paper, GW Center for the Study of Globalization www.gwu.edu/~cistp/research/Tech-BasedGlobIndic_RWR_10.7.02.pdf, accessed 30 October 2006.

Sahlins, M. (2001) *Culture in Practice: Selected Essays*, New York: Zone Books.

Said, E. (2001) 'The Clash of Ignorances', *The Nation*, 22 October.

Salt, J. (2000) 'Trafficking and Human Smuggling: A European Perspective', in Appleyard, R. and Salt, J. (eds) *Perspectives on Trafficking of Migrants*, Geneva: IOM and OIM, pp. 31–56.

Sandholtz, W. and Zysman, J. (1989) '1992: Recasting the European Bargain', *World Politics* 42: 95–128.

San Francisco Chronicle (Tom Abate) (2005) 'The Economy: Struggling to Recover from Dot-com Collapse', 6 May.

Sassen, S. (1996a) 'Cities and *Communities* in the Global Economy – Rethinking our Concepts', *American Behavioral Scientist* 39, 5: 629–39.

Sassen, S. (1996b) *Losing Control? Sovereignty in an Age of Globalization*, New York: Colombia University Press.

Sassen, S. (1998) *Globalization and its Discontents*, New York: New Press.

Saul, J. R. (2004) T*he Collapse of Globalism: And the Reinvention of the World*, New York: Overlook Hardcover.

Scharpf, F. (1999) 'The Viability of Advanced Welfare States in the International Economy: Vulnerabilities and Options', Max Planck Institut Paper 99/9.

Scheff, T. J. and Retzinger, S. M. (1991) *Emotions and Violence: Shame-rage in Destructive Conflicts*, New York: Lexington.

Schisca, R. and Berenstein, D. (2002) *Mapping Jewish Culture in Europe Today: A Pilot Project*, London: Jewish Policy Research Report no. 3, www.jpr.org.uk/reports/jc_reports/no_3_2002/main.htm.

Scholte, J. A. (2002) 'What is Globalization? The Definitional Issue – Again', CSGR Working Paper No. 109/02, www2.warwick.ac.uk/fac/soc/csgr/research/workingpapers/2002/wp10902.pdf, accessed 30 October 2006.

Scholte, J. A. (2005) *Globalization: A Critical Introduction*, second edition, Basingstoke: Palgrave Macmillan.

Schutz, A. and Luckmann, T. (1974) *Structure of the Lifeworld*, London: Heinemann.

Sciortino, G. (2000) 'State Policies Toward Sans-Papiers', in Ruspini, P. (ed.) *Easy Scapegoats: Sans-Papiers Immigrants in Italy*, report prepared for the European project 'Easy Scapegoats: Sans-Papiers Immigrants in Europe', Weinheim, Germany: Freudenberg Stiftung.

Seabrook, J. (1997) *Deeper*, New York: Simon & Schuster.

Seremetakis, C. N. (1996) 'In Search of the Barbarians', *American Anthropology* 98, 3: 489–91.

Shane, S. (1995) *Dismantling Utopia – How Information Ended the Soviet Union*, Chicago, IL: Elephant Paperbacks.

Shannon, U. (2002) 'Private Armies and the Decline of the State', in Worcester, K., Bermanzohn, S. A. and Unger, M. (eds) *Violence and Politics: Globalization's Paradox*, London: Routledge, pp. 32–47.

Shaw, M. (2000) *Theory of the Global State Globality as Unfinished Revolution*, Cambridge: Cambridge University Press.

Siebel, W. and Wehrheim, J. (2003) 'Security and the Urban Public Sphere', *Deutsche Zeitschrift für Kommunalwissenschaften* 42, 1.

Simmel, G. (1971) *Georg Simmel on Individuality and Social Forms*, edited and translated by D. Levine, Chicago, IL: University of Chicago Press.

Simmel, G. (1990) *The Philosophy of Money*, introduced and translated by T. Bottomore and D. Frisby, London: Routledge.

Simmel, G. (1997) *Simmel on Culture*, edited by D. Frisby and M. Featherstone, London: Sage.

Simon, B. (2005) 'The Return of Panopticisism: Supervision, Subjection and the New Surveillance', *Surveillance and Society* 3, 1: 1–20.

Singh, S. (2004) 'Impersonalisation of Electronic Money: Implications for Bank Marketing', *International Journal of Bank Marketing*, 22, 7: 504–21.

Sklair, L. (2002) *Globalization: Capitalism and its Alternatives*, Oxford: University Press.

Skocpol, T. (1985) 'Bringing the State Back In: Strategies of Analysis in Current Research', in Evans, P. B, Rueschemeyer, D. and Skocpol, T. (1985) *Bringing the State Back In*, New York: Cambridge University Press, pp. 3–43.

Smart, B. (2003) *Economy, Culture and Society*, Buckingham: Open University Press.

Smith, J. (1998) 'Global Civil Society? Transnational Social Movement Organizations and Social Capital', *American Behavioral Scientist* 42, 1: 93–107.

Song, M. (2004) 'When the "Global Chain" does not Lead to Satisfaction All Round: Comments on the Morecambe Bay tragedy', *Feminist Review* 77: 137–40.

Sontag, S. (1988) 'AIDS and its Metaphors', *New York Review of Books,* 27 October.

Spence, K. (2005) 'World Risk Society and War Against Terror', *Political Studies* 53: 284–302.

Spencer, R. (2004) 'Global Complexity' *The Sociological Review* 52, 2: 288–90.

Spoonley, P. (2000) 'Reinventing Polynesia: The Cultural Politics of Transnational Pacific Communities', Transnational Communities Programme WPTC-2K-14, Oxford Transnational Communities Working Papers.

Stiglitz, J. (2002) *Globalization and its Discontents*, New York: Norton.

Strauss, M. (2003) 'Antiglobalism's Jewish Problem', *Foreign Policy*, 1 November.

Tarrow, S. (2003) 'Rooted Cosmopolitans: Transnational Activists in a World of States', paper to Amsterdam School of Social Research Workshop on Contentious Politics: Identity, Mobilization and Transnational Politics, 6 May 2002, http://sociology.berkeley.edu/faculty/Evans/evans_pdf/Tarrow percent20RootedCosmops percent204–03 percent20-Soc190.pdf#search= rooted percent20cosmopolitanism, accessed 30 October 2006.

Technology News (2007) 'Microsoft's Vista Set to Sail' 29 January, www.technews world.com/story/software/55439.html.

Thomas, W. and Znanieki, F. (1996) *The Polish Peasant in Europe and America: A Classic Work in Immigration History*, ed. Eli Zaretsky, Urbana, IL: University of Illinois.

Thompson, G. (1999) 'Introduction: Situating Globalization' *International Social Science Journal* 51, 2: 139–52.

Tiffin, M., Mortimore, M. and Gichuki, F. (1994) *More People, Less Erosion: Environmental Recovery in Kenya*, Chichester: John Wiley.

The Times (1951) 'Effects of Reduced Tourist Allowance', 8 November, London.

The Times (1966) 'Holiday Travel Limit £50', 21 July, London.

The Times (1969) 'Minister Condemns Unpatriotic Evasion of Exchange Control', 14 November, London.

Todorov, T. (2003) *Hope and Memory*, London: Atlantic Books.

Tönnies, F. (1971) 'On Gemeinschaft and Gesellschaft', in Truzzi, M. *Sociology: The Classic Statements*, New York: Oxford University Press, pp. 145–54.

Turkle, S. (1999) 'Looking Toward Cyberspace: Beyond Grounded Sociology', *Contemporary Sociology* 28, 6: 643–8.

Turner, B. S. (1981) *For Weber – Essays on the Sociology of Fate*, London: Routledge.

Turner, B. S. (1990) 'Outline of a Theory of Citizenship', *Sociology* 24, 2: 189–217.

Turner, B. S. (1992) *Max Weber – From History to Modernity*, London: Routledge.

Turner, B. S. (ed.) (1993) *Citizenship and Social Theory*, London: Sage.

Turner, B. S. (2006) 'Body', *Theory Culture Society* 23: 223–9.

UK Home Office (2002) *Building Cohesive Communities: a report of the Ministerial Group on Public Order and Community Cohesion*, London: Home Office.

UN (United Nations) (2001) *World Urbanization Prospects: The 2001 Revision*, Economic and Social Affairs Population Division, www.un.org/esa/population/ publications/wup2001/WUP2001report.htm, accessed 30 October 2006.

UNCTAD (2003) *Handbook of Statistics*, New York and Geneva: United Nations.

UN Information Service (2005) 'United Nations Finds Large Reduction in Poverty in Latin America', http://usunrome.usmission.gov/UNISSUES/sustdev/docs/ a5112803.htm, accessed 30 October 2006.

United Nations Development Programme (1998) *Human Development Report*, New York: Oxford University Press.

Urry, J. (2000) *Sociology Beyond Societies: Mobilities for the Twenty-First Century*, London: Routledge.

Urry, J. (2002) 'The Global Complexities of September 11th', *Theory, Culture and Society* 19, 4: 57–69.

Urry, J. (2003) *Global Complexity*, Cambridge: Polity.

Veltz, P. (1996) *Mondialisation: villes et territoires: l'économie archipel*, Paris: Economica.

Wade, R. (1996) 'Globalization and its Limits: Reports of the Death of the National Economy Are Greatly Exaggerated', in Berger, S. and Dore, R. (eds) (1996) *National Diversity and Global Capitalism*, London: Cornell University Press, pp. 60–87.

Wagner, D. (2006) 'The Impact of Terrorism on Foreign Direct Investment', International Risk Management Institute, www.irmi.com/Expert/Articles/ 2006/Wagner02.aspx, accessed 30 October 2006.

Waters, J. (2003) 'Flexible Citizens? Transnationalism and Citizenship amongst Economic Immigrants in Vancouver', *The Canadian Geographer* 47, 3: 219–34.

Waters, M. (1996) *Globalization*, London: Routledge.

Watts, M. W. (2001) 'Aggressive Youth Cultures and Hate Crime', *American Behavioral Scientist* 45, 4: 600–15.

Weber, M. (1978) *Economy and Society*, translated and edited by Guenther Roth and Clauss Wittich, New York: Bedminster Press.

Weber, M. (1984) *General Economic History*, New Brunswick, NJ: Transaction Books.

Wei, S.-J. (2002) 'Is Globalization Good for the Poor in China?', *Finance and Development*, a quarterly magazine of the IMF, 39, 3, www.imf.org/external/ pubs/ft/fandd/2002/09/wei.htm, accessed 30 October 2006.

Weigert, A. (2003) 'Terrorism, Identity, and Public Order: A Perspective from Goffman', *Identity* 3, 2: 93–113.

Weiss, L. (1998) *The Myth of the Powerless State: Governing the Economy in a Global Era*, Cambridge: Polity.

Wellman, B. and Hampton, K. (1999) 'Living Networked On and Offline', *Contemporary Sociology* 28, 6: 648–54.

WHO (World Health Organization) (2004a) *Tobacco and Poverty: A Vicious Circle*, www.who.int/tobacco/communications/events/wntd/2004/en/wntd2004_b rochure_en.pdf, accessed 30 October 2006.

WHO (World Health Organization) (2004b) *Poverty Reduction Strategy Papers: Their Significance for Health*, second synthesis report, Geneva: WHO, www.who. int/hdp/en/prsp.pdf, accessed 30 October 2006.

World Bank (2000) *East Asia: Recovery and Beyond*, Washington, DC: World Bank.

World Bank (2006) *World Development Indicators*, Washington, DC: The International Bank for Reconstruction and Development/The World Bank.

World Development Movement (1999) 'Deadly Conditions? Examining the Relationship Between Debt Relief Policies and HIV/AIDS', www.wdm.org.uk/ campaigns/cambriefs/debt/aids.htm, accessed 30 October 2006.

Yar, M. (n.d.) 'The *Other* Global Drugs Crisis: Assessing the Scope, Impacts and Drivers of the Trade in Dangerous Counterfeit Pharmaceuticals', unpublished.

Zelizer, V. (1994) *The Social Meaning of Money*, New York: Basic Books.

Žižek, S. (1998) 'Hysteria and Cyberspace', *Telepolis*, www.heise.de/tp/r4/artikel/ 2/2492/1.html, accessed 30 October 2006.

Žižek, S. (n.d.) 'No Sex, Please, We're Post-human!', http://lacan.com/nosex. htm#top, accessed 30 October 2006.

Zolberg, A. R. (1999) 'The Politics of Immigration Policy: An Externalist Perspective', *American Behavioral Scientist* 42: 1276–9.

INDEX

Entries indicating whole chapters are in **bold**.

Agrarian Question, the 152–4, 156, 162, 170–1
AIDS/HIV 6, 80, 195–7, 215–16n
Albrow, Martin 2, 27
anti-globalization movements 4, 12–13, 15, 33, 87, 185–7
antisemitism and anti-globalism 186–7
Araghi, Farshad A. 140–1, 148–9, 156–8; *see also* global depeasantization
astronaut families 64–5
asylum seekers 95, 96, 191, 193–5
Auschwitz 7, 98–9, 204, 211n

Barber, Benjamin 177–8
Bauman, Zigmunt 59, 81, 82–3, 101, 132, 191–2
Beck, Ulrich 37, 45, 49–50, 57, 60–1, 62, 75–6, 78, 102, 215n; 'container theory of society' 16, 50, 101, 201; cosmopolitan democracy 30, 95, 96–101; first and second modernity 53–4, 56, 57, 69; global risk society 180–8, 195; reflexive modernization 52–4; reflexive individualization 53, 55, 60, 72–3, 83–4; risk society 51–2, 97; terrorism 183, 184; 'zombie categories' 50–1, 101, 172, 201
Berlin Wall 36, 205
borders 7, 16, 18, 19, 20, 25, 27, 31, 32, 34, 35, 49, 50, 65, 66, 68, 74, 75, 82, 94, 96–7, 102, 158, 172, 174–5, 180, 187–8, 190–4, 201, 208n, 209n, 210n; and disease 194–9
Bové, José 13, 175; *see also Confédération paysanne*
Brandt Commission 156
Bretton Woods Agreement 78, 139
British American Tobacco (BAT) 156; British American Tobacco (Kenya) 162–7, 214n

Calhoun, Craig 41–2, 109
capitalism 8, 16, 17, 22, 23, 29, 33, 36, 38, 46, 47, 52, 59, 61, 71, 77, 79–80, 86, 90, 102, 121, 140, 146–52, 165, 170, 174, 177, 179, 200, 201, 209n
Castells, Manuel 2, 35, 77, 111, 113–17, 167, 211n
China 5, 27, 65, 106, 112, 118–19, 142, 146, 207n
clash of civilizations thesis 175–6, 179–80; *see also* Huntington, Samuel
coffee growing 158–62; Fair Trade 162; Kenya 161–2; primary commodity prices compared 161; Tanzania 158, 163; Uganda 159–60
Cold War 3, 8, 38, 80, 97, 174, 175, 176, 177, 180, 185, 199
Comte, Auguste 16, 17

Confédération paysanne 13, 175; *see also* Bové, José
cosmopolitanism 16–17, 20, 30, 37, 44, 60, 72, 75, 76, 82, 95, 105, 137, 184, 185, 187, 199, 201, 204–5; cosmopolitan memory 97–101; *see also* Beck, cosmopolitan democracy; Levy and Szneider

Del Monte 156
Durkheim, Emile 18, 19, 46–7, 72, 90, 100, 109, 200, 207n, 209n

Eisenstadt, Shmuel 21, 59
end of History thesis 174–5; *see also* Fukuyama, Francis
end of patriarchy? 167–9
European Union (EU) 25, 32, 68, 75, 79, 87, 88, 191, 208n; constitution 175, 210n; farm subsidies 144
everyday life: concept of 29, 38–43, 48, 63, 72, 86, 97, 107, 108, 111; and Internet 125–36; and global inequalities 140, 147, 149; and global money 66–71; and global risks 172, 184, 185, 188, 189, 190, 198–9

foreign direct investment (FDI) 25, 26, 34, 71, 95, 157, 184, 213n
France 79, 90, 175, 185, 210n
Friedman, Thomas 7, 8, 9, 117–19, 174, 177
Fukuyama, Francis 174–5, 214n; *see also* end of History thesis

gender relations 53, 55, 58, 69, 70, 78, 102–3, 124, 126, 145, 154, 165, 166–9, 170, 173, 192, 188, 200
Giddens, Anthony 1, 4, 5, 7, 8, 10, 27, 37, 60, 75, 80, 101, 153, 158–9, 209n; individualization 63, 72; new forms of intimacy 131; runaway word 45, 109; structure-agency 36; symbolic tokens 38, 66; time-space distanciation 9, 147, 209n; tradition and reflexivity 57–9, 59,
global; cities 7, 135, 145, 147, 158, 171; civil society 30, 60, 174, 187, 201; culture 6, 2, 4, 7, 27, 28, 29, 30, 54, 60, 61, 63, 82, 97, 108, 135, 169, 174, 177–8, 192, 205;

complexity 15, 28, 41, 35–8, 59, 141, 196, 209n; depeasantization 140–1, 157–8, 170–1, 190, 203; inequalities 21, 37, 90, 92, 109, 114, 116, 117, **139–71**, 185, 195–6, 197–8, 203; poverty levels 140, 143–5, 152, 154, 158, 169–70, 195, 197, 198, 203, 213n; risks 6, 27, 42, 51, 52, 55, 58, 60, 63, 72, 75, 80, 81, 97, 103, **172–99**, 202; wealth distribution 143–4
globalization: and classical sociology 15, 16, 17–21, 23, 35, 46–8, 50, 71, 72, 109, 139, 200, 201; definitions of 1–2, 4, 11, 12, 13, 15, 28; embedding in everyday life 38–43, 61; end of? 32–4; and hybridity 19, 102, 111, 193, 204; theories of 2, 4, 5, 7–14, 16, 24–38, 49–50, 54–5, 61, 77, 82, 84, 87, 89, 116, 120–1, 148–9, 202–4; unevenness of 2, 30, 113, 114, 117, 141, 146, 153, 154, 164, 167, 170, 184, 203, 206; and welfare 6, 31, 51, 53, 54, 55, 75, 78–9, 80, 83, 91, 102, 145–7, 149–50, 155–6, 158, 171, 185, 202
glocalization 35, 154, 209n
Goffman, Erving 173, 175, 188–9
Granovetter, Mark 42, 46, 150
Guéhenno, Jean-Marie 49, 82
Gulf States, migrant labour in 145–6

Habermas, Jürgen 48, 57, 59, 63, 122, 174; constitutional patriotism 31, 76, 100–1; steering media 66, 108; system and lifeworld 39–41, 93–4, 195
Hannerz, Ulf 39, 95, 178
Hardt, Michael and Negri, Antonio 178–9
Harvey, David 1–2, 7, 10, 188
Held, David 7, 12, 45, 77, 139, 184, 185, 208n
Hirst, Paul and Thompson, Paul 25, 33
Holocaust, the 97–9, 211n
Huntington, Samuel 175–6, 179; *see also* clash of civilizations thesis

India 146, 155, 157
International Labour Organization (ILO) 168–9
International Monetary Fund (IMF) 3, 13, 80, 139, 143, 156, 184, 197, 213n
Internet 3, 13, 42, 68, 104–38, 202–3, 211n; dating 130–4; and decline of

community debate 120–5; and democracy 117–20; digital divide 111, 113–17; email 131–2; and everyday life 125–36; and face-to-face interactions 107–110, 134–36; multi-user environments (MUDS) 128; racism on 128–30; S-diffusion model of 211–12n; and social solidarity 107–10, 125–8; and virtual self 123–5
Irish Republican Army (IRA) 181–2
Islam 2, 171, 172–7, 179–80

James, Harold 32–4
Jessop, Bob 61–2

Keynes, John Maynard, Keynesianism 90, 149–50, 154–8, 171, 209n
Kobrin, Stephen 2, 26, 33–4, 80–1, 82,
Kondratieff (K-wave) cycle 22, 104, 207–8n

Levy, Daniel and Sznaider, Natan 97–101
Luckmann, Thomas 39–40
Luhmann, Niklas 67, 193

McDonald's 28, 38, 82, 121, 177
McWorld vs. Jihad' thesis 177–8; see also Barber, Benjamin
marketing boards, developing countries 157–8
Marx, Karl, and Engels, Frederick 4, 5, 16, 17, 41, 47, 51, 59, 72, 109, 146–7, 148–9, 152–3, 200, 209n
Microsoft 8, 119, 137
migration, migrants 4, 6, 18–19, 25, 31, 32, 49, 64–6, 86, 94, 95–6, 103, 115, 133–4, 145–6, 157, 158, 161, 167, 170, 191–4, 195, 198, 202, 205; and media reporting 193–4; see also asylum seekers,
mobility 5, 11, 30, 44, 55, 61, 62, 84, 94, 96, 103, 105, 133, 151, 168, 175, 187, 190–8, 204, 212n; see also migration
modernization theory 9, 21, 22, 23, 28, 52, 58, 59, 60, 139, 147
money 7, 8, 9, 16, 20, 27, 39, 40, 55, 66–71, 73, 77, 81, 105–7, 141, 149, 159, 166, 187, 202, 208n, 210n; Barclaycard credit scheme 68; cross border

remittances 28, 66, 71, 145–6, 158, 167, 204, 213n
Moore's Law 110–11

nation state and globalization 4, 11, 17, 18, 22, 24, 26, 31–2, 49–50, 52–3, 54–5, 61, **74–103**, 118, 155, 175, 178, 181, 183, 193, 199, 201
neoliberalism 62, 83–4, 88–9, 90, 96, 102, 145–6, 151, 184, 188
Nestlé 8, 156, 159, 160, 161,
Nixon, Richard 28, 110

Ohmae, Kenichi 7–8, 35, 49,
Organization of Economic Cooperation and Development (OECD) 78, 85, 90, 114, 146, 151, 152

Pahl, Jan 68, 70,
Parsons, Talcott 19–20, 90
path dependence 87, 210–11n
Perrons, Diane 5, 61, 83, 104, 114, 115, 117, 145, 167, 168, 214n
Philip Morris 160, 163
Poland 98–9, 204, 208n
Polanyi, Michael 39, 149–51
postcommunism 3–4, 174, 214n
Postdam Conference (1945) 31, 76, 208n
Poster, Mark 117, 123–5
post-Fordism 4, 79–80
poverty and illness 116, 195–7, 198

Quah, Danny 3, 207n; see also weightless economy

Rheingold, Howard 126–7, 186
Ritzer, George 120–2
Robertson, Roland 2, 7, 11–12, 25, 45, 85, 173
Russia 38, 69

Saint-Simon, Henri 16, 17
Sassen, Saskia 7, 77, 94, 95, 192
Schengen Agreement (1998) 191
Scholte, Jan Art 28, 50,
September 11th 2001, xiv, 94, 174–5, 180–4, 186, 187, 189, 191, 193, 197, 198–9
Simmel, Georg x, 45, 59, 66–7 104–6, 109, 123, 135, 190, 200

Sklair, Leslie 21, 23
smallholder production 22, 140–1, 147, 154, 157–60,; and contract farming 158–67, 214n
social capital 30, 39, 89, 93, 120, 125, 127, 128, 202
social class 38, 46–8, 50–4, 64, 69, 70, 77, 83, 90, 92, 97, 143, 152, 162, 173, 183, 185, 193, 200
social cohesion 46–7, 60–3, 84, 89–90, 93–4, 202
social solidarity 2, 15, 18, 44, 45–8, 51, 60–6, 74, 77, 83, 101–2, 107–10, 148, 154, 170–1, 201–2
social welfare see globalization and welfare
society, sociality, concepts of xiv, 10, 15, 16, 18, 19–20, 23, 24, 34–8, 48–51, 76, 83, 89–96, 101, 169, 173, 201, 202; as an object of governmentality 89–96
Soviet Union (USSR) 3, 35, 36–7, 85, 118, 155, 156, 176, 191, 208n; see also Cold War, postcommunism, Russia
space, concept of 7, 9, 10, 11, 20–1, 27, 29–30, 35, 38, 42, 50, 61, 62, 63, 64, 66, 77, 83, 124, 133, 140, 147, 153–4, 175, 189–90, 198, 208n; space–time compression xiv, 2, 5, 7, 10, 11, 110, 136, 202
state, the see nation state
structural adjustment 13, 140, 156, 168, 197, 198, 213n; see also IMF
surveillance 41, 86, 87, 118, 124–5, 186, 188–9, 190, 191, 201

tacit knowledge 39–43, 137–8, 150, 202, 203
telegraphic communication 68, 111–12
television 41, 110–11, 112–13, 116, 126, 183
terrorism xiv, 6, 8, 49, 52, 80, 83, 117, 179–90, 194, 196, 201, 215n; and everyday life 188–90
Third World 21, 151; debt crisis 139, 156, 213n; neo-patrimonial state 155; see also coffee growing, marketing boards, tobacco growing,
Thomas and Znanieki 18–19

tobacco growing, Kenya 162–7; alleged impact on deforestation 165–6; see also British American Tobacco (Kenya)
Tönnies, Ferdinand 15, 120,
tourism 6, 99, 191–2, 197, 215n
transnational communities 18, 28, 30, 49, 60, 63–6, 71, 87, 94, 97
transnational corporations (TNCs) 5, 8, 12, 21, 23, 25, 37, 140, 164, 191, 203, 205; see also British American Tobacco, BAT (Kenya), Microsoft, Nestlé, Philip Morris
trust 9, 42, 47, 62, 66, 69, 73, 107, 110, 125–7, 132–6, 151, 175, 180, 188, 189, 198, 203, 209n

UK 5, 25, 56, 67, 68, 70, 95, 145, 193, 194, 210n; British Empire 31–2; violent disturbances in North England (2001) 92–3
United Nations (UN) 3, 81, 85, 143, 158, 207n, 213n
United States (US) 3, 6, 13, 21, 31, 33, 34, 65, 70, 87, 88, 95, 110, 114, 118, 120, 122, 127, 143, 144, 155–6, 176, 179, 184, 187, 196, 198, 208n, 214n
Urry, John 2, 4, 5, 7, 10, 34–5, 36–7, 40, 45, 48–9, 50, 62, 84, 111, 173, 181, 212n

Veltz's paradox 61–2

Weber, Max 16, 17, 18, 20, 36, 59, 100, 107, 108, 109, 120, 213n
weightless economy 3, 4, 207n; see also Quah, Danny
Whole Earth Electronic Link (WELL) 126
work flexibilization debate 54–5, 56–7, 61, 145
World Bank 3, 13, 80, 139, 141, 142, 143, 156, 213n
World Intellectual Property Organization 119–20
world systems theory 2, 15, 16, 21–4, 139
World Trade Organization (WTO) 3, 33, 88, 186, 211n
World Wide Web see Internet

Yugoslavia (and NATO intervention) 97
Žižek, Slavoj 130–1